The Western Mail

# The Century
# Collection

The
Western
Mail

# The Century Collection

An anthology of best writing in The Western Mail
through the 20th Century

## Edited by John Cosslett

The Breedon Books
Publishing Company
Derby

First published in Great Britain by
The Breedon Books Publishing Company Limited
Breedon House, 44 Friar Gate, Derby, DE1 1DA.
1999

ISBN 1 85983 172 9


Printed and bound by Butler & Tanner Ltd., Selwood Printing Works, Caxton Road, Frome, Somerset.

Colour separations and jacket printing by GreenShires Group Ltd, Leicester.

# Contents

# Foreword

NEWSPAPERS have an all-too-brief shelf-life; within a day, perhaps hours, they are read and then discarded. They have performed their task – to inform, to educate, to entertain – and soon their contents will be largely forgotten. Their ephemeral nature is a cause for sadness, because although much of the writing they contain may not be worthy of preserving for posterity, there are some articles which deserve a longer exposure.

I was, therefore, pleased when I was asked to put together this anthology, for it gave me the chance to bring back from oblivion some worthy pieces. Some of them I recalled myself; others were half-remembered by retired members of the staff; the rest were found in the countless reels of microfilm or bound volumes of the paper through which I trawled in Cardiff's Central Library or the National Library at Aberystwyth.

The selection is essentially a personal, subjective one. But I believe it gives a picture of a newspaper that has a special relationship with Wales and its people, of a paper that has a respect for the past and a hope for the future, a sense of responsibility and a sense of humour.

The articles cover a wide range of writing styles: from the overblown hyperbole of Owen Rhoscomyl on the investiture of the Prince of Wales in 1911 to the impassioned grief of Richard Burton on the death of Stanley Baker; from the quiet understatement of Edward James reporting his adventure during the Tonypandy Riots to the rich eloquence of Gwyn Thomas writing about valley sheep; and from Gordon Parry's clinical dissection of the car crash in which he nearly died to the pure, clever fun of John Greally's literary discoveries.

And as Gareth Jones writes about his flight with Hitler, one is aware that here was an immensely talented journalist with a real understanding of events. His early death was a great loss to the profession.

The pieces follow one another chronologically, with one exception. Although the story of the production of the first edition of *The Western Mail* was not told until 1919, it seemed appropriate that it should lead the procession.

I should like here to thank Mrs Mair Jones and the Saunders Lewis literary estate, Felix de Wolfe and the Gwyn Thomas literary estate, the John Morgan estate, Sally Burton, Bryn Jones and his colleagues at Cardiff Central Library, Dr Gwyn Jenkins and Vernon Jones at the National Library of Wales, Gareth Jenkins, John O'Sullivan and Meic Stephens, all of whom were helpful to me in my task.

*John Cosslett*

The first edition of *The Western Mail* was printed in a dilapidated old salt store behind a Cardiff public house on May 1st, 1869. Fifty years later, in the paper's golden jubilee supplement in 1919, the story of the acquisition of the first press – and the nightmare of the birth of *The Western Mail* – was told by S W Allen, then the only man still alive who had been actively associated with the production of the first copy.

# The First Issue
## By S W Allen

ONE OF THE blessings bestowed on me is a retentive memory. I have cherished and strengthened it by constant resort to it and helped it by a lifelong habit of making notes of outstanding occurrences within my experience. That is why I am able to recall in detail the incidents surrounding the issue of the first edition of *The Western Mail* in 1869.

There is no pleasure in recording the fact that I am the only survivor of the little group who were present in the improvised old machine-room on that occasion – an occasion that has proved of infinite importance to Welsh public life ever since. But it is a pleasure to be able to produce notes and sketches carefully made by me at the time, because they make easy the task set me by the Editor to recount some of the troubles and anxieties that beset the small beginnings of the dear old *Mail*.

I was in my twenty-fourth year, and engaged by the Marquess of Bute as mechanical engineer at the Docks. The Marquess had decided upon a venture as a newspaper proprietor and appointed a Mr Adams as editor of *The Western Mail*, which was to espouse the Conservative cause. Mr Lascelles Carr was appointed as sub-editor, and the literary staff was settled. The Marquess determined upon the plot between St Mary Street and the present Great Western Lane as the site of the offices, and an old salt store, a dilapidated building standing behind the Cornish Mount public house, which has long ago disappeared, was fixed upon for the housing of the printing machine. The Cornish Mount stood on the spot now occupied by the spacious vestibule of the *Western Mail* buildings, there being an appreciative declivity from the level of the roadway in St Mary Street. The salt store was, therefore, still further back from the street, and almost on the old quay wall which skirted the Taff before the bed of the river was diverted to its present position. So much for the site.

In those far-off days the Bute Docks civil engineer and my chief was Alderman John McConnochie, and he it was who was deputed by the Marquess to carry out the work of installing the machinery. One day, calling me to him, he asked bluntly, "Have you ever seen a printing machine, Allen?"

I may be pardoned for remarking now that I have never acknowledged my own shortcomings when put to any test! Youth and a will to make good possibly accounted for my reply at that moment, and I promptly answered, "Yes sir, of course I have," although the love of truth must now extract from me the statement that the only thing in the printing line I had seen was an ordinary lever platen press in a small office – a simple old-time affair for jobbing work that made an impression from the type when an iron slab, pressed down by a hand-lever, brought the paper in contact with it.

"Very well," said Mr McConnochie, "I want you to go to the *Western Morning News* office at Plymouth to take down two printing machines which you will find there and bring them back to Cardiff. They have been purchased for *The Western Mail*, which the Marquess is about to start here".

"Very good sir".

Drawing £5 towards my expenses and putting a hammer and spanner in my pocket, I took the job on without dismay. I looked upon it as a pleasure trip, but it proved a serious business, as events will show.

Taking a train on the old broad gauge to Port Skewett, I boarded the paddleboat *Christopher Thomas* and crossed the New Passage to Bristol. The *Christopher Thomas*, which was named after the well-known Bristol soap manufacturer (who, by the way, was a Welshman) had side-lever engines, and was afterwards converted into a screw-boat by Messrs Finch & Co of Chepstow, for Mr Bland, the Cardiff timber merchant. It was an unforgettable experience to cross the New Passage on her on the top of a flood tide, especially if the weather was rough, but one redeeming feature was the big round of beef and other comestibles that were always to be had at her buffet. Arriving at Bristol, I put up for the night at a coffee tavern near Old Market Street, paying 1s 6d. for my bed and breakfast. Next morning the Flying Dutchman conveyed me to Plymouth, the carriage being no better than a present-day cattle truck as far as comfort was concerned.

At the *Western Morning News* office I was introduced to a Mr Macadam, who asked me my business. I told him, and he took me into the machine room. There I was shown a four-feeder printing machine and a two-feeder contraption of a size and complexity that nearly took my breath away. There were seven miles of tape on them, and the machines weighed over sixteen tons. I had never seen anything like them before, but it was not in me to exhibit my perturbation.

"There you are. What are you going to do with them?" he asked with a broad smile.

"Take them to pieces," was my cool reply.

"How are you going to do it?" he continued.

"With my hammer and spanner, of course," came the answer as I took out my tools, and Mr Macadam stared at me as if he had seen a monstrosity.

Squaring my shoulders, I asked if he could find some handy men for me. His wonderment seemed to gradually change into admiration of my cheek, and he kindly offered to do all he could for me. There were some antiquated sailors and soldiers on the spot, old fogies who were employed in feeding the presses at the office, and he said I could make use of their services. He also introduced me to a Mr Symons, a builder who had some wooden packing cases to dispose of, and matters were settled for commencing the job.

Next day I tackled the machines. Piece by piece, they became dismantled, and each part was carefully marked and sorted before being packed. It was a serious job owing to the innumerable parts and the miles of tapes, with their endless windings, but I made many sketches and got along very well. My handy men seemed to be parting with old pals as they carried out my instructions, for the machines had been installed there for years, and had already become almost obsolete. But that was no affair of mine.

I was more concerned with the fact that my £5 was running out, and I was in danger of being stumped financially. Fortunately, Mr McConnochie arrived suddenly on the scene, and he advanced me another £2 to carry on. Feeling like a kind of millionaire once again, I swanked about the Plymouth streets that evening and turned into a draper's shop to buy a necktie. Plonking a sovereign on the counter, I was amazed to see the shop-man bang the coin against the counter and look suspiciously at me as it gave out a dull sound, without the semblance of a ring. Taking the sovereign between his fingers, he gave it a twist and, to my horror, it broke in two. Explanations were of no avail, and I had to go with him to a neighbouring jeweller's shop. Here the two pieces were tested and, to my relief, the jeweller reported that they were good gold, but that the coin was cracked, and when he offered me 19s for them I closed with him mighty quick. The loss of a shilling was a far better prospect than a night in the police station, which was the fate I had pictured for myself.

To return to the machines. The four-feeder weighed ten tons and the two-feeder six tons, and occupied a deal of room. When they arrived in packing-cases at the old salt store in Cardiff, I began to take dimensions and found that they could not be accommodated without sinking the floor two feet and digging pits three to four feet deep lower still. This brought us into contact with the old quay wall of what is referred to in some of Speede's maps as Porth Llongay. We worked at top speed, for the first issue of *The Western Mail* had been widely advertised for May 1, and

Mr Abel Nadin, who had been appointed general manager of the office, was getting flurried.

At last the machines were in position and ready to be driven with power from an old vertical engine and boiler brought up from the Docks and installed by me in the corner of the salt store.

On the night of April 30 the type formes were brought in and placed on the four-feeder. Everyone was on the tip-toe of expectation as to how things would go. Standing by were Mr Adams (editor), Mr Lascelles Carr (sub-editor), Mr Nadin (general manager), Mr McConnochie, Mr Lewis Vincent Shirley, the Bute solicitor, myself, Sullivan the machinist and his assistants. Having finished their part of the job on the editorial side, Mr Adams and Mr Carr had come in with some bread and a chunk of cheese, into which they kept digging with a pocket-knife whilst the preliminaries were in progress.

At last, everything being in readiness, Sullivan shouted the warning, "Look out!" which, in printers' parlance, means, "Keep your anatomy clear; the press is about to start." Then came the squeak of a slipping belt, followed by an infernal rattle and din, and the machine was on top speed.

Not many copies were printed, however, before a tape flew off. Then a few sheets lost their way and went wandering into the internal recesses of the press. There was a shout, and the machine was stopped. Sullivan wormed himself between the wheels and tape to clear the sheets, little more than the soles of his boots being visible, yet, much as he was hidden from view, he succeeded remarkably well in making his voice heard, though with some difficulty understood, for he suffered from an impediment in his speech. But this little peculiarity did not in the least prevent him from ejaculating epithets more calculated to stagger than stimulate the thinking powers of his assistants.

Such incidents, with slight variations, were from time to time repeated and the contour of the faces of some of the gentlemen present quickly changed from the horizontal to the vertical ellipse. But perseverance and determination won, and *The Western Mail* was from that day an acknowledged power.

That first publishing night's experience taught us many things. It convinced us that the old four-feeder was a back-number as far as efficiency and clean printing went. It rattled so much that the type, however tightly clamped down, persisted in running loose, with the result that the "spaces", which should not have shown at all on the sheets, came up and pock-marked all the impressions with little black smudges. Worse still, many of the "spaces" showed up plainly with the name of Figgins, the type founder, so that the letterpress was interlarded with Figgins, Figgins, Figgins, all over the pages. The first subscribers of *The Western Mail* must have been puzzled as who or what Figgins was. They know now, if there are any of them alive to read my tale. Before me as I write is the memorandum book that I carried at the time, and on two of its pages are impressions that I made from the type before the first newspaper sheet was printed. I therefore claim that the very first impression of *The Western Mail* is in my possession.

It did not take long to realise that the presses from Plymouth were not good enough for a progressive newspaper. One of the first to appreciate this was Mr Lascelles Carr. So thoroughly did he impress the proprietor with his organising and administrative abilities that the entire control and management of the paper was after a short period placed in his hands. Then things began to hum. In thirteen years from the time *The Western Mail* was started he was responsible for the building of magnificent offices, which he equipped with efficient and up-to-date machinery, and shortly afterwards he actually started on the premises the first central electric lighting station in Wales, having previously obtained the sanction of the local authorities to run overhead wires across the streets to supply consumers at a distance.

Much more equally interesting stories to the friends of *The Western Mail* could be told by me, but my allotted task has been to recall what I know personally of the initial troubles that had to be encountered in the establishment of a paper which has long since come to be looked upon by the people of South Wales as almost as indispensable as their morning meal.

*The Western Mail, May 2, 1919*

The end of the 20th century brought the great debate on whether the second millennium would end on the last day of 1999 or that of the year 2000. The end of the 19th century raised a similar argument, and the *Western Mail* leader-writer reviewed the pros and cons in the last issue of 1899.

# Writing "18" for the last time

DOES the new century begin with Monday next, or a year later? The Kaiser has approved of a law for Germany declaring that the twentieth century begins on January 1, 1900, and our own Lord Kelvin is of a similar opinion. On the other hand, it is asserted that not till 1901 will the new century dawn. Most people, we suppose, believe this latter view to be the correct one, and many pity the "confusion" of mind which allows anyone to end the centuries with the 99's. But, really, who is to decide the matter? It is held that the very people who ridicule the idea of a year 0 would object to their own ages being reckoned on any other plan. A child, they point out, is not one till it has lived twelve months or till the second year of its life is beginning. Thus, it is the second year of a child's life that is called 1, and is it any more ridiculous to assume that the second year of the Christian Era was named 1, and that, therefore, a hundred years, i.e. a century, would have passed away by the end of the year 99? The whole matter really resolves itself into a decision as to whether the first year of the Christian Era was called 1 from the first day of that year, or whether the first year is a year 0 and the second year the year 1.

The founders of the Christian Era may have taken either course, and the difficulty is that as to which they took there appears to be no conclusive evidence either way. The Prayer Book, however, certainly defines the present century as "from the year 1800 till the year 1899 inclusive." Sir Courtenay Boyle, the Permanent Secretary to the Board of Trade, writing to the "Times", thinks the question may be safely dealt with from the point of view of expediency only, and that we may, therefore, follow the example of Germany, and treat Monday next as the first day of the twentieth century. He thinks, too, it would gratify at the earliest moment those people who desire to reach the new century as a "record" matter. But, after all, we like to be certain, and a possibly bogus "record" would be no more satisfying than a bogus windfall.

In the estimation of a great many persons, all of whom represent the highest intelligence, the present year forms the last which goes to build up the nineteenth century. The question is looked at simply from an arithmetical point of view by a great many, and thus settled. At the same time, it is only fair to say that there is much to say on both sides of the question, and even those who have pronounced in favour of next year being the real keystone to the century's arch speak with a little reserve when they find that such an authority as Lord Kelvin is on the opposite side. However, the question as to the commencement of the next century is one of little moment, comparatively speaking. It is now given to us and to all Christendom to write the familiar "18" for the last time. The present year, as, indeed, the present century, has been a momentous one in our history. The most far-sighted among us a twelve-month ago did not foresee the peculiar position in which we are placed today. It occurred, no doubt, to very many who followed the trend of events and endeavoured to read the signs of the times that a war between this country and the Transvaal was not an improbability, but no person dreamed of the possibility of two small South African States attempting to annex British territory and defying the whole power of the greatest Empire either in ancient or modern times. The thought was ridiculous, and yet at the close of the year it is in that position Great Britain finds itself.

However, we shall not dwell further on this subject, for with the New Year, a notable change will, no doubt, come over the great chess-board in South Africa, and those who now smile and jeer at Great Britain will have good cause to feel astonished at the situation when the tide of fortune turns. Speaking generally, this country, notwithstanding the difficulties with which it has to cope at present, stands very much higher in the estimation of Europe than it did at the commencement of the year. Germany, Russia, France, Austria, Italy, and other European countries, which are onlookers and follow every movement on the board, must be well aware of the magnitude of the power which lies at the command of Great Britain. They cannot fail to appreciate the energy and promptitude, however slow the movements may have appeared to outsiders, with which this country has despatched the greatest and best-equipped army in the history of the world seven thousand miles from home with a view to assert its authority and defend its subjects from wrong and injustice. Whatever may be the outcome of the present conflict, the gigantic effort which Great Britain has put forth in connection with South Africa will always stand out as a remarkable fact in the history, not only of this country, but of the world. It is difficult to dissociate our thoughts at the present moment from the one topic which has engrossed public attention for the last two months, or one might refer to the highly flourishing condition of Great Britain at the end of the year. Figures do not deceive, and those which have been compiled with great care and studied with due deliberation go to show that this country at present is in a more prosperous condition than at any previous time in its history. This fact alone should suffice to inspire every member of the community with hopefulness in regard to the future.

Greatly, however, as a State is to be admired by reason of its vast commercial prosperity, there is another consideration which weighs much more in England's balance at present. Divided as the country is in normal times into sects and parties, politically and religiously, that is no longer the case. The British people in this crisis are one, and present a united front to the enemy and to the world. During the last three weeks a perceptible change has come over the dream of Europe, and to no other cause can it be attributed than the remarkable unity of feeling, of object, and of endeavour which the country shows. Whatever its shortcomings, or whatever misfortunes it has met in the tented field, the fact is patent that England now stands infinitely higher in the estimation of the world than at the commencement of the year which is about to expire.

*The Western Mail, December 30, 1899*

When the Royal Welsh Fusiliers arrived in Southampton in 1903 after four years' campaigning in South Africa, they were told by the Board of Agriculture that they could not bring their regimental goat ashore – and that he would be put to death the next day. A request by the officers that they should be able to pay at their own expense for the goat to be quarantined was turned down. *The Western Mail* became involved, as these editorials and reports show, and the goat's life was spared.

# The Fusiliers' Goat

WHEN WELSHMEN learn today that a distinguished and patriotic countryman of theirs, newly arrived from the war, lies under sentence of death at Southampton we feel sure that they will not be able to restrain a tear. If the hero were a confounded traitor like the notorious Lynch, or even a pro-Boer like Mr Lloyd-George, something might be said in extenuation of the cruel fate that awaits him. But there is nothing of the kind that can be laid to his charge. On the contrary, his whole career forms an eloquent argument why his life should be spared. He volunteered to serve his Sovereign and country in South Africa, and has seen arduous campaigning for nearly four years. As Providence would have it, he escaped the deadly bullets of the Boers, the evil consequences of forced marches and of poisonous water and short rations, and the thousand and one other dangers of the war. He bore a charmed life, and was not for a day inside a hospital. His soldierly bearing and fine physique were the pride of his comrades. When other soldiers were allowed to return home he still remained on, serving his King and country, and he has only now been allowed to return... But this is not to be. A draconic edict has gone forth preventing this faithful subject of his Majesty setting foot on England's soil. His comrades have protested and even prayed on his behalf, but to no purpose. Poor Billy today must die the death. Billy would have courted his fate on the battlefield – where he could have like a soldier fallen – but the thought of dying like a felon, of being strangled with a piece of red-tape, must break his heart. Mr Hanbury made a pilgrimage to Aberystwyth the other day, but we are afraid that he must make two pilgrimages to St David's after this before Welshmen will forgive or forget the Southampton tragedy.

*The Western Mail, February 11, 1903*

WELSH PEOPLE will learn with pleasure that the life of the regimental goat of the Royal Welsh Fusiliers, who lately returned from South Africa, but who were not permitted to disembark their pet, has been spared by the Board of Agriculture. In due course he may be expected to leave his condemned cell on board the ship for his regimental depot.

The "reprieve" has been granted in deference to representations made to the President of the Board of Agriculture. As soon as we were informed of the heinous plot, hatched in the secret places of the board, to ruthlessly murder the goat, we placed ourselves in communication with the Right Hon. R W Hanbury MP, and told him in a telegram on Tuesday night that much feeling existed in Wales against the Board of Agriculture's order to kill the Welsh Fusiliers' goat, and asked whether it was possible to have the animal spared.

At Southampton the time of execution, fixed for twelve noon, was approaching, but a deadlock had meanwhile occurred, and the execution was to be delayed. This deadlock, according to our Southampton correspondent, had arisen out of a controversy with the Board of Agriculture as to allowing the head and horns of the goat to be preserved. This last despairing request had been made by the officers of the regiment, and it was thought granted; but on Wednesday morning the Board of Agriculture wired forbidding even the head and horns to be removed from the ship, and declaring that they must be destroyed with the remains of the body. The agents declined to permit the animal to be slaughtered under these conditions and telegraphed to the board to that effect. This hitch in the proceedings saved the goat's life, at any rate for a time.

By this time the Right Hon R W Hanbury appears to have interfered in response to our telegram, and he used his influence on behalf of the goat. The Board of Agriculture also began to think that the goat may after all be the authorised regimental pet of the Fusiliers, and on this point they sought information with which any man in the street could have supplied them. In the afternoon we received the following telegram from the secretary of the board of Agriculture:

"Editor, *Western Mail*, Cardiff. Action of board depends on whether particular animal in question is the regular and authorised regimental pet. In communication with War Office on this point. Hope to be able to arrive at decision in course of this afternoon."

To carry the matter further, one of our London representatives paid a visit to the offices of the Board of Agriculture, and secured an important and exclusive statement from a high official, who received him courteously. The official appeared somewhat amused at the alarmist assertions made with respect to the future of the goat, and, asked to explain matters, he made the following statement:

"The whole of the statements that have appeared in the newspapers with respect to the pet goat of the Royal Welsh Fusiliers are premature, unauthorised, and incorrect. The goat has not been killed; it has not been landed from the transport Ortona; and it is exceedingly unlikely that it will be landed yet. As to what will be done with the animal, that is still sub judice, and is under the consideration of the Board of Agriculture."

Good results could not fail to be achieved when the Board of Agriculture and the War Office put their heads together. For two hours they discussed the question, and anxiety was finally set at rest at 6.47pm on Wednesday, when the Secretary of the Board of Agriculture courteously sent us the following telegram:

"Editor, *Western Mail*, Cardiff. Board have now heard that animal in question is regular and authorised regimental pet, and its landing will be authorised on veterinary examination."

Thus was the life of the Royal Welsh Fusiliers' goat spared.

Telegraphing on Wednesday night, our Southampton correspondent says there has been a unanimous chorus of disapproval from all quarters of the intention to slaughter the goat. Among the embarkation staff, which includes several men of Welsh regiments, the utmost indignation was felt, the more so as it was known that hundreds of monkeys and other animals have been brought home by troops and allowed to land. The most notable instance was the case of the 1st Battalion Royal Dragoon Guards, who brought home a wild beast for presentation to the King. This beast was allowed to be landed, and to accompany the regiment to its depot, nothing being said by the Board of Agriculture officials.

With regard to the rumours that orders were not given to destroy the pet, I am in a position to state positively that orders were received at Southampton from the Board of Agriculture that the goat was to be destroyed, and had it not been that the fact came to light that such an outrage was about to be perpetrated, the goat would undoubtedly have been killed. It may be taken for certain that after the visit of the veterinary surgeon tomorrow, and the goat being pronounced free from contagious disease (of which there is no doubt) it will be at once sent to the regiment's depot.

A *Westminster Gazette* representative was informed at the Board of Agriculture

Offices that the reason why the animal was not allowed to land was because the War Office had given the officials to understand that the goat was not technically a regimental pet, but only an adopted pet, and that as the regulation decrees that only bona-fide military mascots can be landed, the Board had no option but to carry out the letter of the law. Although the poor goat is officially regarded as only a "substitute," it has endured the rigours of the whole war, and faced death on endless occasions.

At Wrexham, the headquarters of the Royal Welsh Fusiliers, indignation is keen. The animal, it seems, is not the historic goat presented to the regiment by her late Majesty Queen Victoria. That regimental pet sailed with the battalion when it left for South Africa, but died in Natal in 1900, and his successor, the goat so stupidly detained at Southampton, was purchased at Krugersdorp in the same year.

*The Western Mail, February 12, 1903*

DOTTED HERE and there throughout the country are insatiable altars where victims are periodically sacrificed to the god of red-tape, who reigns supreme in the regions of Pall Mall and Whitehall.

The Board of Agriculture demanded a victim in no less a personage than the historic goat of the Royal Welsh Fusiliers, and yesterday morning death appeared inevitable for the unoffending animal. At the eleventh hour, however, a "reprieve" arrived, and "Billy" is still alive, and, for all we know, oblivious of his narrow escape, for as Mr Lloyd-George would say, he has been literally "snatched from the burning." A regiment holds its pet in affection before all things, and to reward the Welsh Fusiliers' goat with unceremonious death after a few years' hard campaigning in South Africa would have been not only a cruel thing to do to the animal itself, but an insult to one of the most famous regiments in the British Army. The action of the Board of Agriculture was resented not only in Wales, but in England, and especially in military circles, where it was well known that other regiments returning from the Cape had been permitted to land with collections of animals little short of menageries. With the Welsh goat the case was the harder, because "Billy" was the authorised pet of the regiment, and as such had accompanied the battalion and endured all its hardships at the front – hardships to which the goat of the 41st Welsh Regiment, by the way, had succumbed.

Telegraphing to the Right Hon. R W Hanbury on Tuesday night, we pointed out that considerable feeling existed in the Principality, and asked if it was possible to have the animal's life spared. Our intervention proved successful, and now the

Board of Agriculture are making arrangements for the restoration of the goat to the regiment. But it is an extraordinary thing that such a step as the destruction of the goat should ever have been contemplated. It must have been known to the Board of Agriculture that the pet was authorised and regimental, and as such, after fulfilling reasonable quarantine requirements, if necessary, there ought to have been no question about allowing it to land.

*The Western Mail, February 12, 1903*

Arthur Mee, as so many of the editorial and reporting staff in those days, came from Llanelli. A journalistic all-rounder, he was happy with any sort of assignment. Under the name of Idris, he penned poems for *The Western Mail*. And he was also a Fellow of the Royal Astronomical Society, which enabled him to write with authority on the subject. He was not the Arthur Mee who compiled the *Children's Encyclopaedia* and launched the *Children's Newspaper*. On this day, a number of *Western Mail* reporters covered the series of ceremonies at University College, Cardiff; Mee provided the colour piece.

# University Day at Cardiff

## By Arthur Mee

I T WAS amid a heavy shower of autumn leaves varied by gleams of bright sunshine that the ceremony of laying the memorial stone of the new university buildings took place at Cathays Park. The conditions were typical – the falling of the leaves recalled the passing away of the old order, and the sunshine the new educational era which is dawning over Wales. Those who came to witness the ceremony had an hour to wait, and were beginning to note the chill of the November air when the advent of a posse of mounted police and of a tumultuous throng of students, accompanied by their "band," heralded the commencement of business.

A dais had been erected with the appurtenances usual on such occasions. The lady students were separated from the sterner – or shall we say livelier – collegiates by a narrow gangway, up which to the dais marched the chief participants in the ceremony – the authorities of the university, the mayor in full robes of office, with his aldermen, councilmen, and staff, including the inevitable bearers of those silver poker-like ornaments inseparable from civic functions.

The ceremony was not a long one. A good deal of what was said was quite lost in the melody made by the collegians, though they actually did listen to two or three of the orators, chief among whom were Principal Griffiths, Dr Isambard Owen and last, but not least, "Cochfarf," whose few sentences in the vernacular received a truly Welsh welcome. The large block was lowered into its place amid ludicrous vocal exercises from the students and calls of "Mind his toes," and "Give him a drink!" Thus the stone was duly laid and by and bye the spot where now it stands will be occupied by a building as imposing – and shall we say even more momentous – than the stately structures that are now rising in the park.

The scene at the Andrews Hall in the afternoon was a very animated one, the hall being crowded long before the time for the commencement of the proceedings. A choir of students in caps and gowns occupied the platform, and discoursed music, some of which was sweet and some best described briefly as "otherwise." At times in a side gallery a scion of alma mater did some execution on a tin horn and there were other accompaniments of a similar nature. An occasional hymn varied the programme. As time wore on the proceedings became more and more animated, while professors and other dignitaries, many in brilliant robes, took their places in the body of the hall. Mr Austin Jenkins received some delicate attentions from the students, and the Anglo-French alliance was handsomely signalised on the entrance of Professor Barbier.

A minute or so before the stroke of half-past three, a fanfare from the orchestra heralded the entry of the chiefs of the senate, and among them him whom all had met to honour – Lord Kelvin. The great physicist looked well and stalwart in his robes, carrying his weight of years in a way that filled those who saw him with a lively hope that he would yet be spared many winters to the grateful country on which he has conferred such signal benefits.

Dr Isambard Owen, with his keen, intellectual face, occupied the central position; on his left Mr Marchant Williams, Mr Ivor James and Sir Alfred Thomas, MP, looking very fatherly and venerable. On the vice-chancellor's right were Principal Griffiths in his scarlet and ermine robes and the soldierly Sir James Hill-Johnes, while nearby were the mayor and corporation and opposite to them Lord Kelvin, who sat beside Lord Windsor. Lady Kelvin sat by Mrs Griffiths and the Bishop of Llandaff in the gallery, and took intense interest in the proceedings, whilst the good bishop looked as bright and buoyant as a man of a third of his years.

After a melodious rendering of *Hen Wlad Fendigaid*, the well-known graduation ceremonial commenced, and the candidates for B.A. – ladies and gentlemen – were escorted forward by the marshals, receiving their degrees and diplomas according to the time-honoured formula, pronounced in sonorous Latin, very little of which, however, was heard, thanks to the efforts of the students.

The latter were in fine form, and as the recipients of university honours stepped up, escorted by the marshals, they were greeted with such observations as, "Well, Johnny, how are you?" "Well done, Johnny!" "Good old Tudor!" "What have you done, Stanley?" "Good old sospan!" and the like. As the vice-chancellor shook hands with each there were shouts of "How are you, mun?" As Sir Isambard Owen distributed the awards there were more ejaculations, and the blushing graduates retired amid good-humoured yells of "Six months!" or "Blacklist!" or "Discharged with a caution!" or "Hard labour!" or "Take 'em away, Hawkins!" or "Good-bye now, whatever!" The highest degrees came last, and one or two of the recipients received a perfect ovation from their fellow-students.

So far it was the turn of the young folk; last of all came the veteran, the hero of a hundred scientific triumphs. The address to Lord Kelvin was a model of conciseness and good taste. When the aged philosopher came slowly forward to receive his degree he was the subject of a rousing welcome, which culminated when Sir Isambard Owen addressed him as he did with considerable emotion and in ringing words that echoed through the building, and were followed by thunders of applause. There were loud cries of "Speech", but his lordship felt compelled to decline and there was keen disappointment. But all present must have fully understood the reason.

The function as a whole was far and away the most successful in the history of the University of Wales. It was pregnant with significance. Not least was the fact that most of these graduates were racy of the soil. Many had won their laurels by hard effort and self-denial. It was a brilliant throng that welcomed their success, but there were others far away who were present in spirit, and one thought of the little cottage by the mine or on the moorland where sat a father with proud heart, or a mother with glad, glistening eyes.

*The Western Mail, November 14, 1903*

A series of reports in *The Western Mail* in November 1904 covered the beginning of the Great Revival led by the charismatic young preacher Evan Roberts. Spreading through the South Wales valleys and to parts of North Wales, the fervour lasted for a year before fading when Roberts had a nervous breakdown.

# Mission at Moriah

A REMARKABLE religious revival is now taking place at Loughor. For some days a young man named Evan Roberts, a native of Loughor, but at present a student at Newcastle Emlyn, has been causing great surprise by his extraordinary orations at Moriah Chapel, that place of worship having been besieged by dense crowds of people unable to obtain admission. Such excitement has prevailed that the road in which the chapel is situated has been lined with people from end to end.

Roberts, who speaks in Welsh, opens his discourse by saying he does not know what he is going to say, but that when he is in communion with the Holy Spirit the Holy Spirit will speak, and he will be simply the medium of His wisdom. The preacher soon after launches out into a fervent and at times impassioned oration. His statements have most stirring effects upon his listeners, many who have disbelieved Christianity for years again returning to the fold of their younger days.

One night so great was the enthusiasm invoked by the young revivalist that after a sermon lasting two hours the vast congregation remained praying and singing until half past two o'clock next morning. Shopkeepers are closing earlier in order to get a place in the chapel, and tin and steelworkers throng the place in their working clothes. The only theme of conversation among all classes and sects is "Evan Roberts". Even the tap-rooms of the public-houses are given over to discussion on the origin of the powers possessed by him. Although barely in his majority, Roberts is enabled to attract the people for many miles around.

He is a Methodist, but the present movement is participated in by ministers of all the Nonconformist denominations in the locality. Brynteg Chapel, Gorseinon, is to be the next scene of his ministrations.

Our Llanelly reporter writes: The ancient township of Loughor, near Llanelly, is just now in the throes of a truly remarkable "revival," the influence of which is spreading to the surrounding districts. Meetings are being held every night attended by dense crowds, and each of them is continued well into the early hours of the next morning. The missioner is Mr Evan Roberts, a young man who for some years worked at the Broadoak Colliery. He has spent the whole of his life in the place, and was always known as a man with strong leanings towards religion. He is now preparing for the ministry at a preparatory school at Newcastle Emlyn. Whatever the source of his power may be, there can be no mistaking the fact that he has moved the whole community by his remarkable utterances, and scores of people who have never been known to attend any place of worship are now making public profession of their conversion. During my visit to Loughor I found that the "revival" was on everyone's tongue. Colliers and tin-platers, shopkeepers and merchants, in fact, all classes of the community are to be found among the auditors of this fervid young enthusiast, who declares that the message which he brings to the people is that which is revealed to him by the Holy Spirit. At the close of the remarkable service which is described below, I had a short interview with Mr Roberts. This was at the unearthly hour of 4.30 a.m. after I had gone through a unique seven hours' experience. In answer to my questions, Mr Roberts said that the only explanation of what was now taking place in Loughor was that the spirit of God was working among the people. Recently death in a very terrible form has come home to the people of Loughor in the wrecking of the express train, and I inquired of Mr Roberts whether that might account for their readiness to receive the message. He did not, however, think that that was at all likely. Asked as to whether he intended devoting himself exclusively to mission work in the future, Mr Roberts said that in that matter he was in the hands of God.

The meeting at Brynteg Congregational Chapel on Thursday night was attended by those remarkable scenes which have made previous meetings memorable in the life history of so many of the inhabitants of the district. The proceedings commenced at seven o'clock and they lasted without a break until 4.30 o'clock on Friday morning. During the whole of this time the congregation were under the influence of deep religious fervour and exaltation. There were about 430 people present when I took my seat in the chapel about nine o'clock. The majority of the congregation were females, ranging from young misses of twelve to matrons with babies in their arms. Mr Roberts is a young man of rather striking appearance. He is tall and distinguished looking, with an intellectual air about his clean-shaven face. His eyes are piercing in their brightness, and the pallor of his countenance seemed to suggest that these nightly vigils are telling upon him. There was, however, no suggestion of fatigue in his conduct of the meeting. There is nothing theatrical about his preaching. He does not seek to terrify his hearers, and eternal torment finds no place in his theology. Rather does he reason with the people and show them by persuasion a more excellent way.

I had not been many minutes in the building before I felt that this was no ordinary gathering. Instead of the set order of proceedings to which we are accustomed at the orthodox religious service, everything here was left to the spontaneous impulse of the moment. The preacher too, did not remain in his usual seat. For the most part he walked up and down the aisles, open Bible in hand, exhorting one, encouraging another and kneeling with a third to implore a blessing from the throne of grace.

A young woman rose to give out a hymn which was sung with deep earnestness. While it was being sung, several people dropped down in their seats as if they had been struck and commenced crying for pardon. Then from another part of the chapel could be heard the resonant voice of a young man reading a portion of Scripture. While this was in progress, from the gallery came an impassioned prayer from a woman crying aloud that she had repented of her ways and was determined to live a better life henceforward. All this time Mr Roberts went in and out among the congregation offering kindly words of advice to kneeling penitents. He would ask them if they believed, the reply in once instance being, "No, I would like to believe, but I can't. Pray for me." Then the preacher would ask the audience to join him in the following prayer: "*Anfon yr Ysbryd yn awr, er mwyn Iesu Grist. Amen.*" ("Send the Holy Spirit now, for Jesus Christ's sake. Amen.") This prayer would be repeated about a dozen times by all present, when the would-be convert would suddenly rise and declare with triumph, "Thank God, I have now received salvation. Never again will I walk in the way of sinners." This declaration would create a new excitement, and the congregation would joyously sing:

> *Diolch iddo, diolch iddo.*
> *Byth am gofio llwch y llawr.*

I suppose this occurred scores of times during the nine hours over which the meeting was protracted. A very pathetic feature of the proceedings was the anxiety of many present for the spiritual welfare of members of their families. One woman was heartbroken for her husband, who was given to drink. She implored the prayer of the congregation in his behalf. The story told by another young woman drew tears to all eyes. She said that her mother was dead and that her father had given way to sin, so that she was indeed orphaned in the world. She had attended the meetings without feeling her position, but on the previous day, while following her domestic duties, the Spirit had come upon her bidding her to speak. And she did speak! – her address being remarkable for one who had never spoken before in public. Yet another woman made public confession that she had come to the meeting in a spirit of idle curiosity, but that the influence of the Holy Ghost worked within her, causing her to go down on her knees in penitence.

It was now long past midnight, but still there was no abatement in the fervour of the gathering. Fresh fuel was added to the religious fire by Mr Roberts, who described what had appeared to him as a vision. He said that when he was before the throne of grace he saw appearing before him a key. He did not understand the meaning of this sign. Just then, however, three members of the congregation rose to their feet and said that they had been converted. "My vision is explained," said Mr Roberts, ecstatically; "It was the key by which God opened your hearts."

One of the most remarkable utterances of this remarkable night was that of a woman who gave a vivid description of the vision which she had seen on the previous evening. "I saw," she said, "a great expanse of beautiful land, with friendly faces peopling it. Between me and this golden country was a shining river, crossed by a plank. I was anxious to cross, but feared that the plank would not support me. But at that moment I gave myself to God, and there came over me a great wave of faith, and I crossed in safety."

At 2.30 o'clock I took a rough note of what was then proceeding. In the gallery a woman was praying and she fainted. Water was offered her, but she refused this, saying that the only thing she wanted was God's forgiveness. A well-known resident then rose and said that salvation had come to him. Immediately following a thanksgiving hymn was sung, while an English prayer from a new convert broke in upon the singing. The whole congregation then fell upon their knees, prayer ascending from every part of the edifice, while Mr Roberts gave way to tears at the sight. This state of fervency lasted for about ten minutes. It was followed by an even more impressive five minutes of silence, broken only by the sobs of strong men. A hymn was then started by a woman with a beautiful soprano voice. Finally, Mr Roberts announced the holding of future meetings, and at 4.25 o'clock the gathering dispersed. But even at this hour the people did not make their way home. When I left to walk back to Llanelly I left dozens of them about the road still discussing what is now the chief subject in their lives. They had come prepared with lamps and lanterns, the lights of which in the early hours of darkness were weird and picturesque.

In the course of a conversation with our representative on Friday afternoon, Mr Roberts said that he believed we were on the wave of one of the greatest revivals that Wales had ever seen. All the signs of this were present. It was time for us to get out of the groove in which we had walked for so long. He himself was converted twelve or thirteen years ago and ever since then he had been praying for the Holy Ghost to come upon him. That it had come he was certain. It was one thing for a man to be converted and quite another to receive the baptism of the Spirit. The meetings they had had were glorious experiences. When they opened a meeting they had no idea when it would conclude. Only one thing could be said, and that was that it would not conclude until some definite point had been gained.

Asked how many converts had been made, Mr Roberts said that he did not call it conversion, nor did he believe in the counting of heads. Some people had said that he was doing good work. It was not his, however. He was simply an instrument in the hand of God and he wanted men to receive the joy of religion as he had found it. Our fathers had their religion, and too often it made them gloomy. In those cases the "joy" of religion had not been experienced.

*The Western Mail, November 12, 1904*

After six years of negotiations with the Marquess of Bute, the forward-looking burgesses of Cardiff bought the 59-acre Cathays Park for £161,000 in December, 1898 and decided to build the new Town Hall on the site. City status was awarded in 1905, when the building was completed. This editorial of 1906 looked forward to the eventual establishment in the park of the national buildings of Wales. And so it came to pass… the National Museum, University College, Cardiff, the Temple of Peace, the Welsh Board of Health (later the Welsh Office) completed the civic centre – and in 1998 the City Hall came close to being chosen as the home of the National Assembly of Wales.

# The City Beautiful

YESTERDAY was a proud day for Cardiff. After much delay and after much criticism of the undertaking, the new City Hall and Law Courts in Cathays Park were opened, the former by the Marquess of Bute and the latter by the Lord Mayor. When the Corporation entered upon the enterprise of the Cathays Park, and purchased that magnificent centre for the purpose of erecting public buildings, they did not foresee much of the expense that would have to be incurred.

But, having pledged the name and fair fame of their city to a great enterprise, they have followed it out unflinchingly, and Cardiff is today in possession of a pile of public buildings which must ever be a source of pride and inspiration to the citizens.

The enterprise which decided upon the purchase of the Cathays Park deserves a high reward, not necessarily in material wealth, but rather in the moral and intellectual advancement of the people.

Of all the arts, high architecture is the one which most impresses the masses of the people. Its sister – sculpture – is too cold and chiselled to appeal to the popular imagination, unless it be allied to great buildings erected for the public service. Painting must ever appeal to a limited circle, though thousands may treasure beautiful pictures and draw morals from them. Music makes its appeal to the emotions rather than to the intellect.

But who has stood in the presence of a great work of architecture, whether it be under the lofty dome of St Paul's Cathedral or amidst the great memories of Westminster Hall, without feeling enriched in thought and stimulated in intellect? It is because the new City Hall and Law Courts, by reason of their own design and also by reason of the beauty of their surroundings, must exercise an elevating influence upon the people of Cardiff that we attach so much importance to the ceremony yesterday.

It is to be regretted that the weather was so unpropitious; but, in spite of that, the ceremony passed off in a manner that reflected the highest credit on the Lord Mayor, Lord Bute, and the city council.

Yesterday was not the day for counting, still less for bemoaning, the cost. Rather was it the day to rejoice that a great enterprise, full of splendid possibilities for the future, is drawing to completion.

The Lord Mayor, in his admirable speech, reminded the public of the historic surroundings of the site. Much of that history to which he alluded is closely associated with the family of the Butes, and it was, therefore, in the highest degree appropriate that the important ceremony should have been performed by Lord Bute, who, as his lordship reminded us, followed the example of his ancestors, the Lords of Cardiff.

But something more than the associations of the past must have been present in the minds of the great gathering yesterday. They, probably, looked forward to the future, when the Cathays Park will become the appropriate site of the national buildings of Wales. The site was, surely, preserved by Providence for such a destiny.

The Corporation of Cardiff have set a magnificent example of what the future buildings should be architecturally. More than that, they have raised a monument to the civic spirit of Cardiff, which should exercise a lasting influence over the people of today and tomorrow, and lead by gradual events to the making of the city beautiful.

*The Western Mail, October 30, 1906*

A bitter dispute over wages involving miners working in the pits of the Cambrian Combine finally boiled over on the night of November 7, 1910, when pickets brought the Glamorgan Colliery to a halt. The next day, shops in the main street of Tonypandy were wrecked by thousands of striking miners and their families. Violent clashes between strikers and police continued for weeks, with many casualties on both sides, and police reinforcements and cavalry were sent to South Wales on the orders of Winston Churchill. It was into this cauldron of bitterness and confrontation that Edward James, a 25-year-old *Western Mail* reporter, ventured when he took the train from Cardiff to investigate the damage wreaked by strikers on the home of a colliery official. James, a Welsh-speaker from Porthcawl, was appointed London correspondent of *The Western Mail* in 1914, and was to spend 45 years there for the paper, most of them as London editor, before retiring in 1959. He died in 1971.

# In the Hands of the Mob

## By Edward James

I HAVE just emerged from my first experience of what is so fondly described by a certain section of people as "peaceful persuasion." I have it on the reliable authority of a mid-Rhondda picket that luck has been distinctly in my favour in that I have emerged from the delicate process without a cracked skull.

About nine o'clock on Friday night I left Tonypandy for Penycraig to make a few enquiries with reference to some disturbances. A quarter past nine found me in Library Road, where an attack had been made by the strikers on the residence of a man who was alleged to have continued working at the Cambrian Colliery.

In the moonlight I was able to determine something of the character of the crowd. It included a number of sharp-tongued women and several men who were half the distance to a state of inebriety. I stood for a moment only surveying the damage which the strikers had wrought, and as I was leaving I was accosted by a half-intoxicated fellow who was brandishing a huge stick in a most threatening manner, although sixteen Metropolitan policemen were standing within a radius of twenty yards. He did not conceal, on the contrary he was loudly decanting upon, the part which he had taken in the depredations of a few minutes previously. He was equally emphatic about what he proposed to do with the man whose house had been ransacked. I broke away from him as diplomatically as possible, and as I was on my way down the hill I exchanged a greeting with one of the London policemen.

Thereupon the man I had just left came rushing at me, his stick held in the air, and demanded to know what right I had to speak to a policeman. Realizing that, having regard to the man's state of frenzy, some trouble might arise if I remained to argue the point with him, I continued my way, explaining as I left that I only bade the officer "Good night". "You're a spy: you're a blackleg," the fellow shouted, and immediately I was surrounded by a menacing crowd of strikers, all armed with heavy sticks. The pickets were shouted for, and down the hill they ran, together with a number of dangerous looking fellows, who, disinclined to hear an explanation, proceeded to bundle me unceremoniously down the hill. One of the pickets was good enough to use his influence on the unruly mob, some of whom used language which was anything but Parliamentary, and whose fierce brandishing of sticks caused my blood to run cold.

I told them who and what I was and pointed out to them that they had not the faintest justification for thinking me a blackleg. But it was of no avail, and after I had told the pickets where I had stayed the previous night, I was marched down the road at the head of a crowd of men and youths, whose derisive cries and booing was an unpleasant augury of what might happen. I was given definite instructions to speak to no one on the march through the crowded streets, and one of the two pickets who walked on either side of me was so fearful of the danger to which I was being laid open that he insisted on my taking his arm. To that man I shall ever be indebted. He was, however, in other respects, unreasonable, as is indicated by the fact that he called me a liar, emphasized by a strong adjective, because I could not tell him the name of the landlord of a certain hotel.

Several hundred men and women were in the vicinity of the Pandy Pit. They had not long previously been indulging in stone-throwing at the police, and were waiting for the blacklegs who were alleged to be at work in the colliery. With the suspicion of being a blackleg hanging over my head, I was uneasy at the prospect of being marched by the pickets through that ominous congregation, who stood in the roadway in defiance of the police. There were several police officers whom I knew personally in the strong force who had formed up on either side of the road. But it was perfectly clear to me that if I had made any kind of protest or any effort to enlist the services of the police in any way anything might have happened. Indeed, one of my escort suggested the possible consequences of my saying anything.

I was entirely at the mercy of the strikers, and held my peace. Fortunately, the pickets had, at my earnest request, persuaded a large proportion of those who had taken a boisterous interest in my case not to follow in my wake, as they had done for a considerable distance, and I had a small escort as I was marched, tremblingly, between the lines of policemen who were holding the crowd back on either side of the road. For some inscrutable reason the police looked calmly on, as if they were oblivious of the fact that a citizen who had a right to their protection was the helpless victim of a dangerous mob. I emerged from the crowd without molestation. I attribute this entirely to the fact that I opened not my mouth and to my having taken the arm of one of the pickets. What might otherwise have befallen me I prefer not to think of.

From here to the square above Tonypandy Station I had as escort, in addition to the pickets, a crowd of youths, each carrying a big stick and each using the full power of his lungs in my execration. We passed several groups of police-officers, who took not the faintest interest in my case. It was the avowed intention of my "gentle persuaders" to take me to the address I had given them in order to substantiate the account of myself which I had afforded. The pickets now spent most of their time in foreshadowing the dreadful consequences which might occur to me if what I had said turned out false. One of them gave me the comforting assurance that in that event he would not give "tuppence for yer life."

On reaching the square our progress was stopped by a large body of strikers, who gave me that kind of reception one has usually associated with a row at an Irish fair. Big swordsticks were brandished in the air, and I was entertained to a more fluent string of epithets than I have ever previously heard. The crowd was augmented by a general rush from refreshment shops and supper bars, and their demeanour was such that one of the pickets told me afterwards he "thought it was all up." Some of those who were just beginning to take an interest in me were anything but sober, and the sticks they were brandishing were sometimes brought dangerously near to my face. The pickets tried to assure the mob that they were going to investigate my story, but the newcomers would not listen to reason or argument, and there was continuous maniacal shouting of, "To the railway station," and, "Back to Cardiff with him."

Without ceremony, I was led to the railway station. On the way I saw a local police officer, but he kept his eyes on the ground. At ten minutes to ten I found myself a prisoner confronted with a howling mob, who kept up a perfect din of obnoxious remarks, while one of the hooligans – he quite deserved the title – adopted a threatening attitude. I was put in the waiting-room, where one of the railway officials, who knew who I was, whispered something to me. A ruffian in the crowd went up to him, and in angry tones asked him what right he had to speak to me. There was a brief, but vicious altercation between them, the strikers contending that no one had the right to converse with a prisoner of the pickets. During this quarrel the crowd indulged in continuous hooting, and they continued to force their way into the small waiting-room.

My escort made it clear that I had to return to Cardiff by the next train, and that two of their number would accompany me. But we had an hour and twenty minutes to wait. The station officials were good enough to order all the strikers off the station premises, with the exception of the two men who were to be my escort to Cardiff. The crowd waited in the vicinity of the station until they realized that the fun was over, as the two pickets had given an assurance to see me out of the valley. I was a prisoner at the railway station for nearly an hour, during which time I endeavoured to point out to the pickets the folly of the proceeding. I showed no inclination to comply with the suggestion that I should purchase a ticket for myself. Whether my attitude in that matter affected my escorts' frame of mind I do not know, but shortly afterwards they agreed to take me quietly to the address I had given them so that I could prove my identity. This was easily accomplished, and at eleven o'clock I was no longer a prisoner. Be it said to the credit of one of the pickets that he congratulated me on having escaped without injury! Both, however, took it as a matter of course that they had a perfect right to pounce upon a well-meaning and innocent citizen and to compel him to run the gauntlet through streets crowded with strikers.

It is mob law with a vengeance in the Rhondda Valley, and one is amazed at the composure with which the authorities tolerate interference with the liberty of individuals, as instanced by an experience which I am never likely to forget.

*The Western Mail, November 21, 1910*

The adventurer and writer Owen Rhoscomyl won fame as a dashing cavalry commander in the Boer War and went on to write a series of books for boys and the unashamedly nationalistic *Flamebearers of Welsh History*. He also wrote the script for the National Pageant of Wales held at Cardiff Castle in 1909. His pride in Wales was shown in this colourful and romantic report for *The Western Mail* on the investiture of the Prince of Wales (later Edward VIII and, after his abdication in 1936, Duke of Windsor) at Caernarfon Castle in 1911.

# Investiture of the Prince

## By Owen Rhoscomyl

### CARNARVON, Thursday.

IT IS DONE. He that is Chief and King of us all, English, Scots, Irish, or Colonial, stood up today and made himself champion of Welsh nationalism against the world. Hereafter whosoever in the Empire will deny Welsh nationalism must deny his King, for today the King brought his first-born son to Carnarvon to take up the story of Welsh nationalism again on the very spot where once it seemed that Welsh nationalism had been cut across for ever. Whoever else may doubt King George, there will always be one land that will never turn its back on him, never doubt him, never fail him, and that land is Wales.

No man who saw the scene today will soon forget it. As we waited in the grey old castle hearkening for the guns to tell us when the Prince was nearing, we had reminders enough of the days of storm and struggle long ago. The towers and battlements that ringed us in told of the vain attempt to stamp out Welsh nationalism, and round the stands and round the battlements ran a long frieze of the grim coats-of-arms of all the old chiefs and clans of Wales, made famous in red battle for their land. And ever and anon the splendid choir broke into some strain of song, which proved that those old chiefs had not fought in vain. Over all there was one point which emphasised still more the triumph of Wales. Had such a ceremony to be held in England, it would have been held in some great building. Being in Wales, it was held "in the face of the sun and the eye of light." So runs the bardic formula, and as we saw the Prince invested, we saw the sunlight flashing on his purple robe and coronet, on the beautiful sword, and on the golden rod of his Dominion "in the face of the sun and in the eye of light." It would not have been Welsh had it not been that.

But now that the glitter and the guns are gone, now that the singing and the cheering are all passed, what note is it of it all that remains, and with insisting dominance returns again and again? Not the pomp of triumph, not the insolence of armed might, but those feelings of hearthside emotion that go deeper and deeper within us all. Triumph! This was our triumph: that after nigh on seven centuries of exile we have brought our own ceremony home. And as we looked on it we found that we had brought more than our ceremony home. We had brought home a young lad and his father, him and his mother, and his sister, as it might be our neighbour or our kinsman, quick to feel the things we feel with them. Prince and King and Queen and Princess they were, but which of us remembered that when the shouting and the trumpets brought the Prince's procession slowly and stately up from the Eagle Tower, until, behold! the last of the train of councillors in velvet, last even of the tall men in scarlet, between two that walked on either hand of him came a young lad in middy's rig. As he turned with controlled eagerness to the shelter of the Chamberlain's Tower, where he was to rest awhile from the blazing sun, what father in all the crowd but felt his heart go out at once to the boy as if to one of his own? How many of us whispered unconsciously, "Good, good boy; you're doing well, that's it, you'll pull through all right."

And when later the guns and the shouting brought the King and the Queen and the Princess, how right and true was the note of it when we saw that they brought no blaze of Coronation splendours with them to dim the splendour of the Prince's part. Today they reckoned it as his day, not theirs. The King looked an admiral, and gave you the effect of being much more, yet one felt that he was standing back as much as possible from between his son and the glory of the day. And the Queen. Has she ever looked better than today? Or Princess Mary? Simple, genuine, unaffected girlhood, all charm and sweet seriousness. Small wonder that one grey old Cymro called for three cheers for her own self. Yea, one cannot shake it off. The King and Queen and the Princess were like ourselves – all come there hoping that everything would go well for the boy.

Has anyone told the King yet that it is not Welsh to cheer? Someone should tell him, in order that he may not measure our welcome today by the raggedness of our cheering. We seem to feel too deeply, or else to be too shy for cheers. Moreover, there was a world of emotion to us in the very fact of his coming. It is not so long ago that we saw little of Kings in Wales. What we saw today will make us want to see him more and more. We shall soon learn to cheer if he will come.

But now for the story. When the Prince in his midshipman's uniform halted before turning aside into the Chamberlain's Tower, one was struck most of all by the youthfulness of his face. It was so youthful that there seemed a forlornness in his situation – more as if he were a captive Prince being paraded in some triumph. We all knew that the men in uniform beside him would have defended him at all costs, but yet we felt the impulse to step out and draw blade and rank ourselves around him, and so bear him through the rest of the day because he was so young a lad, and there were so many folk watching him, and so great a ceremony to be gone through. But after he turned and stopped between the two flags that guarded the Chamberlain's Tower we experienced the feeling no longer. When he came out there was a new spirit in his face.

At the door of the tower stood two standard-bearers, Sir Watkin Williams-Wynn on the right bearing the Red Dragon flag; Sir Marteine Lloyd on the left bearing the Gelert banner. As the two flags came down there was no one to call the Prince's attention to the strange thing that had happened with them. When the King ordered that these two standards should be part of the ceremonial, Garter King-of-Arms made drawings of the dragon flag as it was when it floated o'er the victory of Bosworth. Some artist, however, intervened, with the result that when the flag was unfurled today, behold! instead of the dragon passant on a field of white and green, outshone the red dragon-rampant on a field of gleaming white, and the Prince was saluted, not by the dragon flag of his ancestor, Henry Tudor, Henry the Seventh, but by the flag of Owen Glyndwr. Against this castle of Carnarvon Glyndwr laid siege in vain. Every other castle in Wales he won, but this one in its might defied him to the end, and we have special record that when he laid the siege he unfurled his banner of the Red Dragon on a field of white. Under that banner fought Meredydd ap Tudor, great-grandfather of Henry the Seventh and ancestor of the Prince of Wales today. And so the flag of Welsh nationalism, which could not get entrance to Carnarvon Castle then, was brought into a place of honour to grace the triumph of Welsh nationalism today! Still more, it was brought in to grace the apotheosis of a descendant of one of the captains who fought for it, and was borne by the descendant of the man who defended the castle against it.

Strange touch of poetic completeness! Inside that Chamberlain's Tower the full regalia lay ready for its bearers and its wearers. The coronet was something far more in keeping than the conventional Prince's coronet of the last few centuries.

But crowns have little beauty ever, and it was in the sword that artistry had achieved a real triumph. The massive gold of its hilt was wrought in beautiful shape; the gold and velvet of the scabbard were perfect. I have seen many swords of State, but never one that showed such beauty and yet never lost the sterner beauty of a real sword for action. It looked and felt a weapon fit for the hand of a young Prince in his first battle. The ring is beautiful, too. No part of the regalia is not beautiful – even the golden rod has its own triumph – but the sword outdoes them all.

While the Prince was preparing within, outside we heard the guns begin again, with the running and cheering and the music of the State trumpeters high up on the turret tops. Then down came the Prince's flag, the Royal flag of Wales, from its pride on the Eagle Tower, and out broke the Royal flag of the empire in token of the coming of the King. Slowly, slowly, with music and with cheering, came the King's procession up from the Eagle Tower, along the green carpet between the crowded stands. In the sunshine every touch of gold and scarlet flashed and counted for its full worth. Stately and beautiful it was to see, all splendour and all bravery. But it did not make us forget that earlier procession, when the white-robed Archdruid came with the bards of the Gorsedd leading the way for the Prince – our Prince. Slowly past us filed the ranks of Ministers, officers, and officials, and then suddenly one saw the King, the Queen with him, and Princess Mary just behind. There was not much cheering here in the outer bailey. We were all too full of what was to happen, now so soon, so near us, under that beautiful canopy of green and gold where those three thrones were waiting, the King's in the centre, his son's on the right and the Queen's on the left. At the foot of the dais the procession parted, and each component element of it took its place in a due and ordered picture. The King kept on till he came to his throne, handing the Queen to hers upon his left. Heralds and Ministers bowed to the King as he took his seat, and then we heard the quiet command to summon the Prince to his presence. Then out came the nobles whose privilege it was, as peers of Wales, to bear the regalia of the Prince – baron and earl, marquess and duke. Quietly they came, and after them out stepped a figure that flashed the whole scene into the romance we all had waited for.

Out from the dark portal stepped the Prince. Prince, indeed, he was now. Though his coat was of purple, yet he seemed to be all in white silk and silver rather than in any colour. Bareheaded now, he looked stronger built and more vigorous in this garb. Wearing the Garter, he stepped forth into the sunlight like a Prince of old romance. Men held their breath, and women's bosoms rose and fell quickly as they watched the boy pass on. Then peers and retinue took their positions. The Prince came to his place, the Earl Marshal set the picture into motion again, leading the movement with the precision that comes by centuries of inheritance, and all in a breath the Prince is making his obeisance to the King.

The King speaks, Lord Mostyn comes up with the mantle, and the Prince stands robed in purple and ermine to the heel. A peer brings forward the sword in its beauty. The King takes it and hangs it about the neck of his son. And so the ceremony goes on. The Prince kneels, the King puts the coronet upon the bowed head, and up goes a shout from all the stands, for that act is taken as the crowning point of all.

The ring and rod follow, and then we come to the moment when the King lifts his son from where he kneels and kisses him on both cheeks.

Then the King leads the Prince to the throne on his right hand, and all the folk along the inner bailey seem to see him stand taller and stronger than ever. Next come Sir John Rhys and the Archdruid to read the address of the people of Wales in Welsh to their Prince, and gallantly the grey old scholar does his part. Gallantly, too, the Prince replies, and for the first time we hear his voice, as it comes out, boyish, yet distinct and firm. Then follows the religious service in Welsh and English, bishop and Nonconformist divine taking part alternately; but the one hymn is in Welsh. It is not one of those hymns which fire Welsh singers into such wonderful effect. Next comes the presentation of the Prince to the people. And here comes the touch which will remain, because it was the latest thing we saw. As the King and Prince came down the steps of the dais we saw the King lead the Prince by the hand. All the way to the three presentations, the King on the left still holds the Prince on his right, and on the right of the Prince again is the Queen, his mother. Close behind is his sister, Princess Mary. It is as if the King presents his son to us to guard and support him through the years to come, and we – yea, we do so take him. Whatsoever may come to him, sunshine and storm, there will always be one land the lad may turn to for help and comfort, one folk he may look to for faith to the finish. That land is the land which he himself today did rightly call "Hen Wlad fy Nhadau". Our land, his land. Wales, the land of his fathers and ours. God be good to it and to him.

*The Western Mail, July 14, 1911*

The editor of *The Western Mail* in 1913 was William Davies, the paper's first Welsh editor. Although appointed to the post in 1901, he had effectively been editing the paper since 1894 as assistant editor under Lascelles Carr. Under Davies, *The Western Mail* helped raise a total of £26,000 (a fortune then) towards Capt Scott's ill-fated expedition to the South Pole. Scott sailed from Cardiff in the *Terra Nova* on June 15, 1910. He and his party (Dr Wilson, Capt Oates, Lieut Bowers and PO Edgar Evans, a Swansea man) were beaten to the Pole by Amundsen, and died on the return journey in March, 1912. The Commander Evans referred to in this article is E R G R Evans, Scott's second-in-command, who became known as Evans of the Broke after an episode in World War I when his ship *Broke*, in company with *Swift*, defeated six German destroyers. He became Baron Mountevans in 1945. Here, William Davies reveals that the 1910 expedition might have been all-Welsh.

# Wales and the South Pole

## By The Editor

COMMANDER Evans' appearance in Cardiff next Tuesday to lecture on Scott's expedition furnishes an opportunity to disclose an interesting fact which has so far been known to only a small circle. This is that in the summer of 1909 Commander (then Lieutenant) Evans was himself preparing an Antarctic expedition.

Sir Ernest Shackleton hinted at this fact in a short speech at one of Commander Evans' lectures at the Queen's Hall a couple of weeks ago. There was an earlier hint in Sir Clements Markham's article in the *Cornhill* for April. "On July 8, 1909," wrote Sir Clements, "Evans came to me with a well-thought-out scheme, and I told him to join forces at once with Captain Scott." In this Sir Clements has made a slight mistake in the exact chronological sequence of the facts, but the statement shows that at that time Lieutenant Evans was busily engaged on his plans for fitting out his own expedition to the Antarctic. From my own knowledge, I am in a position to throw further light on the project.

It was almost exactly four years ago that I received a telephone call from Mr W. L. Griffith, the permanent Secretary to the High Commissioner for Canada in London. He wanted me to run up the following day to discuss a matter which he considered to be of importance and interest – "both to you and Wales," he put it. Mr Griffith is not a man who wastes either his own or anybody else's time, so the following day I was in his room in the London office of the Dominion Government. There he told me of Lieutenant Evans, of whom he had clearly formed a very high opinion.

"He is going out to the South Pole," Mr Griffith said, "and it is my belief that anything that young officer undertakes he will carry through. It struck me that as he is a Welshman – his forebears came from Cardiff – it ought to be possible to make it a Welsh expedition and, therefore, it is a matter for the *Western Mail*. Anyhow, it seemed to me worth your consideration."

And considered it was that evening in the Devonshire Club. Lieutenant Evans explained his plans. These, it may be mentioned, differed from those subsequently followed by Captain Scott, and as it is not impossible that they may yet be put to the test by the author of them, I need say nothing further here than to note that the first objective was the exploration of King Edward VII Land.

The possibility of fitting out a Welsh expedition was carefully considered, and it was agreed that the prospect was not unfavourable. Subsequent developments conclusively proved that this was not too sanguine a view. Anyhow, the encouragement which Lieutenant Evans received at this informal conference decided him to go ahead, and he was given an assurance that Wales would support him with both enthusiasm and subscriptions.

From this point Lieutenant Evans threw himself into the prosecution of his scheme. Then came a surprise. He found that Captain Scott was planning an Antarctic expedition for the following year.

As Lieutenant Evans had by this time made his own scheme known to certain authorities on exploration, he thought it right immediately to see Captain Scott. The result of the interview was that Captain Scott asked the young Lieutenant to join forces with him. Scott would be in control of the expedition and Evans would be second-in-command and captain of the ship. It was also agreed, so I always understood, that Evans would be in the last dash for the Pole. Indeed, Captain Scott mentioned this in his Cardiff speeches.

This arrangement was made on the 16th of July 1909, and the hustle for getting the expedition ready for the following year was begun with characteristic vigour. Captain Scott estimated that he wanted £40,000 and both he and Lieutenant Evans set out on a mission to collect funds. Wales was assigned to the second in command, and he soon had the heather ablaze.

Lieutenant Evans' activities are well-known and need not be repeated here. But it is well to place on record that out of the £36,000 in the coffers of the expedition when it started South, Lieutenant Evans himself had been instrumental in obtaining £26,000. This is proof of the soundness of the belief that if Captain Scott had not decided to return to the South Pole, Lieutenant Evans would have succeeded in carrying out the projected Welsh expedition, and that the whole of the money would have been forthcoming from the Principality – including, of course, the Government grant.

For it is not an unnatural assumption that since Wales did so well on behalf of an expedition which was not distinctively Welsh, it would have done still more, and a great deal more, if the expedition had been wholly Welsh.

It is no secret that the whirlwind success obtained by Lieutenant Evans in Cardiff and South Wales took Captain Scott by surprise. He could not conceal – indeed, he did not attempt to conceal – an impression that Celtic exuberance was responsible for the assurance that Wales would do great things for the expedition. Certainly, he did not eagerly accept my suggestion to allow Lieutenant Evans to come down to South Wales to place the matter before our countrymen. After pondering on the suggestion for a few moments he said: "I don't want Evans to go down to Cardiff for £25 or so."

I assured him that if I did not think the result would prove substantial, I should not have made the suggestion.

The lieutenant came, with what consequences in support for the movement and in a now historical association between Cardiff and the expedition we all know…

On the night before the *Terra Nova* left Cardiff on its long voyage, Captain Scott said at a public banquet:

> "We would not have faced the strain of preparation except for the support we received from South Wales. When we entered upon the preliminary work of the expedition nine months ago, I secured the services of a Welshman (Lieutenant, now Commander, E.R.G.R. Evans) whom I knew well, and I sent him down to Cardiff to canvass. The result of that canvass was that we have been able to fit up a jolly good expedition and I cannot find words to express adequately my appreciation of Lieutenant Evans' services."

One may be permitted on this occasion to recall also a passage or two in a letter which on June 18, 1910, Captain Scott addressed to the editor of the *Western Mail*:

> "I should be lacking in gratitude if I did not, even at this late moment,

express my appreciation of the particular service which has been rendered to our cause by the *Western Mail.*

"Throughout the preparation of the expedition you have freely used your great influence to interest the public in the venture and to gain its support for our needs.

"I most gratefully acknowledge that this great assistance has been given freely from a patriotic desire to advance a national undertaking.

"Believe me,

"Yours very truly,

"R. SCOTT"

*The Western Mail, June 28, 1913*

The worst British mining disaster occurred on October 14, 1913, when an explosion ripped through the Universal Colliery at Senghenydd – a village at the top of the Aber Valley, near Caerphilly. A total of 439 men and boys were killed in the blast and the underground fire which followed. The *Western Mail's* pages were full of reports of the tragedy, but none of them painted as graphic a picture as this – an early example of what modern-day news editors call a colour piece.

# Raging Sepulchre of Senghenydd

## By a Special Correspondent

SENGHENYDD, Tuesday

BETWEEN Cardiff and Senghenydd there are four stations, and between them slow trains have been dragging all day. Since the first news of the disaster was sent over the wire early this morning the trains have been full, crammed full, with silent men and pale women with swimming eyes.

Drawn up at a platform they have seen an engine and a single carriage rattle past at intervals, bearing to the hospital at Cardiff men who may yet die before they enter its doors. Finally, after what seems an interminable journey, the train clanks into Senghenydd and stops, and they plod patiently along the black, unlevel road up to where, in the fork of the valley, the stacks and sheds of the great colliery stand out grimly.

The uneven roads are full of people – more silent men, more women with drawn faces and moist eyes. The slopes of the mountains, either side green enough, despite the blackness of the village, are spotted with groups. Police begin to be in evidence, good-naturedly keeping the road clear to the great tragedy.

Then the gaunt, straddling mechanism of the huge winding wheels, a general ugly confusion of wire and wood and brickwork, feathery tufts of steam sizzling here and there continually, black greasy mud underfoot, a silent crowd, with constant movement in the midst of it, nurses with the Red Cross on their breasts, ambulance men, motor cars, more police, cinematograph operators… over all a grey sky and a faintly acrid reek in the air, like rotting wood. That is the taste of the fires below.

It is terrible to think that underneath us as we stand, even though the scene be hideous, 400 men are lying twisted in a hell of smoke and fume and poisonous gases. There is nothing to see yet, save a monotonous procession of men with the red grenades which are to fight the raging devils below with chemicals. They brought up 11 corpses this morning – you can see them in that shed at the furthest end of the row, poor, cold, mangled fragments of flesh which make you physically sick to see, so shattered and torn are they.

No more rescue work can be done till the brave, blackened fire-fighters have conquered in the struggle below our feet… One of them, perspiring, coal-black, pushes into the shed, where there is a fire burning brightly and where food and drink may be hastily despatched.

"Well?" says a grey bearded man to him. "No more yet, doctor," he says, wiping his face. "Fire and smoke worse than this morning. But I think we're getting at them in the west – don't know if they're alive or dead"; and he pushes out again.

In this way the grey autumn afternoon passes. The crowd thickens, the workers come and go, until by five o'clock (God be praised!) there is news that the fire is under control at last and the rescue work may begin.

The crowd is very quiet. The men, apathetic and stolid in the face of Death, a frightful death which may come to each of them in his turn and sweep them to destruction, converse hardly at all, and then in low voices.

It is the women who talk, not violently or idly, but with a sense, perhaps, that talk will save them from going mad. They tell how in one house a father has been swept away, in another a son, in another two sons and two brothers, in yet another a husband, two sons, and two brothers. They talk also of women who have fainted before the feared news has been told them, seeing death in the informant's eyes. They tell of young lads, pallid with fright under their outer skin of coal grime, collapsing in the rescuers' arms. They tell of a woman who has drowned the memory of a dead husband in drink, and who raved and shouted and cursed at all things in heaven and earth in her madness… But for the most part they are stonily quiet, showing only the torture they are enduring by the lines under the eyes and the strained look of despair.

So the day wears wearily away in bleak Senghenydd, and still there are 400 men, by this time beyond all hope, dead in the raging sepulchre of flames and smoke underground. And of all this, there is only the faint acrid smell of the air to paint the whole horror on the imagination.

*The Western Mail, October 15, 1913*

The wartime National Eisteddfod of 1917 is remembered chiefly for the emotional moment when it was announced that Hedd Wyn, the winner of the Chair, had been killed in France. In silence, the chair was draped in black. Hedd Wyn (Ellis Humphrey Evans) had left for France with the 15th Battalion the Royal Welch Fusiliers in June of that year and was killed in the battle for Pilkem Ridge on July 31. In 1992, a film telling his story and scripted by Alan Llwyd won international acclaim.

# The Black Chair

BIRKENHEAD caught the Eisteddfod fever on Thursday, and there were repeated scenes reminiscent of past enthusiastic national gatherings. On Wednesday the town was largely indifferent to the invasion of Welsh bardism, although it paid tribute to the Gorsedd. Yesterday it surrendered unconditionally. The spirit of bardism possessed the place from early morning, and strengthened its hold as the day wore on. Dyfed had cause to be proud of his procession, swelled as it was by the reinforcements of Celtic delegates from Scotland, Ireland, and Manxland. Among those initiated into the Gorsedd circle were some of the most distinguished scholars and nationalists of the sister Celtic nationalities.

Mr Llewelyn Williams, MP, called attention to the fact that they were assembled within a dozen miles of Offa's Dyke, the barrier raised more than a thousand years ago to confine the Welsh within the recesses of the mountains. But Offa's Dyke was in ruins, and the Saxon policy of exclusion and repression had failed. Despite the disabilities of centuries there was more Welsh spoken today than ever before. (Applause)

At the Eisteddfod itself the crowds were so crushing that three sides of the pavilion were taken down and seats in many rows placed outside, facing inwards, more than doubling the capacity of the pavilion, and yet leaving row on row standing beyond the chairs.

The day was so crowded with Eisteddfodic incidents which appeal to the bardic heart and mind that conductors were in high fettle, the platform scintillating with Eisteddfod characteristics. Time and again in the course of the day some generous and frequently unknown spectator readily contributed to increase – in some cases doubling – the prize offered, and in others giving consolation prizes to competitors praised by the adjudicators.

Two incidents in particular appealed to the tenderest feelings of the audience, each illustrating the devastating effect of the war on the Eisteddfod. The audience first awakened to something unusual happening when, in response to a call from the conductor, a wounded soldier was seen limping to the platform, followed by Brigadier-general Sir Owen Thomas, with his newly-won Gorsedd honours upon him. The interest took tragic form when Llew Tegid, in explaining the circumstances, said he had a most painful duty to perform, at once interesting and sad. Three years ago at Bangor National Eisteddfod two military choirs from the Welsh Army, under the fostering wing of General Owen Thomas, competed. One of the choirs was from the 16th Battalion, the other from the 17th. The prize was awarded to the 17th Battalion, which went out shortly after to France, and every one of those gallant fellows, musical sons of Wales, with the single exception of the conductor, had rendered the supreme sacrifice for his country. (Profound sensation) The conductor was present that day, but, as they saw, maimed for life.

The families of two of the members of his choir had sent rosettes to be placed on his breast at the National Eisteddfod. The rosettes were white to represent the untarnished honour of those brave fellows; black to represent a nation's sorrow for her dead heroes.

There was hardly a dry eye in the great audience when General Thomas pinned the little rosettes, telling so big a story, on the wounded hero musician's breast.

The second incident was equally tragic and unusual, when at the chairing of the bard the name of the successful competitor was called and no response was forthcoming. Rumours were already current that something unusual was about to happen, and they gained credence when the Archdruid, after consulting the records of the committee, announced that the successful competitor was Ellis Evans, Trawsfynydd, who sent in his composition July last. Since then he had been sent with his draft to France, and there, like many thousands of others, had laid down his life for his country. There could be no question of investing any representative, and instead of the usual chairing ceremony the chair was draped in a black funeral pall amidst death-like silence, and the bards came forward in long procession to place their muse-tribute of englyn or couplet on the draped chair in memory of the dead bard hero.

Cemlyn, commenting on the pathetic incident, writes:- It is only a few months since a young soldier in training in this country expressed his grief as follows, at the death in action of a friend from Festiniog:-

*Ei aberth nid a heibio – a'i wyneb*
*Annwyl nid a'n ango,*
*Er i'r Almaen ystaenio*
*Ei dwrn dur yn ei waed o.*

That young soldier, who has now also made the great sacrifice in France, was Private Ellis H Evans (Hedd Wyn), Trawsfynydd, Merionethshire, who was on Thursday declared the winner of this year's bardic chair. Hedd Wyn, who was 29 years of age, was one of the most promising bards at the present time in Wales. He was accorded second place for premier honours at Aberystwyth National Eisteddfod; indeed, one of the three adjudicators (the Rev J J Williams) placed him first. Five chairs at the principal eisteddfodau in North and South Wales had fallen to his lot of recent years.

Lord Mostyn made an excellent chairman of the morning meeting, contenting himself with the briefest address, whilst Mr Lloyd George, who was accorded a right royal reception, delivered an address on the lessons of the Eisteddfod in this war, ending up by saying that while the British Empire was a great Commonwealth made up of many nations, they were all one in purpose, action, hope, resolve, and sacrifice, and, please God, he added, one in triumph and victory.

*The Western Mail, September 7, 1917*

Throughout the General Strike of 1926, *The Western Mail* and its sister paper the *Evening Express* continued to publish, using a skeleton staff composed of overseers, journalists, girl typists and apprentices. Together they sold more than two million copies during the strike – and the *Mail* was the first newspaper selling in Fleet Street with the news that the strike was off. The Prime Minister, Stanley Baldwin, wrote to Sir William Davies, editor of the *Mail*, "I was very glad to see that the general strike did not prevent you from bringing out every day a normal copy of the paper. It is an achievement of which you may well be proud, and reflects the highest credit on the emergency staff who made it possible." The TUC ordered the strike following a lock-out of the miners, whom they had pledged to support in a dispute with the coal-owners. But the government organised the emergency movement of supplies and mobilised middle-class volunteers to maintain skeleton services. The armed forces and police remained loyal and made 5,000 arrests. The TUC, losing control of the situation, called the strike off on May 12 – but the *Mail* printers did not return to work for another week

# When Girls Mastered the Linotypes

THE PRODUCTION of *The Western Mail* and *Evening Express* during the nine days of the strike has been a pleasurable romance of loyalty. We feel sure our readers will share with us the pride in an achievement unique in the history of the press during the last nine days, and will join in paying tribute to the small but loyal band of workers who made it possible.

When it seemed inevitable that the general strike must be called, plans were made for emergency production. We knew the men who could absolutely be relied upon, and we were not mistaken. But so far as the general body of employees was concerned no intimation at all was available of their attitude towards a general strike, which meant the breaking of contracts which they had solemnly entered into with the firm.

There were grave faces and mysterious conferences, comings and goings between one office and another. The effort of making up the collective mind of the local branch of the Typographical Association was evidently a laborious and elaborate procedure. Eventually it was decided, with a good deal of reluctance, to obey the unlawful mandate of the TUC.

Let it be said here to the credit of the men who went on strike, that to a man they finished their night's work and finished it well and when, soon after dawn, in the absence of trains that could be relied on, a great fleet of motor lorries passed out of the *Western Mail* lane, heavily laden with copies of Tuesday morning's paper for all parts of the country, the strike pickets already posted on duty gave a sympathetic cheer.

Fortunately there was none of the silly and impudent interference with editorial policy that marked the beginning of the general strike in some of the London newspaper offices.

The Cardiff men were too wise to indulge in any attempt at censorship; if they had attempted it it would have made not the slightest difference to *The Western Mail*, which would have appeared as usual, but it is worth noting that they did not attempt it.

When Tuesday morning came, we were still doubtful as to whether any of the linotype operators of the *Evening Express* staff would report for duty, but it was not long before it became evident that the members of the chapel had taken the plunge and gone on strike.

Immediately the emergency arrangements began to work. They started off like clockwork, and like clockwork they have been in operation ever since. Except for a few extra hands who dribbled in on Tuesday, these emergency arrangements were responsible for the production of the *Evening Express* yesterday and they are responsible for the production of *The Western Mail* today.

Our readers can judge for themselves their efficiency and the rapid progress towards the production of a perfect newspaper made by a "strike" staff, which at a moment's notice took on skilled work with which most of them were wholly unfamiliar.

It may almost indeed be said that in nine days we have enlisted and trained a staff that can carry on with a vast amount of credit, or, in justice, we should explain that they trained themselves.

When we started to produce the *Evening Express* on Tuesday, the Linotype staff consisted of the overseers and a few headmen in different departments. They were men of experience, some of them had been in the service of the Western Mail Limited for very many years; but occupying the positions they did they had not for some years tapped at the keyboard of a Linotype machine. Before many minutes had passed, however, they had renewed all their old cunning and resource, and from these few men came column after column of matter sufficient to enable the *Evening Express* to go to press at very much the same hour of the day.

Going to press was no mean performance. In the numerous processes that go to make the modern newspaper, there is none more delicate and important than the stereotyping, the making of flongs, and the casting of plates from molten metal heated to a certain degree. This all-important job was tackled by works managers and amateurs with a somewhat superficial knowledge of its complexities. But they succeeded beyond expectations, and when the great presses began to roar and rattle out the first paper produced in Cardiff, perhaps in the whole country, during the strike, the music was like a song of triumph to those loyal workers who made the stereo plates and ran the printing machines.

Outside the city was silent. The trams had ceased. Their clangorous noise no longer made day hideous. Corporation buses were nowhere to be seen. People walked about in almost apprehensive silence. There were many gloomy, anxious faces. Suddenly, swarming into St Mary Street came the rush of newsboys, shouting "*Evening Express!*" The familiar music of the newsboys' shout was never more welcome. Many people cheered the lads as they dashed through the streets. One newspaper at any rate had refused to be muzzled or stopped, and this first visible evidence of the determination of the public to carry on had as cheering an effect upon the citizens as a whole, as it was plainly depressing to the strikers who were walking the streets in hopeless idleness.

When the *Evening Express* had published its last edition on Tuesday – the Second Pink, as usual – the self-same staff that produced it set about preparing for the still larger task of producing Wednesday morning's *Western Mail.* No thoughts of an eight hours' day, still less a seven hours' day, troubled these fine workers. They had resolved to do it night and day until the strike was over. Beds were provided in the office. The kindly caretaker had converted parts of the office into a veritable hotel with comforts that challenged comparison with the Cecil. With every hour their output on the Linotype machines increased in speed as well as quality.

In order to cope with the important news matter that had somehow to be given, the services of the process block department and the lady typists had to be requisitioned. Carefully prepared typewritten sheets containing the news were as carefully photographed and reproduced in half-tone, and with the aid of these a four-page *Western Mail* was published as usual on Wednesday morning when other papers had stopped publication altogether.

Not only Cardiff but London and the whole of the country were astonished and gratified, London especially because its own great newspapers were momentarily stopped and the sight of a provincial journal on sale in thousands in Fleet Street at breakfast time was so unusual and unexpected.

Encouraged by this initial triumph our little skeleton staff rose from their temporary beds on Wednesday determined to achieve greater things still. The cheerful faces in the Lino-room, the stereo foundry and the machine room were a delightful contrast to the gloomy and disappointed faces of the strike pickets outside; but the latter could not refrain from paying a secret tribute to their former colleagues and wondering how they had accomplished the seemly impossible.

The workers inside knew how it was done and there is no great secret about it. It was loyalty and the Britisher's determination to win. Soon the skeleton staff began to receive accessions from unexpected quarters. The lady typists were no longer satisfied with typing news for the photo-etcher to reproduce in block form. They volunteered to man the Linotype machines. Some of the experienced hands had their doubts. A printer has to serve a seven-years' apprenticeship to his craft. How could these young girls, fresh from school some of them, hope to be of any useful service? However, offers of help were not to be despised, and when the first of the lady operators brought up her "take" and asked for more "copy" to set-up, the overseer had the surprise of his life. The girls had mastered the machines in the course of a few hours, and soon they were merrily turning out column after column of good matter, much of it actually with fewer mistakes than are committed by experienced hands.

As the days wore on the technical capacity of the staff increased, and further accessions of strength came from other departments. There was no lack of volunteers eager to learn and perform, and editors, reporters, advertisement clerks, accountants, all tried their hands with surprising good results. But the palm must be given to the lady typists who, day and night, worked with a happy enthusiasm and increasing efficiency that made the nine-days strike a nine-days pleasure to the skeleton staff of *The Western Mail* and *Evening Express*.

With a staff growing so rapidly in efficiency it was possible on Friday, the fourth day of the strike, to increase *The Western Mail* to eight large pages – at that time probably the largest strike edition in the country – and it has remained this size ever since. From the very beginning, too, the *Evening Express* has been an eight-page paper – not merely an emergency sheet, but a newspaper.

If the unceasing publication of *The Western Mail* and the *Evening Express* has had anything to do with breaking down the strike – as we believe it has – that is sufficient recompense for the small and loyal band that made their production possible.

In every department, from the Linotype room to the machine room, the men and women have been splendid. Nor must we forget the packers and the publishers and the lorry drivers and news agents, who, sometimes at great peril, carried the papers through crowds of hostile demonstrations and sold them to people waiting eagerly for the news. It is a triumph in newspaper production under the greatest difficulties imaginable – greater even than the difficulties that were surmounted when the *Western Mail* premises were burnt down. To have come through the strike without the loss of a day's publication is an achievement of which *The Western Mail* and the *Evening Express* are legitimately proud. We are prouder still of the staff that made it possible.

*The Western Mail, May 13, 1926*

When Cardiff City beat Arsenal at Wembley to win the F A Cup in 1927, no club outside England had ever held the trophy before. The *Western Mail's* soccer writer Citizen said that Cardiff captain Keenor was the proudest Welshman in the world when he received the Cup from the King. But another Welshman, he said, was the saddest man on earth. This was Daniel Lewis, Arsenal's Welsh goalkeeper, who allowed a 75th-minute shot from Ferguson to twist out of his fingers and roll over the goal line. When the victors returned to Cardiff, they were given a heroes' welcome. An editorial said, "…they could hardly have envisaged so splendid a Roman triumph on their return. It was a democratic demonstration, an unrestrained idolatry of popular heroes. The victors' chariot was a storm-centre: it progressed through a hurricane of joyous clamour and a carnival of colour… Those who honour Cardiff by their prowess are in turn worthy of honour."

# Stirring Moments at Wembley

## By Our Special Correspondent

"NINETEEN-TWENTY-SEVEN – the year Cardiff City first won the Cup". That is how Welsh football history and, perhaps, some other history too, will come to be dated in the future. And no one who was present at Wembley on Saturday can easily forget the scenes or the singing, the tense anxiety of the closing minutes of the game, the great Welsh shout of triumph when the referee shrilled out the final and Keenor, captain of Cardiff City, followed by his men, went up to the King to receive the FA Cup, which, for the first time in its half-century of history, has been taken out of England.

The winning goal came when many of us had almost resigned ourselves to a re-play. Neither side seemed to be playing sufficiently good, clever and finished football to win, or to deserve to win. Then the unexpected happened. Ferguson shot into the goal-mouth. The Arsenal goalkeeper caught it. Len Davies was not far off, but still far enough away to be no cause of anxiety. Lewis, the goalkeeper, had plenty of time apparently to clear. He bent to his knees to gather the ball, and in bending he turned away from Davies, who was racing up. Everybody expected to see him rise and get the ball away. Nobody really expected a score. The silence was tense all the same. Then Lewis fumbled – that is how it seemed to spectators in the stands: Cup-tie nerves, perhaps. It is said that the ball was spinning and was difficult to hold, and that may be, of course, the explanation. At any rate, we saw the ball slip out of his hands and roll, all too slowly, it seemed, towards the net. There were Arsenal shouts of dismay and Cardiff shouts of joy. Lewis tried to grab the ball. Too late: it had crossed the line. Len Davies was leaping high in the air; a leap of triumph. Lewis, a rather pathetic figure, went slowly into the net to get the ball. It was destined to be the winning goal, and Lewis, who had played so well, had seemingly let his side down.

When the great crowd, close upon a hundred thousand, realised what had happened, such a shout went up as Wembley had never heard before. The crowded tiers of the vast amphitheatre became a stormy sea of tossing, waving hats and blue and white favours. Everywhere people were standing up, shouting themselves hoarse. In the Royal Box the King was smiling. Behind his Majesty the face of Mr Lloyd George was wreathed in patriotic smiles. Behind him again Mr Winston Churchill was smiling over to his old colleague of Coalition days little messages of national congratulation.

The Lord Mayor of Cardiff, excusably forgetful in the circumstances of the decorum of the Royal Box, joined the throng in a demonstration of enthusiasm that has rarely been equalled on a football field.

When the shouting had ceased and the game was re-started, there were many who, on reflection, qualified their enthusiasm with sympathy for the Welshman who was keeping goal for the Arsenal. And let it be said at once that a misfortune which might have unnerved most players seemed only to stimulate the Arsenal to greater efforts and to make Lewis himself rise to great heights again and again to avert further disaster. Cardiff City's supporters lived through anxious moments in the last fifteen minutes of the game. There were keen, desperate attacks and thrilling saves. Experts may call the quality of the football poor, but there was no denying the tremendous pace, the eager attack, the stern defence…

At the start it seemed as if both sides were suffering from nerves. Arsenal were playing the better football – their passing was infinitely superior. Buchan was always in the picture leading attacks, and Hardy was always in the picture, too, breaking them up and making magnificent clearances. As the game proceeded the pace increased, and when Cardiff scored it gave them just the tonic and the confidence they seemed hitherto to lack. Desperately anxious and thrilling though the close was, Cardiff City were now clearly the winners and they played a sporting open game to the end. There was none of that futile, unsportsmanlike waste of time that has spoiled many a good match after the first score. Up to the very call of the whistle, both sides were striving hard, one to equalise, the other to increase its lead. And so, whatever the experts may say of the quality of the football and the nature of the goal, Cardiff City's victorious Cup Final will be remembered as amongst the most sportsmanlike and the cleanest on record.

It will be remembered, too, for many other things. Some will call it the singing Cup Final. If this community singing is persevered in, it will not be necessary soon to come to Wales to hear singing. For many hours before the game began the crowds waiting in the Stadium were singing, and as the people surged into the great amphitheatre the volume of sound increased until, when the King came in, the National Anthem went up with a fervour that recalled the heroic, loyal days of 1914. It was a great crowd of sportsmen, more than half red, perhaps a third blue and white, judged by the favours that were shown about, and a very large section neutral, but whether the warp and woof were red or blue the result was a web of happy, loyal sportsmen gathered to witness a great contest. Instinctively they all turned to the King after the National Anthem, and spontaneously they sang the old song of democratic greeting and good-fellowship, *For he's a jolly good fellow.*

Then, as the crowds continued to pour in, favourite old hymns and songs were sung. As Welshmen we longed for *Cwm Rhondda*, with its thrilling, almost barbaric, beauty of swelling harmony, but *Hen Wlad* satisfied our national pride; and most beautiful and wonderful of all was *Abide with me*, sung with all its pleading tenderness by ninety thousand people. Not even the thrills of the game, nor the shouts of triumph, can efface the memory of that great hymn sung by so many, and yet sung so tenderly. Let it not be said that the English are not an emotional race. The Welsh men and women in the crowd were moved as one expected them to be; but so were the English; and many an eye was dimmed with tears, the memory carried back, perhaps, to heroic days of peril and sacrifice and unfaltering trust.

The memory of this deep emotion stands out against a background of joyous festival. For the English Cup Final is much more than a great football contest – much more than the climax of the football year, the conflict between the two teams that survive the ordeal of the rounds. It is a tremendous festival, and this year to an occasion hitherto – with one exception, and that again Cardiff City – exclusively

English was added the flavour of an international: something of the flavour of an England v Wales Rugby contest at Cardiff or at Twickenham.

From Wales the men and women went up to London in legions. All through the Friday night and the early hours of Saturday morning the streets of London were musical with Welsh hymns and songs. The leek and the daffodil were almost as abundant, worn as favours, as the City's colours. It was not merely a Cardiff City occasion. It was an all Wales occasion.

*The Western Mail, April 25, 1927*

To this day, no one knows the identity of The Junior Member for Treorchy, *The Western Mail's* star political columnist from 1910 until the outbreak of World War II and for another five-year period from 1959. His speciality was the imaginary interview, and *Western Mail* readers knew this. But the editor of *The Times* didn't, and when the Junior Member "interviewed" Lloyd George on his 68th birthday, and quoted his remarks concerning the attitude of the Liberal Party, *The Times* solemnly dealt with the matter in a leading article. The *Western Mail* leader writer gleefully wrote, "For twenty years this licensed genius, whose identity is probably the best-kept secret in journalism, has entertained readers of the *Western Mail* with imaginary interviews with public men, and a mention, favourable or unfavourable, in his articles has come to be regarded as a passport to fame. It is one of the peculiar qualities of his wit that his victims enjoy his penetrating irony as much as those who rejoice in their supposed discomfiture, and his uncanny prescience, his knowledge of the inner thoughts of men and the hidden significance of events, have given to his articles the spice of reality that is the essence of great satire. All his victims are made to "speak" in a manner exactly like their own. But nobody, so far as we know, ever accepted one of his imaginary interviews until *The Times* walked boldly into the Junior Member's trap." *The Times* apologised to its readers, Lloyd George issued a statement making his position clear, and he congratulated "his old friend the Member for Treorchy" on his "real triumph."

# Mr Lloyd George
# and
# his Future

## By the Junior Member for Treorchy

O NE OF the most illustrious of ancient philosophers was so oppressed with the gloom and the gravity of human existence that he was never tired of maintaining that if only men could see life in its true perspective they would regard the phenomenon of birth with an unutterable sadness and that of death with real joy. According to his interpretation of the riddle of human existence, it is infinitely better to pass out of life than it is to come into it.

Happily, so sinister a theory has never succeeded in making any sort of appeal to mankind. On the contrary, there is in human nature an instinct, the persistence of which manifestly demonstrates its validity, which leads us to hail a birth as an occasion for genuine joy. It is something which is fraught with glorious possibilities. And so it has come about that the birthday figures for most of us as a conspicuous date in the calendar. Its significance, as it comes round year after year, is self-evident. It serves the purpose of a visible milestone on life's journey. It registers a retrospect. On the one hand, it marks the distance that has already been traversed, while, on the other hand, it is the starting point for fresh effort.

Such were some of the reflections which occupied my mind when, a few days ago, I paid a special visit to Lloyd George on the occasion of *his* birthday.

"Ah, my dear fellow," he exclaimed as he gripped me by the hand in hearty welcome, "it is indeed fitting that you should call upon me on such an occasion. I candidly confess that there have been occasions on which I have been exceedingly anxious to avoid you. I have had plans in the offing, and while delicate machinations were being resorted to behind the scenes I have been apprehensive lest, in your characteristic eagerness for secret and exclusive information, you might spring the mine. Or, if I may put it in another way, an immature scheme is like a photographic plate. It must not suffer exposure before it has been fully developed if it is to turn out a success. Now, Treorchy, I cannot forget that there have been occasions on which you have succeeded in gaining access to some of my plates, with the result that they were held up to the light of publicity before they were really ready. I could cite several instances of this kind, but I will content myself with just one.

"It was on the celebrated occasion on which I entertained the Welsh Liberal members to a most sumptuous dinner at the House of Commons. After they had regaled themselves to the full and the waiters had left the room I took them into my confidence in regard to the tactical dispositions which I had, in the exercise of my resourcefulness as an old Parliamentary hand, devised for their benefit. Every one of the assembled members readily, and even eagerly, submitted to the seal of absolute secrecy. You can, therefore, imagine my unutterable astonishment a couple of days later when I read in the *Western Mail* a full account from your pen of what had transpired at that meeting."

"But, surely," I remarked, "you must realise that information is to a journalist what public opinion is to a politician – it is the raw material with which he makes his bricks."

"Quite so," remarked the Wizard in ready reply, "and I do not complain of your astuteness on that occasion. As a matter of fact, I admired it, for, as I said at the time, it conclusively proved that the Intelligence Department at the *Western Mail* office displayed far greater perspicacity than the Welsh Liberal members could command. However, there is no need for any subtlety of method on this occasion. You have been good enough to visit me on my birthday, and I am ready to answer, without evasion or mental reservation of any kind, any questions that you may choose to put to me. Let me, however, emphasise the significance of this all-dominating fact: I have attained my 68th birthday, and I am still going strong."

"That is very evident," I remarked with a smile which reflected his own. "But tell me," I continued, "what are your plans for the future?"

"Well," he replied, as his countenance wrinkled afresh into the most whimsical of his smiles, "I would just like to remind you that when Mr Gladstone attained his *sixty-fifth* birthday he retired from the leadership of the Liberal Party on the ground that when a statesman embarks upon the mid-sixties he ought to withdraw from the noise and the dust of the political arena in order to devote the remainder of his days to the contemplation of the world to come. Now, Treorchy, I am already three years older than was the illustrious statesman when he first retired from the Liberal leadership, but can even you, with any stretch of the imagination, picture me retiring from political warfare in order to spend the remainder of my life in a passive contemplation of the world to come?"

"Knowing you as I do," I remarked, "I cannot bring myself to envisage even the possibility of such a step."

"Of course you can't," said the little Wizard in the most triumphant of tones.

"And let me add this," he went on; "There would be far more justification for the contemplation of such a step on my part than there was in the case of Mr Gladstone when he announced his retirement from the Liberal leadership after the general election of 1874. It is quite true that at that election the Liberal Party suffered a heavy defeat, in consequence of which it found itself relegated to the cold and sterile shadows of the Opposition benches. Still, although depleted in its numerical strength in the Commons, the party was united in spirit and in purpose."

"That is certainly more than can be said of it at the present time," I murmured.

"That is perfectly true," he asserted. "In fact," he continued, "it would be futile to close one's eyes to the fact that never in its whole history has the Liberal Party been at so low a figure in its Parliamentary numbers as it is in this Parliament. Its ranks have been literally decimated and its traditional prestige has gone.

"You have doubtless heard of the traveller from Hindustan who arrived at an Eastern city where tattooing constituted a social cult. With the view of being in the fashion, he requested the professional tattooer to tattoo on his back the image of a lion. When, however, the professional proceeded to prick the skin with the needle the traveller inquired in pain what part of the lion he was doing, and when the tattooer replied that he was doing the ear, the traveller commanded him to draw the lion without the ears. The pricking continued, when the traveller inquired in renewed anguish what part was then being done, and when he was informed that it was the tail he insisted that the tail should be omitted. 'What part are you at now?' asked the agonised traveller a few minutes later as the operation was being continued, and when the professional replied that he was portraying the belly of the lion the traveller commanded him to omit that part also. Then, in his despair, the tattooer threw down his needle as he exclaimed, 'Why, even the Almighty could not make a lion without ears, tail and stomach.' And yet," continued the little Wizard, "I am expected to accomplish the impossible with the Liberal Party. It has lost its *heart* as well as its tail. Between ourselves, I sometimes feel that its *stomach* has also gone, and yet I am being held responsible for its emaciated and truncated appearance.

"Although I am the official leader of the party, men like Grey, Runciman, John Simon, and Donald Maclean, who in past days used to urge loyalty to the skipper as the first duty of every member of the party, are deliberately and even sullenly holding aloof from me and publicly flouting my authority. In the circumstances, I should be fully justified in emulating the historic example of Gladstone by throwing up the responsibility of the leadership in order to find leisure for contemplating the glories of the world to come."

"But you are certainly not the man to do that," I observed.

"I certainly am not," was his emphatic reply. "To a man of my temperament, with my passionate love for the fray, 'the world to come' is too remote and intangible to engage my activities. I live for what these eyes can see: this old earth is quite enough for me. And so in spite of the ruptures and cleavages with which the party is riven I mean to stick to its leadership."

"But what about the future?" I inquired, eager for information. "I observe," I continued, "that some of the newspapers have lately been speculating whether you are likely to go to the Right or drift to the Left in that fresh alignment of parties and of policies which the exigencies of the political situation are so palpably bringing about; indeed, one of the most devoted of your henchmen has recently been asking whether *you* can lead into another Promised Land. It is an interesting speculation. It would be interesting to know what in your inmost heart you really believe your future is likely to be. You must surely have cast your own horoscope."

"Of course I have," he replied, "but I must frankly admit that I am an enigma even to myself. I have always believed that he is the wisest mariner who, in view of the fact that the wind bloweth where it listeth, is content to wait to see which way the wind *does* blow before he unfurls his sails. As I may remind you, I was at one time the head of a government which was predominantly composed of Conservatives, and at the present time I am keeping the Socialists in office. Although I have thus boxed the political compass, I can justly claim that I have never lost sight of the *direction* of the wind. Believe me, that is the all-essential factor in political navigation."

"But what about *your* future?" I again inquired.

"Ah, Treorchy," was his reply as his face relapsed afresh into a characteristic smile. "Let me answer your challenging question under cover of a true story. Two shipwrecked sailors were adrift on a raft when one of them, in a spasm of panic, began to offer up prayer, in the course of which he was about to promise to reform his life if only Providence would spare him, when he was suddenly prevented from uttering his vows by the exclamation of his companion, who cried out, 'Hold on a minute. Dinna commit yerself. I think I see land.' And so, Treorchy," continued the little Wizard, as his countenance became corrugated afresh with his quizzical smile, "I can only say in reply to your question that I am not prepared to commit myself *just yet* in regard to my future destiny. I may go to the Right or I may drift to the Left. My decision will be determined by circumstances. In the meantime I must wait until I can discern *where the land lies.*"

*The Western Mail, January 23, 1931*

THE ORDER OF RELEASE.

J M Staniforth's cartoons first appeared in the *Evening Express*, sister paper of *The Western Mail*, in the late 1880s. But from 1893 he produced a daily cartoon for the *Mail*.

*Left:* Staniforth showed a triumph for outraged Welsh sentiment when the Agriculture Board decided that the regimental goat of the Royal Welsh Fusiliers would have to be put down. The *Mail* took up the animal's cause, and it was reprieved. *February 13, 1903.*

# Out of the World.

MISS ABERYSTWYTH: Boo-oo-oo; I want the National Library!

DAME CARDIFF: Hadn't you better wait, dear, until flying machines are a practicability?

When a Government commission decided that Cardiff should have the National Museum, but that the National Library should go to Aberystwyth, the *Mail* mocked the chosen location. The paper said that putting the Library in that absurdly remote site would dissipate the dignity of the Welsh capital, and comparatively few people in Wales would be likely to see it or use it. *March 27, 1905.*

A strong protest was made by *The Western Mail* at a plan to spend £1,000 on the provision of piggeries at the Cardiff Mental Hospital at Whitchurch. *June 1, 1907.*

## The Cardiff Corporation £1,000 Piggery.

Our Artist gives an impression of what it will be like.

The Lunacy Commissioners later advised the Cardiff Asylum Committee to cut the cost of the piggeries by half. *April 16, 1908.*

## A Vanished Dream.

MR. GRUNTER: Dear me; this is awfully disappointing! Why, they're little better than ordinary sties!

CARDIFF CORPORATION: I am very sorry, sir, but I assure you I am not to blame. It was those wretched, parsimonious Lunacy Commissioners who prevented me from providing you with the beautiful palace I had intended.

## The Danger on the Line.

## The Danger Averted.

Sincere and hearty congratulations to the hero of the hour.

Few people were hopeful of a settlement when a national rail strike loomed. *November 6, 1907.*

Lloyd George intervened, brokered peace, and became the man of the hour. *November 7, 1907.*

# GENERAL VIEW of the CEREMONY.

## Archbishop of Canterbury Escorting the Archbishop of Wales to his Throne.

SPECIALLY DRAWN FOR THE WESTERN MAIL BY J. M. STANIFORTH.

Staniforth also produced many atmospheric drawings. This full-page illustration depicted the enthronement of the Archbishop of Wales at Llandrindod Wells following the disestablishment of the Church in Wales. *June 2, 1920.*

**CARDIFF TO-DAY.**
*No Monday morning feeling this week !*

A cartoon by Leslie Illingworth showed the atmosphere of euphoria after Cardiff City won the F A Cup at Wembley in 1927. Illingworth first drew football cartoons for the *Evening Express* before joining *The Western Mail* as a political cartoonist in 1921, shortly after the death of Staniforth, and spent six years with the paper before moving on. He retired in 1968 after 29 years as the political cartoonist of the *Daily Mail. April 25, 1927.*

**AWAITING DEVELOPMENTS.**

J C Walker drew cartoons for *The Western Mail* and the *South Wales Echo* for nearly 40 years until he retired in 1960. Once offered a permanent post on the *News of the World*, he opted to stay in Cardiff because, he said, he did not want to join the London rat-race. *June 27, 1931.*

Reprinted from the

# HISTORY
# ON YOUR DOORSTEP

## Western Mail
AND SOUTH WALES NEWS

BY GEOFFREY EVANS

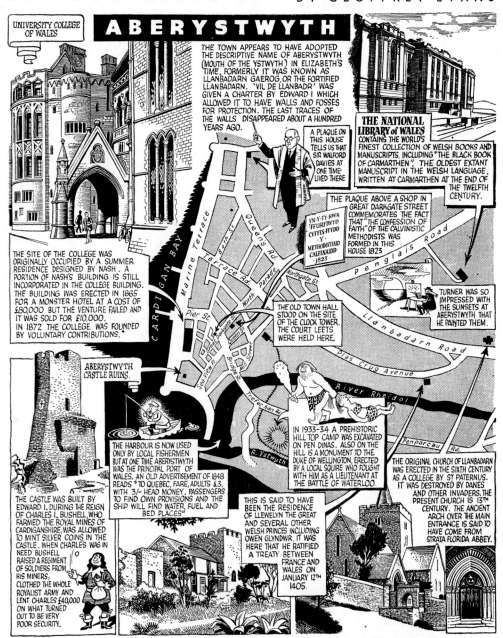

### ABERYSTWYTH

UNIVERSITY COLLEGE OF WALES

THE TOWN APPEARS TO HAVE ADOPTED THE DESCRIPTIVE NAME OF ABERYSTWYTH (MOUTH OF THE YSTWYTH) IN ELIZABETH'S TIME, FORMERLY IT WAS KNOWN AS LLANBADARN GAEROG, OR THE FORTIFIED LLANBADARN. 'VIL DE LLANBADR' WAS GIVEN A CHARTER BY EDWARD I WHICH ALLOWED IT TO HAVE WALLS AND FOSSES FOR PROTECTION. THE LAST TRACES OF THE WALLS DISAPPEARED ABOUT A HUNDRED YEARS AGO.

A PLAQUE ON THIS HOUSE TELLS US THAT SIR WALFORD DAVIES AT ONE TIME LIVED THERE

### THE NATIONAL LIBRARY of WALES
CONTAINS THE WORLD'S FINEST COLLECTION OF WELSH BOOKS AND MANUSCRIPTS, INCLUDING "THE BLACK BOOK OF CARMARTHEN". THE OLDEST EXTANT MANUSCRIPT IN THE WELSH LANGUAGE, WRITTEN AT CARMARTHEN AT THE END OF THE TWELFTH CENTURY.

THE SITE OF THE COLLEGE WAS ORIGINALLY OCCUPIED BY A SUMMER RESIDENCE DESIGNED BY NASH. A PORTION OF NASH'S BUILDING IS STILL INCORPORATED IN THE COLLEGE BUILDING. THE BUILDING WAS ERECTED IN 1865 FOR A MONSTER HOTEL AT A COST OF £80,000 BUT THE VENTURE FAILED AND IT WAS SOLD FOR £10,000. IN 1872 THE COLLEGE WAS FOUNDED BY VOLUNTARY CONTRIBUTIONS.

YN-Y-TY-HWN FFURFIWYD CYFFES-FFYDD Y METHODISTIAID CALFINAIDD 1823

THE PLAQUE ABOVE A SHOP IN GREAT DARKGATE STREET COMMEMORATES THE FACT THAT "THE CONFESSION OF FAITH" OF THE CALVINISTIC METHODISTS WAS FORMED IN THIS HOUSE 1823

TURNER WAS SO IMPRESSED WITH THE SUNSETS AT ABERYSTWYTH THAT HE PAINTED THEM.

THE OLD TOWN HALL STOOD ON THE SITE OF THE CLOCK TOWER. THE COURT LEETS WERE HELD HERE.

CARDIGAN BAY

Marine Terrace · Terrace Rd. · Queens Rd. · Bath St. · North Parade · Northgate St. · Pier St. · Sea View Pl. · Bridge St. · Mill St. · Queens · Trefechan Rd. · Penglais Road · Llanbadarn Road · Plas Crug Avenue · River Rheidol · Penparcau Rd. · R. Ystwyth

ABERYSTWYTH CASTLE RUINS.

THE CASTLE WAS BUILT BY EDWARD I. DURING THE REIGN OF CHARLES I, BUSHELL, WHO FARMED THE ROYAL MINES OF CARDIGANSHIRE, WAS ALLOWED TO MINT SILVER COINS IN THE CASTLE. WHEN CHARLES WAS IN NEED BUSHELL RAISED A REGIMENT OF SOLDIERS FROM HIS MINERS, CLOTHED THE WHOLE ROYALIST ARMY AND LENT CHARLES £40,000 ON WHAT TURNED OUT TO BE VERY POOR SECURITY.

THE HARBOUR IS NOW USED ONLY BY LOCAL FISHERMEN BUT AT ONE TIME ABERYSTWYTH WAS THE PRINCIPAL PORT OF WALES, AN OLD ADVERTISEMENT OF 1848 READS "TO QUEBEC, FARE, ADULTS £3, WITH 3/- HEAD MONEY. PASSENGERS TO FIND OWN PROVISIONS AND THE SHIP WILL FIND WATER, FUEL AND BED PLACES"

IN 1933-34 A PREHISTORIC HILL TOP CAMP WAS EXCAVATED ON PEN DINAS. ALSO ON THE HILL IS A MONUMENT TO THE DUKE OF WELLINGTON, ERECTED BY A LOCAL SQUIRE WHO FOUGHT WITH HIM AS A LIEUTENANT AT THE BATTLE OF WATERLOO.

THIS IS SAID TO HAVE BEEN THE RESIDENCE OF LLEWELYN THE GREAT AND SEVERAL OTHER WELSH PRINCES INCLUDING OWEN GLYNDWR. IT WAS HERE THAT HE RATIFIED A TREATY BETWEEN FRANCE AND WALES ON JANUARY 12TH 1405.

THE ORIGINAL CHURCH OF LLANBADARN WAS ERECTED IN THE SIXTH CENTURY AS A COLLEGE BY ST PATERNUS. IT WAS DESTROYED BY DANES AND OTHER INVADERS. THE PRESENT CHURCH IS 13TH CENTURY. THE ANCIENT ARCH OVER THE MAIN ENTRANCE IS SAID TO HAVE COME FROM STRATA FLORIDA ABBEY.

Apart from his front-page pocket cartoons, Geoffrey Evans produced the *History on Your Doorstep* series, which illustrated towns all over Wales. He said it was the hardest job he had ever done, going from place to place, digging out history, and illustrating events and people on a how-to-get-there map. He once drew three in four days. The series was later reproduced on cards.

# THE ADVENTURES OF TWM SHON CATTI - - - No. 449

Sketches by Geoffrey Evans.
Script by Beryl M. Jones.

| | | | |
|---|---|---|---|
| Furiously did Barty hiss: "I'll clap you all in irons for this!" | But One Ear spat with wicked glee, "And you shall walk the plank!" grinned he. | Twm watched the scene with fuming faces "You dare not take the captain's place!" | "Then fight it out." Now came the cry From every ruffian standing by. |

# THE ADVENTURES OF TWM SHON CATTI - - - No. 450

Script by Beryl M. Jones.
Sketches by Geoffrey Evans.

| | | | |
|---|---|---|---|
| With gleaming sword gripped in each hand, There leering One Ear made a stand. | Twm raised his small sword up on high, While Bob Tail Tim watched closely by. | They darted here and parried there, For One Ear was a swordsman rare. *Another instalment on Monday.* | It seemed as though poor Twm would lose, And Snoozey shivered in his shoes. |

# THE ADVENTURES OF TWM SHON CATTI - - - No. 451

Sketches by Geoffrey Evans.
Script by Beryl M. Jones.

| | | | |
|---|---|---|---|
| Most grim and deadly was the fight As each one strove with all his might. | Then Bob Tail barked with much to do, And Dido screamed, "Quick! Run him through!" | With fresh vigour, Twm gave a dart. His sword an inch from One Ear's heart. | A master One Ear now had found, His two swords clattered to the ground. |

# THE ADVENTURES OF TWM SHON CATTI - - - No. 452

Sketches by Geoffrey Evans.
Script by Beryl M. Jones.

| | | | |
|---|---|---|---|
| "You'll live—since pardon now you seek On bread and water for a week." | "Twm shall be King o' Buccaneers," Deafening now were all their cheers. | Though to escape Twm now did try, They lifted him up shoulder high. | But Twm went up to Barty's side, "Here is your rightful chief," he cried. |

Geoffrey Evans drew cartoons for *The Western Mail* for 38 years until he retired in 1965. He also produced two popular strip-cartoon series — *Twm Shon Catti* (above) and *Lewsin Lloyd*.

# HUMOUR THROUGH THE AGES: By Western Mail cartoonist Dorrien

Dorrien Jones, Kidwelly-born and Welsh-speaking, freelanced for all the national newspapers before joining *The Western Mail* in 1974. His speciality was the pocket cartoon, but he also produced a series of half-page cartoons for rugby-international supplements. This clutch of cartoons entitled *Humour through the Ages* accompanied Ryan Davies's article on Welsh humour in 1976.

*(By Permission of the British Library)*

In an editorial in 1931, *The Western Mail* said that the effects of the great Welsh Revival led by the evangelist Evan Roberts in the years 1904 and 1905 had seemingly passed away, though the memory of it remained. "But there is at least one place in Wales where the spiritual influence, the refining force, which it sent like a flame through the land burns with bright sincerity. Away on the trackless hills of Cardiganshire the people still gather on one day in the year – usually mid-summer day – to hold a prayer meeting in the old Revivalist manner… It is the outcome of the simple, steadfast faith of the men and women of a quarter of a century ago who were caught up by the influence of the Revival and who, through all the changes of the years between, have remained faithful to their vows." The man who was sent to capture an impression of the meeting for *Mail* readers was Clydach-born Sam Jones, who started writing for newspapers when he was at University College, Bangor, and joined *the Mail* as a staff writer in 1927. In 1932, he moved to the BBC in Cardiff, and in 1935 went to the BBC's new regional office at Bangor, where he was responsible for its development and expansion over the years until he retired in 1963.

# An Echo of the Great Revival

## By Sam Jones

TWENTY-SIX years ago, when the sound of the Welsh Revival was still clear in the land, two farmers and a sea captain of North Cardiganshire conceived the idea of an open-air prayer meeting among the hills of their home.

Who would come or whether anyone would come did not concern them much. They had faith, and merely announced along the countryside that on a certain day "Cwrdd Gweddi'r Mynydd" would be held. They even announced that food would be provided.

On that memorable day 120 women were required to provide food for the multitude. And "Cwrdd Gweddi'r Mynydd" has been a great feature of North Cardigan life ever since.

Those three pioneers are still alive. They have attended the meetings ever since, and old age has but added to their enthusiasm and increased their faith. They were present at last Friday's meeting – Daniel Jones, Hafod Las; Richard Jones, Maeneli, and Captain David Rees, Llanon. Captain Rees is a brother of the recently-elected Bishop of Llandaff. The Rev Timothy Rees comes of good Nonconformist stock, and Cardiganshire stock at that.

The morning session of last Friday's meeting was held at the tiny chapel of Bethel, which nestles among the hills some 10 miles from Aberystwyth. This was in the nature of a preparation for the great events of afternoon and evening.

We climbed countless hills as we drove to Bethel on Friday morning. The white-ribboned road meandered in and out of the green fields, topped many a ridge and plunged into numerous steep little valleys. Bethel was reached, and as we approached the tiny building there came the familiar strains of that delightful old hymn tune "Llydaw," and on the morning air were borne the words that have inspired Welsh gatherings all over the world:

O! tyred Iôr Tragwyddol,
Mae ynot Ti dy Hun,
Fwy moroedd o drugaredd
Nag a feddyliodd dyn...

The stern, square little chapel was soon full. Cars had brought visitors from distant parts, but the inhabitants of the countryside, like John the Baptist of old, had tramped all the way. How had those old fellows and old ladies negotiated the hundred and one hills?

How can that morning's meeting be explained to the uninitiated? A prayer meeting? Yes, it was that – and more. There was singing, in plenty, and also a "Seiat". That last word is difficult to surmount. A confessional? A recounting of experiences? It is all that and more, and one is forced back to the original word, so peculiarly Welsh – "Seiat".

There was no order or system at this meeting, and yet it was ever so orderly. An old fellow – 80, if he is a day – stands there and prays. His body is bent with toil, his face is furrowed, his hands are gnarled, and he speaks of strange experiences with an exultation torrential in its eloquence and soul-stirring in its emotion.

An old lady in the corner, dressed in a fashion as old, if not older, than her years, offers up prayer. Her high-pitched, sing-song voice rings clear in the morning air, and her deep-rooted convictions, expressed in startlingly eloquent language, move her hearers to loud approbation and acclamation. And what English word can convey the meaning of "porthi"!

Now a girl in her early 20s speaks, her face aglow with exultation. And then comes a strange note. "Even though I've lost my mother tongue I've not lost the faith of my mother!" and the accent of London strikes a startling and well-nigh alien note in that peculiarly Welsh atmosphere.

Many took part in that morning's meeting; the women, curiously enough, were easily in the majority – and what eloquence was theirs! The narrow dialect of the Rhondda Valley cut across the broader Cardigan speech, and the soft burr of Carmarthenshire also intimated the wide area from which that congregation was drawn.

Great emotional heights were reached, the bursts of song were full-throated and hearty, and I, who am too young to remember that amazing Revival of the early part of the century, obtained an insight into the astonishing religious emotion that swept our country in those days. It has to be experienced to be understood.

How changed the scene that afternoon! On the slopes of Pant-y-Gwair a crude platform had been built – a couple of farm wagons and a few planks. A steep mountain towered above our heads, and over the brow of the hill lay the lovely mountain lake – Llyn Eiddwen. The land swept in a wide vista to the broad valley below.

Llanon and Llanrhystyd lay in the distance and a range of low-lying hills topped the distant and misty horizon.

High up on the breast of the hill the congregation clustered – many hundreds; and from all points of the compass came small groups, down the hillsides, up from the valley, to swell that strange congregation.

Could any words better describe "Cwrdd Gweddi'r Mynydd" than the words of one of the hymns sung that afternoon:-

*Mae'r Jiwbil dragwyddol yn awr wrth y drws,*
*Fe gododd yr heulwen, ni gawsom y tlws,*
*Daw gogledd a dwyrain, gorllewin a de,*
*Yn lluoedd i foli Tywysog y Ne'.*

Nature was at her best and a warm sun was tempered by the sweet mountain breeze. A reading from the Scriptures (Joel ii.), a hymn, and again the meeting was open to whosoever was moved to take part. The older folk – and how old many of them were! – gathered at the foot of the improvised pulpit, all dressed in sombre black and in fashions that spoke of another age. The higher one looked up the hillside the brighter the dresses, until the eye reached the uppermost fringes, where knots of brightly garbed little children shared the curiosity of an occasional sheepdog at this amazing gathering.

There were many eager to take part in the meeting, and women were again prominent. Some amazing experiences were related, and well-nigh each speaker had a strange tale. Many of the speakers and those who took part in prayer might be, according to our standards, badly educated, but what an amazing native culture they revealed! Pithy and startlingly appropriate quotations from the Bible came readily to the lips, extracts of hymns were recited with telling effect, all bespoke a natural wit and culture of which the nation may well be proud. But, what is more, they possessed a Faith that our age is but blindly seeking for.

One old lady, so humbly dressed, and bearing the marks of a long and arduous life, thrashed the assembly into enthusiasm with a peroration that one has seldom heard on public platform or pulpit. "*Ches i 'run diwrnod o ysgol erioed,*" she said, with the tears streaming down her rugged features, "*ond ysgol Iesu Grist!*" She had learned to read her Bible in her mother and, it is certain, her only tongue. She quoted verse after verse, recited the hymns of Pantycelyn and spoke with an eloquence racy of the soil. That was a memorable address, and from one of the humblest of that humble gathering.

Well into the afternoon the meeting lasted, and figure after figure stood on the crude platform or spoke from amongst the assembly, and no pen on earth could give a faithful record of the strange, emotional stirrings roused or brush paint in true colours the ecstasy those simple, sincere people experienced in that strange meeting in "Cwrdd y Mynydd" on the slopes of Pant-y-Gwair.

An even larger assembly gathered for the evening meeting. We stood on the upper reaches of the gathering, and looked down upon the assembly, which stretched right away into the hollow below. Now snatches of prayer, delivered in the sing-song manner peculiar to the Welsh people perhaps, would reach us, scraps of "confessional" couched in oratorical terms, and then the swelling notes of a hymn that swayed the multitudes of the Revival of 1904. Sheep wandered over the hillside unperturbed. A sheepdog with lolling tongue waited patiently for its master, and figures could still be seen in the dim distance making for this Seion of the hills.

It was a matter of very livelihood for those farming folk to tear themselves away from crops badly needing attention in these rare fine days. But they did it that they might praise their Maker among the lonely hills, under the canopy of Heaven.

We are a strange people, and even if "Cwrdd Gweddi'r Mynydd" is but an echo of a Revival of years ago, among those hills the echo is still marked and clear.

*The Western Mail, June 29, 1931*

On March 1st, 1932 *The Western Mail* reported that Mr Ormsby-Gore, the Commissioner of Works, had refused to allow the Red Dragon to fly from the Eagle Tower (the highest) at Caernarfon Castle on St David's Day. On the day, the Union Jack was hauled down and the Red Dragon nailed to the mast. The Dragon was removed by officials, but it was then flown from the Eastern Tower by Bangor students, who again hauled down the Union Jack from the Eagle Tower and tore it up in Castle Square. Mr Ormsby-Gore later ruled that the Union Jack and the Red Dragon should fly from the Eagle Tower on separate and equal masts on St David's Day and the King's Birthday. Reports and editorials tell the story…

# The Red Dragon and the Eagle Tower

## From Our Own Correspondent

LONDON, Monday

IT IS felt to be a pity that Mr Ormsby-Gore, the First Commissioner of Works, has not seen proper to relax the hard and fast official rules concerning the flying of the Welsh Dragon flag from the Eagle Tower of Caernarvon Castle. If the Welsh flag were given the place of honour for only one day – the National Saint's Day – in the year it would be an appropriate recognition of national sentiment and it would have outraged no principle.

There is naturally a good deal of resentment at what looks more like a piece of official stupidity than anything else, for no one believes that any affront to Wales is intended, but now that a protest has been made, it is not likely that much more will be heard of the matter – this year at any rate.

Several ardent Welshmen approached the Office of Works today to see if anything could be done. Sir William Cope, Bart, who, although no longer in the House of Commons still takes an active interest in Welsh affairs and carries on many of the duties formerly assigned to him as Whip for the Welsh Conservatives, got early into touch with Mr Ormsby-Gore, who gave him the same information as he afterwards gave to the House of Commons when questioned on the matter.

In the House of Commons today, Mr Hopkin Morris (L. Cardigan) asked the First Commissioner of Works a private notice question whether the "Red Dragon" was to be flown from Caernarvon Castle tomorrow (St David's Day) and what were the rules governing the flying of flags from Royal castles?

Mr Ormsby-Gore said the answer to the first part of the question was in the affirmative. Regarding the latter part, castles appertaining to the Crown, not in the personal occupation of his Majesty, followed the normal rule of all Government buildings, namely that the Union Jack only was flown on a specified list of days which did not include any of the National Saints' days. Exceptions to the general rule had been made, however, in certain instances, of which Caernarvon Castle was one. Since 1922 the Union Jack had been flown on the Western Tower and the Welsh Dragon flag on one of the Eastern Towers on St David's Day. He was not proposing any change in the matter.

*The Western Mail, March 1, 1932*

DRAMATIC incidents marked St David's Day at Caernarvon. The Union Jack, in accordance with custom, was hoisted in the morning on the Eagle Tower of the Castle and the Red Dragon on the Eastern Tower.

When the Union Jack was seen floating over the Eagle Tower a number of people who had regarded the refusal of the Office of Works to accede to the request to fly the Welsh flag on the tower as a slur on Wales decided to take action.

The organiser of the Caernarvon Branch of the Welsh Nationalist Party and a number of members of the party proceeded to the castle and climbed the Eagle Tower. Despite the fact that the wind was blowing at almost gale force, they succeeded in hauling down the Union Jack and nailing the Red Dragon to the standard.

While they were engaged at the top of the tower a crowd of people had gathered in the square facing the castle, and cheered them continuously.

When officials of the castle discovered what was happening they decided immediately to restore the Union Jack. The gates of the castle were so quickly closed that members of the Welsh Nationalist Party were shut in. When they asked to be allowed to go out the gates were promptly opened.

It was not long before the Union Jack was back over the Eagle Tower, while the Red Dragon was restored to the Eastern Tower.

The second incident at Caernarvon Castle occurred as a result of a visit paid to the town by a party of 30 or 40 college students from Bangor.

The students passed through the turnstiles of the castle as ordinary visitors, climbed the stone steps to the Eagle Tower, and carried away the Union Jack.

They carried it first of all to the office of the Welsh Nationalist Party, and subsequently took it to the Castle Square, where the chairman of the Bangor branch, who was carried shoulder-high, addressed his fellow-members and a group of the general public. He protested against the insult offered to the Welsh flag and to the Welsh nationality that morning.

The students then took up the Union Jack and tore it to pieces amid much shouting and singing of *Land of My Fathers*.

A number of ex-servicemen looked on with evident displeasure at the treatment given to the Union Jack, and at one time it seemed likely that a conflict would ensue between the two sections.

*The Western Mail, March 2, 1932*

I T IS a far cry from the red-tape puerilities of Mr Ormsby-Gore to the acts of wantonness and profanation which took place at Caernarvon Castle yesterday, and there is no reasonable connection between the two. Welshmen with any regard for self-respect and any desire for the respect of others would have been content to tolerate the former in the hope that ere long the Office of Works would find some better basis of action than the worship of precedent, or at least acquire a more intelligible habit of reasoning when called upon to explain or justify its conduct. The pressure of sane public opinion ought to tell in the long run; the only danger comes from the conduct of the less reputable and less responsible elements. Stupidities such as those perpetrated at Caernarvon yesterday would ruin the best of causes. Two sets of mischief-makers visited the castle in the course of the day – a number of members of the extremist and irresponsible Welsh Nationalist Party, who took down the Union Jack from the Eagle Tower and replaced it with the Welsh Dragon, and later, members of the University College at Bangor, who took down the replaced Union Jack, ran up the Welsh Dragon in its place and then tore the former to tatters.

To every patriot the national flag is a sacred emblem of nationhood and loyalty, an insult to which must be avenged instantly and without measure, and it was a pity that when these shameful incidents occurred at Caernarvon yesterday nobody felt called upon to administer suitable chastisement to those who had defiled the national emblem. It is a very awkward thing to happen – awkward for the Dewi Sant celebrations, for the Welsh Nationalist Party, and for the Bangor College. The Nationalist party may be beyond hope and so also may be the students, but will not the college do something to clear its reputation?

*The Western Mail, March 2, 1932*


THE OFFICE OF WORKS has made a concession to Welsh sentiment with regard to the flying of the Red Dragon from the Eagle Tower at Caernarvon Castle on St David's Day.

The decision was conveyed in a letter from Mr Ormsby-Gore, First Commissioner of Works, to the Mayor of Caernarvon (Mr D Elliot Alves).

The final letter of Mr Ormsby-Gore is as follows:

"I feel I ought to write to you in regard to the incidents at the Royal Castle of Caernarvon on March 1.

"The question of flying the Welsh Dragon at Caernarvon Castle was first raised by the town clerk of Caernarfon in 1913. A reply was sent that some hesitation was felt in adopting the suggestion, as the Office of Works were advised that the Dragon was strictly speaking a badge and not the Welsh national flag.

"The matter received some publicity locally as a result of which, in the following year, the town-clerk addressed himself to Mr Lloyd George, who was the Chancellor and Constable of the Castle.

"The question was referred first of all to the Heralds' College, who endorsed the fact that there was no national flag for Wales other than the flag of the Union, commonly termed the Union Jack, and that under the Order in Council of November 5, 1900, it was clear that the flag of the Union was the only flag which should be flown at Caernarvon Castle unless the Sovereign was within its walls.

"The subject was discussed in the Caernarvon Town Council, when apparently some dispute took place as to whether or not the Red Dragon was the national flag of Wales. At this stage I myself, then a private member for a Welsh constituency, raised the matter in Parliament without success.

"The question was then dropped, and though again raised in 1916, was not further pursued until 1922, when your predecessor in the mayoralty of Caernarvon, Mr Richards, wrote to Lord Crawford, then First Commissioner, suggesting that the Union Jack should be allowed to fly on the present flagstaff, but that the Dragon flag should be flown on a temporary flagstaff on another turret. Lord Crawford referred the matter to Mr Lloyd George, who, in his capacity both as Prime Minister and Constable of the Castle, submitted it to the King.

"The King approved the proposal, and Mr Richards, the mayor who hoisted the flag, wrote that the King's gesture had given great satisfaction to all the townspeople, and that he desired to place on record their great appreciation of Lord Crawford's action.

"Since then the Welsh Dragon has been flown regularly on St David's Day, and we received no intimation that the wishes of the people of Caernarvon were not met until last Wednesday, when a letter was received from Mr Lloyd George's private secretary.

"To this letter a reply was sent, explaining the Department's general policy in regard to the flying of flags on days other than those authorised by the King. That letter, unfortunately, did not take account of the fact that an exceptional arrangement already existed. When the matter was referred to me on February 29 I felt that I had no alternative but to decide that the practice approved in 1922 should be followed, partly because it was obviously impossible to recommend an alteration to the King in the time available and, partly, because we had received no formal representations from any properly constituted body, or from the Constable of the Castle, on which I could put any recommendation to the King.

"St David's Day is not a day appointed for the flying of flags on Government buildings, and as Caernarvon Castle is already treated exceptionally to this extent I, personally, see no reason why, as the flying of any flag on that day is already irregular, the Red Dragon should not take the place of the Union Jack on the Eagle Tower provided that the Union Jack is also flown on the Watchman's Tower on that day, or, if preferred, both flags could fly from different masts on the Eagle Tower.

"If the Caernarvon Town Council would like this to be done, and would make representations to this effect, I should be glad to consider their suggestion and make the necessary submission to the King."

*The Western Mail, March 4, 1932*

GRACIOUSLY ignoring the scandalous episode of the destruction of the Union Jack at Caernarvon on Tuesday and the truculence of the Welsh Nationalist Party. Mr Ormsby-Gore, the First Commissioner of Works, has come to a favourable decision as the flying of the Red Dragon at Caernarvon Castle on St David's Day. The circumstances, apparently, still present some difficulty to the official mind, for the pundits of Heralds' College are still of the opinion that the Red Dragon flag of Wales has no official existence, and Mr Ormsby-Gore appears to have been enabled to come to his present decision on the basis of the fact that an irregular practice has already managed to establish itself. It would probably be found – Heralds' College notwithstanding – that a great many established practices have an unofficial and even irregular origin, so the irregular origin to which Mr Ormsby-Gore alludes may well be overlooked.

The Red Dragon may have been "strictly speaking a badge and not the Welsh national flag" and "the Flag of Union, commonly called the Union Jack" will always be regarded with honour in Wales except perhaps by a minority of irresponsible and disorderly students, but the former is popularly and universally regarded as the national flag, and it will doubtless ere long enjoy an official standing. St David's Day seems to suffer under a reproach similar to the Red Dragon; it is not, we are informed, an official day of rejoicing on which banners may be hung over the outer walls, but even the official mind is susceptible of enlightenment if the lesson be "drilled into it" with sufficient persistence, and the double recognition may presently be forthcoming.

*The Western Mail, March 4, 1932*

Gareth Jones, born in Barry, was a brilliant student of languages, gaining a first from University College, Aberystwyth, and firsts in French, German and Russian at Trinity College, Cambridge. He became David Lloyd George's foreign affairs secretary in 1930, and three years later joined *The Western Mail*. A gifted writer, he quickly became a respected member of the editorial staff, and travelled widely in Europe as the continent began to move towards war once again. The highest pinnacles of journalistic achievement were in sight when his life was cut tragically short in 1935, just before his 30th birthday. Kidnapped and held to ransom by bandits in Mongolia, he was shot by them when police tried to rescue him. A collection of some of the articles he wrote for *The Western Mail* was published under the title *In Search of News* in 1938.

# With Hitler across Germany

## By Gareth Jones

In Hitler's Aeroplane, Three o'clock Thursday Afternoon,
February 23.

IF THIS aeroplane should crash the whole history of Europe would be changed. For a few feet away sits Adolf Hitler, Chancellor of Germany and leader of the most volcanic nationalist awakening which the world has seen. Six thousand feet beneath us, hidden by a sea of rolling white clouds, is the land which he has roused to a frenzy. We are rushing along at a speed of 142 miles per hour from Berlin to Frankfurt-on-Main, where Hitler is to begin his lightning election campaign.

The occupants of the aeroplane are, indeed, a mass of human dynamite. I can see Hitler studying the map and then reading a number of blue reports. He does not look impressive. When his car arrived on the airfield about half an hour ago and he stepped out, a slight figure in a shapeless black hat, wearing a light mackintosh, and when he raised his arm flabbily to greet those who had assembled to see him, I was mystified.

How had this ordinary-looking man succeeded in becoming deified by fourteen million people? He was more natural and less of a poseur than I had expected; there was something boyish about him as he saw a new motor-car and immediately displayed a great interest in it. He shook hands with the Nazi chiefs and with those others of us who were to fly with him in the famous "Richthofen," the fastest and most powerful three-motored aeroplane in Germany.

His handshake was firm, but his large, outstanding eyes seemed emotionless as he greeted me. Standing around in the snow were members of his bodyguard in their black uniform with silver brocade. On their hats there is a silver skull and crossbones, the cavities of the eyes in the skull being bright red.

I was introduced to these, the élite of the Nazi troops, and then to a plump, laughing man, Captain Bauer, Hitler's pilot, the war-time flying hero. We then entered the great aeroplane and now we sit far above the clouds.

Behind Hitler sits a little man who laughs all the time. He has a narrow Iberian head and brown eyes which twinkle with wit and intelligence. He looks like the dark, small, narrow-headed, sharp Welsh type which is so often found in the Glamorgan valleys. This is Dr Goebbels, a Rhinelander, the brain of the National-Socialist Party and, after Hitler, its most emotional speaker. His is a name to remember, for he will play a big part in the future.

To Hitler's left sits a massive, fair-haired man besides whom Hitler looks dwarf-like. This is Hitler's adjutant. The others in the aeroplane are secretaries, and there are five members of Hitler's bodyguard in their black and silver uniforms with red swastika badges. The only two non-Nazis are another newspaper correspondent and myself and we are the first foreign observers to be invited by Hitler since he became Chancellor to accompany him on a flight.

Next to me sits a scarred, well-built member of the bodyguard, who has a sense of humour and keeps ragging another member who is sleeping. He has already offered me two boiled eggs, two bags of chocolate, an apple and biscuits. There is nothing hard and Prussian about my fellow-passengers. They could not be more friendly and polite, even if I were a red-hot Nazi myself.

The chief of the bodyguard is now drinking to my health in soda-water and grinning. He shows me his silver badge, which he wears on his breast and which shows that he has been a follower of Hitler for thirteen years. He is obviously proud of his uniform and points out his photograph to me in a weekly illustrated newspaper.

The clouds underneath have now cleared, and we can see the Elbe winding below. Hitler is now asleep. The sun is shining upon the engine to the left. I take up a Nazi newspaper and I read: "Tomorrow night Goebbels and Prince August Wilhelm are speaking in the Sport Palace in Berlin."

Prince August Wilhelm, the son of the Kaiser! What relations are there, I wonder, between the Monarchists and Hitler? I recall an item of information which I picked up in Berlin. The Kaiserin had come to Berlin to win over Hitler. A meeting was arranged in a salon. Hitler kept the Empress waiting in the drawing-room twenty minutes while he chatted in the corridor outside. At last they met, but the Empress failed in her mission, and Hitler is not yet converted to Monarchism.

Another item is: "Fifty thousand people hear Dr Goebbels in Hanover." I look at the vivacious little man and see that he is reading Wilson's Fourteen Points. His smile has disappeared, and his chin is determined. He looks as if he were burning to avenge what the Nazis call the betrayal of 1918. I recall the Nazi slogan: "Retribution."

A notice, "In Memoriam," which I next read in the Nazi paper then gives a clue to the emotion which has been let loose in Germany. Beneath the photograph, surrounded by a thick black line, of a handsome young boy in a Nazi uniform I read: "The father of this Storm Troop man, Gerhard Schlemminger, was one of the two million who fell for Germany. The wife he left behind bravely went along her path of duty and educated her son to be a sincere, honourable German citizen in the decadent post-war days of confusion and vice. But Gerhard, who gave all his energy for the freeing of Germany, was yesterday struck dead by a murderous Bolshevik bullet."

This throws a light upon the political passions in Germany. I look again at Hitler. He and his followers feel that the hundreds of Nazis, such as this young boy, who have died in street battles must be avenged, and they will be ruthless in crushing Communist opposition.

Hitler is now turning and smiling to his adjutant. He looks mild. Can this be the ruthless enemy of Bolshevism? It puzzles me.

We are now descending, however. Frankfurt is beneath us. A crowd is gathered below. Thousands of faces look up at us. We make a smooth landing. Nazi leaders, some in brown, some in black and silver, all with a red swastika arm-band, await their chief. Hitler steps out of the aeroplane. But he is now a man spiritually transformed. His eyes have a certain fixed purpose. Here is a different Hitler.

There are two Hitlers – the natural boyish Hitler, and the Hitler who is inspired by a tremendous national force, a great Hitler. It is the second Hitler who has stirred Germany to an awakening.

*The Western Mail, February 28, 1933*

Madame Clara Novello-Davies, mother of the Welsh composer, actor and playwright Ivor Novello, became famous in her own right when the choir she had trained swept to victory in the Chicago World Fair in 1893. She was always grateful for the help of *The Western Mail*, which had helped to fund the choir's trip. Many more triumphs followed, and her popularity grew, particularly when she organised concerts to raise funds for the troops during World War I. Ivor Novello won fame at the same time for composing the tune of *Keep the Home Fires Burning*, and went on to write a series of successful plays and musicals, including *Careless Rapture* and *King's Rhapsody*. Madame Clara died in 1943, her son in 1951.

# A Life of Many Triumphs

## By Glyn Roberts

A SHORT, rubicund woman, with snowy white hair and a comprehensive smile will take the chair at one of this week's gatherings of the National Eisteddfod. It will be the first time she has ever done so, although now for more than forty years she has been an outstanding figure in the musical and even the national life of Wales. It is Madame Clara Novello-Davies, who is, perhaps, the most famous Welsh woman alive, and who is certainly one of the greatest personalities Wales has ever exported to a grateful world.

Those who hear her address a representative gathering of Welsh people this week, and those who see her at Neath before and after her particular hour of prominence, will see a woman who, since first she became an international celebrity in 1893, has made and consolidated with every passing year a reputation approached by no one else. Today there are many who regard Madame Clara Novello-Davies as the greatest teacher of voice production in the world.

Scores of Welsh singers have adopted her system of "tonal physicals", that breathing technique which is the basis of her teaching. Actors and singers all over the world have improved their voices immeasurably – and even their health – by taking it up. Enrico Caruso, the possessor of the most astonishing voice on record, believed in it; many of the most famous screen stars of Hollywood have been able to face the advent of sound without the trepidation their original voices encouraged. The system gave them perfect microphone voices.

When that actress of genius, the late Jeanne Eagels, was shown the terrifically exhausting part she was to act on the New York stage in Somerset Maugham's *Rain* – as Sadie Thompson – she went to Madam Clara Novello-Davies, who was at that time enthroned in New York. Knowing that her voice, as it then was, could stand only so much and no more, she was worried. So she studied under the Welsh magician.

Nearly two years later, when *Rain* had broken all records for a New York run, and was still going strong, Miss Eagels wrote a letter to her teacher. It said: "How right your method must be, when I can, for three hours, talk, scream, yell, and sing in the apparently throaty voice of Sadie, when in reality I only use the throat to liberate the deep sounds I produce with the muscle."

Even Freddie Welsh, one of Wales's greatest boxers, found her system invaluable. In a fight in New York, in which he was defending his world's light-weight championship, he received a staggering punch to the solar plexus, which would have knocked out many much heavier men. The crowd thought the fight was over. Welsh rested for a few seconds on one knee; when he arose he nodded gratefully to a smiling woman in the audience. The rest of the crowd did not understand. Tonal physicals had scored another triumph!

The story of Madame Clara Novello-Davies's astonishing achievement in training a choir and inspiring it to victory in the "World's Championship" at the Chicago World Fair in 1893 has been told and re-told so often to Welsh readers that I need not give it here. She has never ceased to thank the Editor of the *Western Mail* at that time, Mr Lascelles Carr, for making it possible for her to go. He guaranteed most of the choir's expenses. "A young reporter" she says, "raised seven hundred pounds in two days. He gave every ounce of energy and more devoted service than I ever hoped to command. I like to think that he received his reward as the years went by, for that young reporter is now Sir William Davies, the successor to Lascelles Carr."

From the triumph at Chicago, which made her name world-famous, this dynamic little woman went from one amazing experience to another. At once they arranged for a ten weeks' tour of the United States. They returned, to be given a civic welcome at Southampton.

Queen Victoria commanded a performance at Windsor. The choir was consumed with nervousness, but the Queen wept with emotion, presented the young conductor with a magnificent pendant and added the prefix "Royal" to the choir's name.

There followed an appearance at the enormous Trocadéro in Paris. Here again the Welsh choir succeeded, to receive a tremendous ovation. Saint-Saëns made his way determinedly to the platform crying, "I must kiss that magnificent right arm!" and insisted on doing so. Then he crowned its owner with gold laurel leaves, and said: "Your teaching is perfect, your conducting magical!"

Then came miscellaneous triumphs in America, one of the most remarkable being the performance – Madame Novello-Davies directing – of the great Choir of One Thousand Voices in the Metropolitan Opera House, with Alda and Caruso as soloists.

Long spells in New York in the boom years took this remarkable teacher away from Britain. But she always came back. Her theories have aroused enthusiasm in hospitals and attracted great doctors and Cabinet Ministers. Today, more than ever, they monopolise her attention.

But she continues to make spectacular appearances before the public she has delighted for so long. There have been Jubilee celebrations at Cardiff, another Royal Command performance before King George V and the British Singers' Symphony, a remarkable achievement in her seventieth year.

These were all great achievements. But to her nothing has been so wonderful as being "the one and only mother" – her own phrase – of Ivor Novello, one of the most brilliant young men of this generation. The story of Ivor as a baby, and her fears that he would grow into another "Uncle Ebenezer", will provide one of the most amusing chapters in the delightful memoirs which Madame Novello-Davies is at last seriously preparing for the public. The mother's affection was not wasted, for no mother can ever have had a better son than this young man who was destined to become the idol of so many women. It is a very rare thing to see Ivor Novello appear in public without his mother; not a day passes without him visiting or ringing her up.

They are an amazing pair, and the story of their lives and the unexpected turns they have taken – they, the last of a long line of Nonconformist ministers and local musicians – is one of the most romantic of modern Wales. And Madame Clara Novello-Davies has never ceased to surprise and delight Wales. May she long continue to do so!

*The Western Mail, August 7, 1934*

On a summer's night in 1934, American press baron William Randolph Hearst allowed the Gorsedd of Bards to use St Donat's Castle to hold a pageant and feast with a 14th century theme. Among the bards was Cynan (the Rev Albert Evans-Jones), who had already won the National Eisteddfod Crown on three occasions and the Chair once, and was twice to become Archdruid. It was a memorable occasion, as was shown in this report he wrote for *The Western Mail...*

# A Bardic Pageant

## By Cynan

St Donat's Castle,
Thursday Night

*The whiten bread and barlie ale*
*Here is in wondrous store,*
*And fatted flesh of sheepe and kine.*
*No land produceth more.*

S O SANG Sir John Stradling of St Donat's Castle in 1620, as he thought of the fruitfulness of his fair Glamorgan demesne – a fruitfulness that enabled the House of Stradling ever to entertain the bard and the musician right lavishly in their ancient castle hall, and to afford generous patronage to Cymric art and culture.

Of Norman stock the family might be on the one side, holding no better claim to St Donat's and its manors than the title wrested by William de Esterling's raiding sword and preserved by the beetling walls of his craggy fortress, overlooking the British Channel; but Welsh it had grown in sympathy, and indeed in blood on the distaff side, ever since the fourth generation, when Sir Robert Stradling married Hawisia, daughter of Sir Hugh Bryn, the lawful Welsh heiress.

From that day till the death of the last of their line in 1738 the Stradlings successively continued to enrol their names as Welshmen and warm patrons of Welsh literature.

Whoever first conceived the idea of this full-dress state visit of the Gorsedd to St Donat's Castle must have been gifted with a vivid sense of the past, the sort of imagination that hears the very stone cry out of the wall. I will make a shrewd guess that the first suggestion came from Mr Lloyd George's fertile brain, that it met with a most generous and enthusiastic response from our host, Mr W R Hearst, the present castellan, and that the wonderful pageantesque possibilities of such an occasion were fully marshalled and developed by Capt Crawshay, the Herald Bard.

As we left Neath this evening I wondered what old Iolo Morganwg would have said to this Gorsedd invasion of his country. Did he ever imagine in his wildest dreams that the "neo-Druidic" movement, which originated with him, would in a little over a century muster bards from the North, South, East and West to pay tribute to the Glamorgan tradition?

The Gorsedd of Bards that passed through Iolo's country this evening is a Gorsedd that lays no claim to Druidic antiquity, but it does claim that this erratic genius and mystic has outlined for our Eisteddfod a national ritual, so dramatic and effective in its symbolism that even the bitterest critics of the Gorsedd have been gladly chaired or crowned under the Great Sword of Peace "yn ol braint a defawd."

Apart from the valuable services rendered by its literary and musical boards and its council, I believe the Gorsedd's popular appeal today is due to its being regarded as the National Pageant of Wales. Which is why those of us who have its success at heart cannot rest contented until all slackness and slovenliness have been cast out of its ceremonies, and it becomes a truly dignified symbol of the spirit of a nation.

Here at St Donat's Castle, at all events, the Herald Bard had at last been given his opportunity to stage that splendid bardic pageant of which some of us dream – a Gorsedd meeting of pure dramatic ceremonial, not encumbered by the usual tedious speech-making.

As our conveyances approached Nash Point I saw for the first time that hoary pile of St Donat's rising in solitary grandeur above the coastline.

It is one of the few old castles in Wales which have never been left untenanted from the Norman period. In the evening mists I pictured to myself a procession of its distinguished castellans down the ages sallying forth through the main gateway with their retainers to bid us welcome. Norman pennons mingled with Cavalier plumes and Plantagenet chain-mail with Tudor velvet.

Conspicuous amid the brilliant throng were that fourteenth-century Sir Edward Stradling and his son Sir William, both bearing the red-cross insignia of the Knights of the Holy Sepulchre. Sir Harry Stradling, too, who, having made a pilgrimage to Rome and Jerusalem scatheless, had the misfortune to be captured while crossing the Severn by the Breton pirate Colin Dolphin, who held him to ransom for £1,400.

Most interesting of them all to me was a noble figure in Elizabethan doublet and ruff, that other Sir Edward Stradling, traveller, scholar, and patron of scholars, the ablest and most eminent of his line.

I remembered the famous library of ancient Welsh manuscripts which he had built up at St Donat's, and I thought of his friendship with Dr Sion Dafydd Rhys, who called him his "Maecenas."

It was probably in this very castle that he persuaded that old "Cymro of Llanfaethlu and Doctor of Siena" to write his famous "Gramadeg." It was certainly he who paid the whole cost of its publication in 1592 and arranged for several copies to be distributed amongst the gentry "for the encouragement of their study of the Welsh language."

No wonder that Rhys dedicated his great work to this patriotic friend, who persuaded him to render such signal service to that ancient tongue, so dear to them both.

Truly we were on holy ground; and I was not surprised to see that dignified ecclesiastical ghosts walked in that procession, too, by virtue of their association with this historic site – from the blessed St Donatus, founder of the little church in the narrow dell below, to the learned Archbishop Usher, who, after the Battle of Naseby in 1645 found in a little room at St Donat's Castle a refuge and a hermitage for a year to write his book on "The Antiquities of the British Church."

Slowly the ghostly procession seemed to wend its way towards us, and now the Gorsedd procession, looking hardly less ghostly in flowing robes in the twilight, led by the Archdruid and the Herald Bard, went forth to salute the past.

As we approached the castle walls, however, I found them guarded, not by ghosts but by stalwart men-at-arms of flesh and blood, and very formidable they looked in their mediaeval armour. An alarum of trumpets from the main gateway, and the Herald Bard's voice responded in Welsh to their challenge thus:

"Ho there. Is there a porter?"

"Yes. Why askest thou?" came the reply in Norman French from the porter in the keep above (Professor Morgan Watkin, author of this scenario).

"Open the gate!"

"I will not open. None may enter here save the king's sons or bards plying their craft."

"We are travelling bards and we bring song with us."

"Where do you travel?"

"We go to our people's Eisteddfod at Neath. I am Sieffre o Gyfarthfa and here is the Chief Bard Gwili wearing his chaplet and a company of the Bards of the Isle of Britain with him."

"Perchance ye be warriors disguised as bards. Halt while I report to the castellan!"

A short interval and the porter returned with his master's assurance of welcome, after the Archdruid had removed his chaplet to show that he was in truth the Chief Bard and that we all came in peace.

The portcullis was raised and the Gorsedd entered to find a warm Welsh welcome in the court – not from a Norman baron, but from their fellow-bard, Llwyd o Wynedd (Mr D Lloyd George), in Gorsedd robes, and the ladies of his family in charming mediaeval costume.

Followed such a sumptuous banquet as the bards of old loved to describe:

Pysgod, adar mewn bara,
Pasteiod, hen ddiod dda,
Cig ceirw o law cog cywrain...

In short, an unforgettable State meal in the dining-hall, surrounded by priceless tapestry and Gothic stone screens, through which strains of sweet music came from concealed harps and madrigal singers.

The waiters and the guards posted round the hall were all in period costume, and played their parts in this pageant of pageants with gusto, but the life and soul of this lively entertainment of song and dance was the Welsh jester (Gunstone), whose brilliant mimicking was nothing short of the very genius of comedy.

The dinner closed with bardic addresses to Llwyd o Wynedd by Edgar Phillips, Crwys, and others.

But in the outer court more pageantry was yet to come – the Cwmavon choir forming a processional of monks filing through the dusk with their torches chanting the Nunc Dimittis, then the birds of dawn singing in the trees as the scene changed to 1934, when a party of miners moved home from the night shift, their spirits undimmed by adversity, and flaming as courageously as the torch of faith carried by the ancient monks.

Here, indeed, was a pageant that will remain in the imagination of all who were privileged to witness it. A pageant linking the story of the Wales that was with the hope of the Wales that is, a pageant revealing the immeasurable dramatic talent of our people and what the Gorsedd might do in future with pure ceremonial and drama, not only within our castles but at every Eisteddfod meeting.

It was altogether such a charming and colourful Welsh "Noson Lawen", in such a magnificent and historic setting, that it was only on our return journey to Neath that I found time to give a thought to the sneering allusions made to it beforehand by certain English visiting journalists and would-be supreme advisers of the Gorsedd and the Welsh people.

And remembering their gibes at this Pageant of St Donat's – and their misconstruction of a thing which they had not seen, I seemed to hear on the night wind those words of wisdom uttered by Sion Dafydd Rhys in 1592: "This thought

I would leave with you before we part – that nothing has yet been done in this world so peerless and so perfect but some ill-disposed man could take it upon himself to besmirch that fair thing with words of soot."

*The Western Mail, August 10, 1934*

Leonard Mosley was the first newspaper correspondent to parachute into Normandy after the Allied landings in France on D-Day – June 6th, 1944. His reports were carried by newspapers across the free world, including *The Western Mail.* This despatch covers his experiences on D-Day +2 as Allied troops fought their way into France against stubborn resistance.

# Where Every Man Seeks Shadow

## By Leonard Mosley

WITH THE ALLIED FORCES IN FRANCE,
Thursday (Delayed)

THE BRITISH and Canadian Forces driven in from landing areas have made contact today. We are still engaged with the enemy before Caen, at the moment chiefly in gun duels and in skirmishes and reconnaissance patrols.

I have just come back from the area north of Caen, where I accompanied a British infantry battalion moving up and digging out snipers as they went. A German mortar battery was firing on the road as we went along. Two men fell. A man was sent back for stretcher-bearers, and the long line strung out in single file under the shelter of a stone wall. We went forward along the sunken road through a little village.

At a farm on a hill where the village began, my party paused and watched the infantry move doggedly on, towards the unknown country where the Germans wait in the wooded hills to meet our coming attack.

As in most of this war, there are no fixed lines, no entrenched positions. There are strong points, but otherwise the enemy may be anywhere at any time – in front of you, beside you, or even behind you.

But out of all this confusion our commanders contrive an orderly pattern – a pattern of advancing movement. And the enemy left behind in an advance are mopped up gradually by other British Forces coming on behind.

After leaving that village we travelled back along a shelled road and made our way to the headquarters of the airborne troops. They created this flank, and have held it against repeated attacks by infantry and sometimes by armoured forces. They are under constant fire from guns, mortars, and snipers, but they have held on, and even improved their position. When I spoke to their officers and men, they were confident and full of spirit.

They are magnificent fighters, as good under the nerve-racking strain of continued sniping and mortar fire as they are in the exciting first hours of a raid.

Beyond them, holding another part of the flank, are Commando troops who, like the airborne boys, created the front they hold.

There you have the picture this afternoon – our front in this sector, with the Canadians swinging inland to join our infantry, who hold a deeper thrust towards Caen, and then the airborne and other infantry, and the Commandos. Behind this curved front the beaches still clang and drone with the ceaseless activity of unloading and distribution of supplies.

All through yesterday afternoon I was in green Normandy fields and cider apple groves watching Panzer troops making a fierce attack. With Panzer tanks, self-propelling guns and lorried Grenadiers, they have been trying to break through our perimeter and cut us off from the bridges that lead to the beaches.

It has been queer and exciting, for this is a queer and exciting type of war. It is the type of war for which these tough paratroopers have been specially trained – close-quarter war in which every man seeks shadow, trusts no man no matter what uniform he wears unless he has the password, and where a five-yard run from tree to tree may well mean death.

It would be foolish to say that we are fighting on a front, for just as we infiltrated among the Nazis early the other morning so now he is infiltrating among our troops. His snipers are hidden in holes, strapped in trees, hidden in cottages, barns and cattle shippons.

We were naturally unable to find or eliminate all his strong points, and so one or two mortar positions and machine-gun nests have suddenly spoken from where we might well have assumed he was absent. As a result, also, when we have least expected it, there have been bullets whistling past our ears and mortar bombs bursting over our heads, and I have learnt, like the rest of the men of this force, not at all costs to presume that when a twig breaks over the way or some leaves wave, that it is cattle or just a puff of wind.

Yes, it's queer and exciting, and though few men have had more than a couple of hours of sleep since we left Britain on Monday, it is tense enough to keep our eyes wide open.

Now that the Panzers are taking a hand we have begun to find something we can get our teeth and our shells into. They came rumbling up the road from Caen early this morning with light tanks and armoured reconnaissance cars in the lead, followed by lorried infantry and heavy-gunned Panzers.

Our cars saw them first and flashed back the news. Since then it's been pulse-quickening indeed for your correspondent. You freeze behind trees, and feel helpless without arms, and watch the paratroops with you slithering through poppies stealthily tracking down camouflaged enemy virtually in your midst. And then – whoosh – and a shower of dirt and a cloud of smoke bring your mind back to the Panzers again, for you realise he is firing at you.

Actually, at one period yesterday he got near with his Panzers and naturally very much closer to our forward defence localities. Thanks to our cleverly-positioned guns he didn't get any further.

The boys of this airborne force are good. Make no mistake about that. They have been trained on the principle that dropping by parachute, far from being the end of their job, is only the beginning, and they have been putting that into practice today.

What has been particularly refreshing is the officer who commands this force. He has been here, there, and everywhere controlling his forces, positioning his guns. Never, by looking at him, would you guess that the situation has been grim. His boots are shiny, his jodhpurs immaculate, and, come shell or bullet, he has always worn his red Airborne beret rather than his steel helmet.

When he runs over the situation, his remarks are clear, realistic; and the way his finger jabs the map as he tells you what he is going to do is confidence inspiring in itself.

It is obvious that the enemy's intentions are to cut us off from the bridges we captured so dramatically with our shock paratroopers and gliders – bridges that lead us across the canal and the river to the beach-head forced by the sea-borne invaders on our right flank.

I can understand why he would wish to do that. For I visited the beaches yesterday to send off my first dispatch from France, and it was a grand sight. Though it was misty, raining and a high sea was running, landing craft were coming in in streams, debouching men, guns, lorries, tanks and supplies on the sand.

When near the beaches the air was loud with the sound of war, and guns were banging from all sides. Troops were grinning cheerfully. Actually, the Luftwaffe has so far been almost completely absent.

*The Western Mail, June 10, 1944*

This full-length obituary editorial on King George VI was written in 1951 by John Gay Davies, then a young leader-writer, when the King had an operation for lung cancer. But the King hung on, and it was not published until February 1952, after John Gay Davies had left for the *Daily Telegraph*. The then editor of *The Western Mail*, David Prosser, had ordered that the editorial should be kept in type until it was needed. The style and approach of the editorial illustrates the ambience of the time. John Gay Davies returned to edit the *Mail* for two years from 1964.

# King George VI

WITH THE passing of King George VI, Britain and the Commonwealth have lost a monarch beloved as few have been before him. All of us in this great family of many races grew to love his late Majesty for his sincerity and gentleness no less than we admired his unobtrusive strength and courage in the ordeals which, over the years, he insisted on sharing with us. The deep personal sorrow which attended his accession to the throne never obtruded itself on his dedication of himself to the service of his people. His broadcast speech on the night of his coronation set the tone for a reign which glowed with the virtue and charity of Christian kingship. On that occasion, after thanking his subjects for their demonstrations and messages of goodwill, his Majesty said: "I will only say this – if in the coming years I can show my gratitude in service to you, that is the way, above all others, that I would choose." How faithfully and at what cost did he fulfil that great and humble promise.

His accession found Britain uncertain and troubled in mind as the storm-clouds gathered. The legacy of the years of disarmament had left the country without the means to translate convictions into policy in the field of foreign affairs. Some there were who still refused to see the growing menace to freedom and the institutions of democratic Europe. But many others unconsciously and instinctively measured events against the old, the absolute values. King George was among their number. In a speech from Canada on the occasion of his tour of that country in 1939 he showed his abiding reverence for the simple virtues from which our people have always drawn their strength. As long as these things remained sacred to us we need not fear; but we must look also to the future. "Remember," he said, "that the key to all progress lies in faith, hope, and love. Hold fast to all that is just and of good report in the heritage which your fathers left you, but strive also to improve and equalise that heritage for all men and women in the years to come." Timely words, for the nation had need to summon all its faith and hope in the grim, desperate years which followed that fateful autumn.

Of the many services rendered by the late King to his country probably none will be remembered with greater respect and admiration than his inspiring example during the war years. From his unforgettable broadcast at Christmas of 1939 to the supreme moment when he received the homage of his people on Victory Day the King set a standard of stubborn courage and devotion to duty which matched and complemented that of our great war leader. Brushing aside all plans for ensuring his safety, the King stayed by his people in the heart of the Empire, seldom leaving his capital except to visit his troops or the citizens of the bombed towns. Those who served in the forces overseas will remember with gratitude the hazardous visits which his Majesty made to the theatres of war and will recall with affection his patent happiness at being among his forces in the field. Those who endured the merciless German bombing of 1940 and 1941 will treasure the memory of the King's compassion and the gracious sympathy of his Consort. Together they faced with their people the worst that the enemy could bring against us, and at the war's end they found that a new indestructible bond had been forged between them and their subjects.

The peace ushered in no era of ease and prosperity. Fighting for economic survival Britain faced disaster only less potentially fatal than that which had been so recently averted. But in this struggle, too, the King was at his post, supporting and unifying in his quiet wisdom those basic aspirations of his people which have no relevance to political differences. As the international situation deteriorated the King showed once again the steadfastness and power to inspire and console his people which they came to know during the war years. Now that he is gone from among us we feel that we have, indeed, lost an "ever-present help in trouble," a source to which we could always turn for inspiration and example.

To the widowed Queen, to whose help and devotion King George owed so much, our hearts go out in sorrow and in sympathy. May she be sustained by the knowledge of all that her presence has meant in the life of a great and good man. For the new Queen we offer our prayers for her sustenance at a time when her grief must make the burden of accession hard to bear. Through the noble part she has already played in the public life of the realm we have come to know and cherish the qualities of heart and mind which she brings to the task of reigning in her father's stead. Let her be assured of our loyalty and devotion. Should she need reassurance in the stress and conflict of our times let her remember her father's words on the heritage which is hers, "Like the great coral reefs in the Pacific its growth has gone on silently and invisibly, from century to century, strong to resist the surge and thunder of the tides of fortune and of time."

*The Western Mail, February 7, 1952*

After war service in the Royal Navy, Pontypridd-born J B G Thomas joined *The Western Mail* in 1946 as chief rugby writer, a role he filled for 36 years, and became the most renowned sports editor in the history of the national newspaper of Wales. This is his report of the famous Welsh victory over New Zealand by 13-8 in Cardiff in December, 1953 – the last occasion when Wales defeated the fearsome All Blacks. The Welsh team were: Gerwyn Williams; Ken Jones, Gareth Griffiths, Bleddyn Williams (captain), Gwyn Rowlands; Cliff Morgan, Rex Willis; Billy Williams, Dai Davies, Courtenay Meredith, Rees Stephens, Roy John, Sid Judd, John Gwilliam and Clem Thomas. J B G died in 1997.

# When All Seemed Lost

## By J B G Thomas

WALES won a desperate and thrilling international match at the Cardiff Arms Park against her greatest Rugger rivals, New Zealand, by two goals and a penalty to a goal and a penalty. Desperate because for three-quarters of the play Wales looked like losing, and thrilling because our players staged a tremendous revival to gain victory.

For an hour a dull cloud of gloom and disappointment hung over the famous ground. Then, in the final 20 minutes, the Welsh players broke out to dominate. Shaking off an unusual lethargy, which had cramped mind and limb, they first equalised, and then went on to gain the score which brought victory. Thus New Zealand failed again, for the third time in 48 years, to get the better of Wales on the Cardiff Arms Park.

Many Welshmen will say that Wales were fortunate to win. I think not. Down through the years the argument will continue, as it has done about the 1905 disallowed try by Deans. Some will say that New Zealand should have won. Of course they should have, but it was their own errors and not misfortune that robbed them of the prize.

The cup of victory was snatched from their lips as they were about to drink deep. But the basic fault with the All Blacks was their own lack of imagination behind the scrum, coupled with the sudden easing up of their forwards, who had dominated a listless Welsh pack for an hour. Swiftly and surely, Welsh hands seized the cup, and the great crowd gave the final stages of the play a unique atmosphere of tension with their deep-throated victory roar.

In the final 20 minutes the Welsh pack, which had been beaten, pushed and outpaced for an hour, rehabilitated itself. The spark that rekindled the flame of Welsh "hwyl" came from the roar of the crowd. Their strange and uncanny silence for the first 20 minutes of the second half seemed an omen of defeat. Then suddenly they remembered the Cardiff match of November, when the crowd's support helped the club to hold on for victory.

It was "Come on, Wales!" from over fifty thousand voices that broke the Rip Van Winkle spell. The Welsh forwards, for so long fettered and dispirited, shook themselves free to rampage, harass and rattle the whole New Zealand side. It was a great awakening, and in this moment of transformation none did better than W O Williams, D M Davies and C Meredith. These front-row forwards were tireless. Battered though they were by determined New Zealand scrummaging, and with little shove behind them, they still fought magnificently and played their part in the revival.

Wales got ahead early in the match, but as the first half progressed the forwards failed to make headway. The New Zealand pack, inspired by the return of their captain, R C Stuart, played at their best.

The giant White, easily the best forward in the team, Skinner, Clark and Hemi were always on the ball. In the line-out play they held their own with the experts of Wales. At one stage they forced Wales to indulge in the horrible business of tapping the ball back! In the set scrums they produced a magnificent first-shove to give Hemi an initial advantage over D M Davies. All eight pushed in unison while the Welsh scrum moved like a reluctant tortoise back over the turf. Their brakes could not hold the tourists' shove. In the loose they worried the Welsh midfield backs, and only brilliant covering by Willis, Morgan, and Gerwyn Williams kept them out.

K Davis, at their heels, was a great improvement upon Bevan. Quick and elusive, he deceived the Welsh back row time after time until just before the interval, when he was "downed" in the traditional manner!

Haig, at first five-eighth, was too slow to take advantage of his forwards' long period of supremacy, and, though they tried hard, neither Tanner nor Fitzpatrick could penetrate in the middle. Once Fitzpatrick went to the blind side, but G Williams crashed into him on the line. The two wings (Jarden and Elsom) had few chances; none that enabled them to threaten. How lonely it must be nowadays to play on the wing in an international match!

Scott had a fine game. His accurate high punt brought the New Zealand try, but he was no better than Gerwyn Williams, who played his best match for Wales. His display answered the critics and he is back to stay.

The Welsh backs were not as menacing as usual, owing to the long periods of New Zealand pressure and their limited supply of the ball. Griffiths did not have a happy match, for he missed the high punt which enabled the tourists to score their try and later he suffered a painful dislocation of the shoulder.

Still, his courage in returning to the field after the injury was the inspiration his harassed fellows required. Bleddyn Williams was well marked, but always kept his head as a leader and well deserved the honour of captaining two successful sides against the Fourth All Blacks. The two wings had few chances, but they did not waste one of them. Rowlands collected seven points to justify his inclusion as a place kicker, and Jones was prominent in both the Welsh tries. His own was a beautiful effort.

Morgan and Willis were grand. Hampered and buffeted at the base of the scrum, Willis rose above his troubles, and Morgan – the incomparable – was a great and brave little player. The forwards were very bad and very good in turn. The second and back rows played well below form for an hour, and then hit back, with a fury that turned and shattered the threatening All Black forward waves. In that period we saw the Welsh forwards at their best, but we had suffered long in silence.

A word, too, for the referee, Dr Peter Cooper, who did well; controlling a remarkably clean match with comparative ease.

The singing was of poor quality until the teams fielded for the start, then the rich notes of the anthems floated up into the chill air of the first true winter's afternoon of the season.

Fitzpatrick "dummied" the kick-off with Scott and the match was on. The All Blacks soon looked dangerous forward, and appeared to have strengthened their defence, particularly in midfield. Davis was here, there and everywhere, continually probing, but few supported him. The early scrums went monotonously to New Zealand, until after 15 minutes Willis robbed Davis on the blind side, and Judd dribbled away up the right touchline. Ken Jones carried on to boot well ahead, where Scott waited. The full back gathered, only for Jones to crash into him. The ball went loose, and Gwilliam and Judd were up to drive it through.

A yard from the line, Judd scooped up the ball and dived over to score a try at almost the exact point where he had scored for Cardiff in November. Rowlands made a good start by kicking the goal.

After this effort we expected more scores from Wales, but instead the players became strangely subdued and allowed the All Blacks to take the initiative, particularly at forward. Wales were penalised at a scrum, and Jarden kicked a superb goal from near the touchline on the Welsh 25.

Then Rowlands was short with a couple of penalties; Clarke received a cut above the eye, but carried on; Jarden was just wide with another long-range effort, and the New Zealand pressure increased. Finally, they took the lead near the interval. Scott punted high in the swirling breeze to confuse the Welsh backs in front of their own posts. Griffiths misjudged his catch, and the ball rolled loose. Bill Clarke was the first All Black forward on the spot, and though the Welshmen attempted to regather the ball on their line, Clark was given the touchdown for a try. Jarden kicked an easy goal, and New Zealand were ahead at the interval.

There was much nodding of heads and wagging of chins at half-time. Things were not going well for Wales. Would they be beaten? On the restart, the All Blacks pounded away in their attempt to drive the Welsh forwards into the ground.

When Griffiths left the field with a shoulder injury after 10 minutes, they appeared to be succeeding. Surely seven Welsh forwards could not hold eight All Blacks? The siege was on. It was desperate stuff, but the Welshmen held out until Griffiths returned.

Thomas then rejoined the pack, and the fighting Welsh set off to storm the New Zealand line.

An All Black forward refused to play the ball in a loose maul following a half-wheeled scrum, and the whistle went. A penalty to Wales! Rowlands landed a neat goal, and the scores were level. Could the match be won by Wales?

There remained 10 minutes for play as the men in red swept into the attack with a fierceness that caught the All Blacks completely by surprise. It was thrilling now, for the flood gates of Welsh enthusiasm had been opened.

Then came the winning try. Elsom was tackled in possession inside his own 25. Clem Thomas gathered when the ball went loose and, after drawing Scott, keeping out of touch and turning around in one movement, punted accurately across to the right. The area was poorly guarded, and up came Jones at great speed to gather, swerve inside Jarden and race over the line for a magnificent try. Rowlands kicked the goal and Wales were back in the lead.

The final New Zealand challenge was badly directed, and Wales were on top in the closing minutes. The final whistle went and as the crowd cheered, Roy John and Scott wrestled for the ball. John was winning, only for him to relax at the thought of victory and present the ball to Scott.

As the players walked off, shaking hands and changing jerseys, many of them were still bewildered. The revival had shaken everyone, but most of all the tourists!

*The Western Mail, December 21, 1953*

Eighteen months after the death of Dylan Thomas in New York in 1953, actor-playwright Emlyn Williams took to the stage in a one-man production entitled *Emlyn Williams as Dylan Thomas Growing Up*. The show was successful, and ran for three months at the Globe in London's West End. He put the show on again in 1980 – this time at the Ambassadors.

# Emlyn as Dylan

## By Windsor Davies

ONE OF THE most amazing dramatic contests for some years is currrently going on in a London theatre between two Welshmen, with nothing in common save their Welshness. On the one hand, Emlyn Williams – playwright, man about town, and many voiced actor; on the other, Dylan Thomas – poet, social rebel, spinner of improbable yarns, scrub-haired reprobate, unrepentant bibber, genius, and *still* alive.

*Emlyn Williams as Dylan Thomas Growing Up* is nothing less than an excursion into dramatic alchemy, which somehow sublimates the expected clash of personalities and blends them into one. Admirers of the dead poet will be pleased to learn that the personality that does emerge from two hours of enthralling entertainment is demonstrably Thomas's.

Before us is Mr Williams, in a beautiful blue suit, tailored as with a knife; in a beautiful white shirt; wearing a beautiful red tie; with his handsome cat's head and his fur a gleaming, silken white.

One gazes at this apparition, this miracle of suavity and *savoir-faire*, and wonders how on earth such an intellectual ruffian as Thomas can be recreated within this frame. But it is done, and marvellously well done, within the first 10 minutes; and long before the evening ends Dylan Thomas has been glancing sidelong and wicked out of Mr Williams's eyes; and Thomas's words go dancing and shimmering about the theatre, uproariously comic, tragic and pathetic.

And when one least expects it, there comes the slyly calculated stroke of vulgarity, irresistibly releasing more laughter than one can comfortably deal with.

Described in its most prosaic terms, the performance is no more than a series of readings from Thomas's less well-known works. But neither Thomas nor Williams are prosaic people and Mr Williams does not read in the usual sense of the word.

It is true that at the start he carries a threateningly large pile of manuscripts under his arm. These he places on a solitary chair on a naked stage. That is as far as the reading goes. Having, so to speak, demonstrated his willingness to read if anyone asks him, Mr Williams sits down, forgets all about his bundle of papers and talks to us in his sonorous and infinitely flexible voice.

Before one quite realises it, he succeeds in making himself inconspicuous where he should be by right as inescapable as a lighthouse. Thomas's words pass thorough his lips as though they were some facile instrument played by the poet; and the people listen to the music, and not to the performer.

What consummate skill this needs can be known only to Mr Williams, whose own personality is robust enough to resent suppression.

It is Thomas talking about Thomas, as the superb raconteur; and it is easy and pleasant – and disconcerting – to see little boy Thomas on the stage staring through the school railings with polite, infant malevolence at an inoffensive and Panama-hatted fat man in his Swansea garden.

One by one, the whole Colney Hatch of Thomas's real or imagined characters appears to be blasted with irony or to be dissected by him with the curiosity of a naturalist examining a rare and oddly-shaped beetle.

Thomas's younger selves do not escape the scalpel, and the analysis here takes on superb drollery. "I remember myself very well at the age of 17," purrs Thomas-Williams. "A young fellow who talked rather 'fency' and who had a habit of announcing every so often that he would shortly be leaving for Chelsea, to take up a careah as a free-lance journalist. Penniless, but convinced that, in a vague way, he would be able to live" – here Mr Williams stares blandly at us – "off women…"

And so it goes on, through all the wonderful variety of Thomas's moods, until Mr Williams slowly walks off for the last time, speaking, prayer-like, the lovely and touching poem, "And Death Shall Have No Dominion." The last spell has been cast, and it holds one even after the curtain has been rung up for the applause.

For Mr Williams reserves until the last a magnificent *coup de théâtre* which depends for its effect not upon greasepaint and egotism, but upon an extraordinary humility.

*The Western Mail, June 29, 1955*

Gwen Bonner Roberts was a staff feature writer on *The Western Mail* in the 1950s. This is one of a series of weekly articles she wrote under the title *A Woman in Wales*.

# Harmony in Yellow

## By Gwen Bonner Roberts

THE SKY above us was an uneven blue, like the faded folds of a velvet curtain which has hung too long in the same place. Underfoot, the salt-dry stones squeaked unpleasantly; the tide was far out, and there was mud between us and the water.

We were strangers, but we talked together like friends meeting after a long absence; the conversation had the remembered completeness of a familiar unexciting dream.

I had watched her walking towards me, and I had known that she would stop to talk; a tired, middle-aged woman in a yellow dress, too bright, too stiffly new, and wearing gloves.

Suddenly she stopped and took her gloves off. She smiled, and I knew what she was thinking – it had crossed my mind, too. Something about *"O why do you walk through the fields in gloves, Missing so much and so much? O fat, white woman whom nobody loves…"*

But I knew that she was missing nothing at all, she was much loved and she was happy.

She stopped and picked up a pebble, a yellow pebble which she rubbed with satisfied fingers. She sat near me. "I like yellow," she said; and then we were talking about all the homely housewifely things associated with yellow.

Sunshine on wash-day, butter, young chickens, cutseed-cake, beaten eggs, mustard in a glass jar, a bar of yellow household soap, the yellow freckles on her daughter's fair skin, daffodils which grew by her kitchen window, always the first to bloom.

"No one planted them – they are rather like the small wild daffodils you find on the hills in Brecon," she said.

"John's baby curls were as yellow as saffron," she went on affectionately. "Who would have thought he would have grown into such a swarthy ruffian; the dear boy, his eyes haven't changed and his smile is the same."

She told me about the time when John's cousin came to spend the summer at the farm, and John was found with his head under the pump in the yard, trying to wash the curls out because he had just realised that it was only girls who had curly hair.

All that happened was that John had a cold, and he cried and cried until old Twm took him to see the big bull at Hendy, a fine red beast with a curly poll; "Curls for strength, see, John bach."

"When I was a girl at home the carts were painted yellow. My father's name, Henry Lewys – most particular he was about the way it was spelt – and the name of the farm, Hafod Braf, picked out in red and black.

"The wheels were yellow, too. I can see them now, covered in mud, rolling into the yard, and the man shouting at the horses, because he himself had been clumsy and the cart, full of swedes, had scraped against the gate leading into the yard.

"I was leaning out of the window feeling that the world was a wonderful place. I was full of romance, reciting to myself from the Song of Solomon 'My beloved is like a roe or a young hart.'

"My father, I remember, did not care for the Song of Solomon, probably because of the 'threescore queens, and fourscore concubines, and virgins without number.'

"Funny that, wasn't it, in a farmer?"

I agreed, although for the moment I could not see why a Welsh farmer should have taken fourscore concubines in his stride, as it were. Was it possible that she thought concubines were something that grew, had she confused them with columbines?

She told me of Auntie Harriet's attic room, papered from the squares of wallpaper taken from the pattern books, obligingly supplied by the manufacturers. It was a waste, said Auntie Harriet, to buy paper for the attic, but something had to be done about the walls.

The result was "unusual, as you might say, but very pretty, and so neatly done, too. Auntie Harriet papered it herself, using the best flour for the paste."

She went on talking, talking as women do when we suddenly feel the need to talk. We touched on yesterday and today and did not question tomorrow. When she left me, I was sorry.

She walked away clumsily over the unfriendly pebbles, dusting the sand from the skirt of that quite hideous yellow dress. She put her gloves on and waved to me.

*The Western Mail, June 29, 1955*

One of Wales's best-known entertainers, broadcaster and comedian Wyn Calvin comes from a family of Presbyterian preachers. Famed for his portrayals of the Dame in countless pantomimes, he was elected King Rat of the Grand Order of Water Rats, the show-business charity, in 1990. In 1958 he was asked by David Cole, then editor of *The Western Mail,* to write a series of articles on humour. He wrote this article when he was entertaining British troops in Cyprus.

# Humour in the Pulpit

## By Wyn Calvin

A FEW generations ago, anyone connected with the theatre was considered a social outcast. To be "on the stage" was to have "gone to the devil". This attitude lasted long in Wales, and traces of Puritan dislike of anything theatrical still persist, though happily they are now almost non-existent.

In the Nonconformist Wales of the past, therefore, any young man with dramatic or humorous gifts (or both) had only one career open to him in which he could use them – the Church.

The result was that great talents of humour and drama found expression in the pulpit, and there can be no reflection on the sincerity of the preachers who used these gifts – nor on their effectiveness.

Theology and humour may sound strange bedfellows, but every minister of the Gospel will readily acknowledge the help and usefulness of an illustration or story with humorous point.

Every servant of the church acknowledges "humour" as one of God's most precious gifts and one that is supremely useful to them in their work – in the pulpit or out of it.

Which of us has not some moral or parable indelibly engraved on our memory which reached its target in our imagination because it was pointed with humour?

As a child I vividly remember the annual visits to our chapel of a little preacher from North Wales. He literally bubbled with good humour and, more than 20 years later, I can still remember some of his illustrations – and I still value their lessons.

One, in the early days of the war, described a little girl's prayer for the protection of her "mummy and daddy", her new baby brother who had whooping cough, and Laddie, their terrier. "And please, dear God," she concluded, "look after yourself, otherwise we are all sunk."

His theology may not have been the most distinguished, but that smiling little minister was a shining example of good nature – and, to us children at any rate, one of Heaven's finest ambassadors.

Of course, humour is out of place in the pulpit unless it points a greater, deeper lesson. However great man's sense of humour, his spiritual needs are greater.

The great German reformer Martin Luther (who was so aware of the devil's presence that he once threw an inkwell at him – the wall of a German castle still bears the inkstain) said that the two things the devil most feared were prayer and a sense of humour.

On the surface, they appear incongruous, yet theologians agree that both were characteristic of Christ. At first glance it would not seem that Jesus possessed a good sense of humour... we read that He wept, but never that He laughed.

A closer look, however, in the light of our knowledge of the Jewish sense of fun, suggests that no one could describe a, huge, ungainly creature like a camel trying to crawl through the eye of a needle without a trace of laughter, nor give the nickname of "Rock" to a lively, restless and volatile man like Peter without the hint of a smile.

Our great Welsh preachers are so often pictured as sombre, ranting, bearded Bible-pounders; righteously-angry old men. This is unfortunate and unfair to most of them. They knew the value of a smile – in the pulpit and out of it.

Moreover, some of the "greats" like Thomas Chas Williams, Menai Bridge, Cynddelan Jones and Seth Joshua used their comic gifts as well as their acute sense of the dramatic. Their rhetorical impact was heightened (or deepened) by the use of illustration, humorous and penetrating.

Steven Jenkins, of Haverfordwest, preaching on Noah, provides a typical example. He vividly described the entry into the Ark of all the animal couples and then the final closing of the doors when the creatures were safely housed and the threatening heavens began to open.

The preacher portrayed several people who then came pleading for entrance. "Too late, too late" cried Noah (with a heavy West Wales accent!). Then in great excitement Mrs Noah shouted, "Noah, boy, thou'll haf to oopen the door now.

Here is the Mayor of Mesopotamia in his carriage and six."

"Too la-ate, too la-ate," jubilantly cried Noah.

The amusement created by the description of the scene helped the preacher to make his point and stress the finality of God's word that excluded all privilege.

So great was the impact of Steven Jenkins's humour in the pulpit that, after his death, his biography was written and called *Sanctified Humour*.

At one time he was experiencing a trouble, not unusual in Welsh churches, called "cythroel canu" – or "the devil in the choir". (It is strange how unpleasantness and misunderstanding in the work of the Church seems to stem from the music and singing.)

This Pembrokeshire preacher was going on horseback one Sunday morning to preach at a village some miles from Haverfordwest. He had heard that this church, too, was having its musical trouble, and he decided to touch on it in his sermon.

"As I was riding here this morning, my friends," he intoned, "I heard the birds singing in the trees and I said to myself, 'There is a lesson for you, Steven Jenkins. The little birds are praising their Maker and singing; which is more than thou has done today.'

"Then, when I got as far as Cannaston Bridge I beheld two birds fighting hard with feather a-flying, and I said to myself, 'There you are, the devil is amongst the singers here, just like in Haverfordwest.'"

Another humorous illustration that impressed itself on a small boy – and I know how deeply, because I was the boy – came from a sermon of my father's, and it has been a constant reminder ever since.

An old West Wales tramp used to go around the farms every Tuesday to beg. Then each Thursday he would go round the same farms to say "Thank you" for what they had given him on the Tuesday.

"It's a strange thing," the tramp said, "but I always get more on the Thursday when I go to say 'Thank you' that I do on the Tuesday when I go to beg."

The Rev. Seth Joshua, who was founder of the Forward Movement in Wales and a unique evangelist, found his puckish wit of great use in his work. (He used to tell his wife, who had been C of E before marrying, "My dear, you've been inoculated, vaccinated and confirmed, and not one of them took.")

After preaching in Memorial Hall, Cardiff, a man in the gallery got up and attacked his doctrine.

"Wait a minute," said the preacher, "Where did you get your information?"

"In the ninth chapter of Romans," said the man.

"What is that?" asked the Rev. Seth Joshua.

"You know - St Paul's letter to the Romans."

"Oh yes," said the preacher. "But to whom is it addressed? Turn to chapter one my friend. It says 'To all those at Rome, beloved of God, called to be saints.' Are you beloved of God? Are you a saint?"

"Well, no, not exactly," said the heckler.

Then Seth turned on him fiercely. "Well what do you mean by reading other people's letters?... this one is not addressed to you at all, man."

Undoubtedly, one of the most effective uses of humour for the minister is in appealing for church funds, though it is seldom put as bluntly as by a Roman Catholic priest in North Wales recently.

After reminding his congregation that they were his flock, he went on, with Irish twinkle and accent, to say:

"I am the shepherd of this flock, and one of the first duties of a shepherd is to fleece his flock."

There followed an appeal – and a second collection.

The Rev. Cynddelan Jones, as an advocate of the British and Foreign Bible Society, would convulse his listeners with a description, in his dry monotone, inimitable and unvaried, of a little dog running round and round in ever-decreasing circles.

"What for? My dear friends...Oooooh... (in the same monotone)... To do what I am doing here today, trying for to make the two ends meet."

Although some of our greatest preachers have been amusing in their illustrations, the real genius of their preaching was the way in which they used the humour to point to the deeper message. It was a means to an end – to make greater truths better understood.

*The Western Mail, December 4, 1958*

The twelfth child of a Porth miner, Gwyn Thomas won a scholarship to Oxford, where he read modern languages. After working in adult education from 1940 to 1942, he taught French for two years at Cardigan Grammar School, and later Spanish at Barry Grammar School. The first of his nine novels was published in 1946, but it was not until 1962 that he gave up teaching to become a full-time writer. His first – and most popular – play, *The Keep*, was written in that year. The keynotes of his work were his brilliant eloquence, his sharp wit and his ability to picture the absurdities in the life around him. Most of his writings were centred in the mining communities of Glamorgan. He was also at home as a television panellist, where his dry witticisms and rich descriptive turn of phrase made him popular. For some years he wrote a regular Saturday television column for *The Western Mail*, and a selection of extracts from these articles was published under the title *High on Hope* in 1985. He died in 1981.

# The Unquiet Fleece

## By Gwyn Thomas

WE ALL know the sort of feelings aroused in Missouri by the James Brothers, the conflicting tides of anger at joints incontinently cased and stripped and of pity for the everlasting renegade who is a useful hook for the sense we all have of being more or less drastically on the run.

The nearest you are likely to come to that situation in Britain is with the sheep of South Wales.

In judging these creatures you can forget about the sheep you have come across in other parts of the world. These performers have developed instincts and muscles which, alongside Canterbury lambs, put them in the timber-wolf class.

The feud between the sheep farmers who, in terms of social psychology as applied to sheep straying, have still 80 years to go before they catch up with the Rebecca Riots, and the urban authorities in the valleys has now reached Kentucky level.

The councillors say they have the right to impound the flocks that come roaming down the slopes to add a new dimension of fuss and intractable stupidity to the valley villages. And we now have voters with vans whose task it is to corner and corral these animals.

These workers have each a thousand clownish defeats to their credit. Imagine a single tipstaff, unarmed, trying to halt the gallop of Dick Turpin's Bess and you will see that they earn their portion of the rate.

The angrier farmers on the other hand, claim that the councillors are no better than a bunch of no-good rustlers, haters of mutton as well as squandermaniacs, and that they will come high-tailing down and free their cattle by force if there is any more of this impounding nonsense. So it is only a matter of time before the rattle of squirrel guns breaks the moonlit silence of the cwm and those councillors who have not locked themselves in the mayor's parlour will walk abroad with protective wads of four-ply agenda beneath their dark serge.

There is no doubt that the resilient awareness and drive of these sheep leaves many of the inhabitants far behind.

Not long ago I came out of a café at the top of the Rhondda. I was accompanied by a man whose respect for the strength and sapience of our sheep makes him the only man in Glamorgan who really understands the way they feel about the cow in India.

A group of about 12 sheep had just come down from the hillside. Their coats had been torn by headlong trips through a dozen fences, discoloured by journeys up and down a score of tips.

They have a tough hopefulness, these sheep; they nibble at the ghost of grass on tip sides as utterly barren as anything on this earth. Spectral food for spectral lives.

This group stood in a rough semi-circle about 20 yards from the café. Only one or two had their eyes on the café from which, with patience, they knew they might expect a bounty of scraps. They knew, too, that if they stood too close to the shop or stared in chorus the caterer would come to regard them as a kind of grey neurosis closing in on him and a hindrance to people wishing to come in and eat.

So there they were, half showing the roguish and softly savage glint of dignity in degradation, knowing precisely the degree of pressure to exert on the humans now cluttering up the valley-bed if they were to continue existence on the uncertain surfaces of the globe.

"There's no doubt about it," said my friend. "These creatures have really graduated. When they find that the wool they wear is as inferior as the stuff we wear, they'll demand the vote."

There was a period during which my father and I suffered from a joint and waxing insomnia. We would sit in the kitchen, the valley around us quite soundless.

We would each have a volume of Gibbon's *Decline and Fall,* and we would read steadily, lifting our heads and exchanging a wink on every 50th page to show that our insomnia had never been better. At two in the morning, as grimly resolute as Loyola, the parade of the sheep down the High Street would begin.

Outside each door was a loaded ashbin. Down they would go as the marauding platoon worked its way towards the centre of the town.

We could identify each bin by the timbre of the awaited clang. "That's Mrs Morgan's." "There goes Mrs Shanklyn's." "Hullo, that's Waldo Treharne's, twice. Must have tamped."

Sometimes one particular note would be missing, a crash of particular quality expected, but not heard. My father, fussy to the point of mania about all things that happen by night, would often go out to make sure that the bin which had been missed was the one we had imagined. And if it were, he would sometimes drive the sheep back, telling them to tip our own bin, which was heavy and made a noise that woke the dead if heaved over too clumsily.

Domestic gardens the sheep regarded as a kind of bonus. I have seen the leader of the troupe that did our locality for many years peep over a wall and stare at the produce of a particular garden. He wagged his head in a clearly negative way.

A week later he looked in again. His yellow eyes lit up, he nodded his great head in a firm yes and waved on his troupe. They cleared the wall like a Grand National field and every last vegetable was lifted in a matter of minutes.

Year after year my father's garden was given this treatment, somewhere in late May. He wrote a poem for the Birchtown National Eisteddfod on the lines of Markham's *Man With The Hoe,* but written with specific bitterness against sheep, beginning: "I damn thee, ram, progenitor of woe." In Welsh that added up to a fine invective mouthful.

Later he was persuaded that the fence and gate at the top of the garden were too low to keep out invaders. He built them up with a zeal and to a height that would have done credit to a neurasthenic French noble in 1788.

He planted the garden and sang as he did it. He had the Sioux on the right side of the stockade. A lovely May brought each furrow to fat perfection. My father felt fulfilled and secure. He was planning another poem on the ultimate goodness of man and earth.

In the meantime we were keeping our eye on the sheep. They were patrolling the back lane behind the house, and time and again we saw their leader, a most pensive ram, whom we called Attila, pause and stare at the barricade my father had put up.

Attila was working something out, and a sheep more conscious of trigonometry than Attila never lived. He knew that he had the legs to clear the new obstruction but lacked the run to give him the impetus and lift.

One night of full moon he found the answer. He and his friends pushed in the back door of the house across the back lane from us. They filed up the garden path, flexing their muscles and thanking Attila. They lined up for the run, Attila in the van.

At that moment my father had gone to the top of the garden to admire the great blowsy beauty of the mountain under the moon, to savour the smell of lusty beanshoots and rose bushes, to fit a last line of plangent exaltation to his ode, saying how in this moment of peace a pattern of loveliness was emerging from its immemorial scars.

Then Attila, the biggest sheep in the zone, came hurtling out of the night and landed right on top of him. As soon as he got sorted out from Attila another sheep cleared the barrier and laid him flat.

The next day my father tore down the barricade. He sought out the troupe who were sleeping it off on a neighbouring hillock and he told Attila that there were still five or six shoots of this and that he had overlooked in the dark, and that he was now free to go back and finish the job without half-killing the tenant and putting paid to odes.

My father never submitted his poem. But later that year he won the prize for the best bitter epigram awarded by the Philosophy class at the Library and Institute, a short black statement equating Attila, the sheep, with some local politician of athletic turpitude.

*The Western Mail, April 30, 1960*

John Gay Davies, who edited *The Western Mail* in 1964-65, let the readers see that the paper could see the funny side of things when it wanted. He introduced the light-hearted Second Leader on a Saturday, and liked to write it himself when he could make time. This is one of his…

# Good Ball from Pythagoras

NONE of the proposed changes in the rules of rugby will be worth two-pence without a change in the shape of the ball. To pretend otherwise is to trifle with the intellectual crisis with which players from Felinfoel to Fiji are now bravely contending.

A round ball is out of the question, for reasons which need not be adduced here. A square ball, while it would undoubtedly add to the interest taken by more sluggish supporters, would lead to vexatious disputes between teams at half-time as to whether the four angles were still all 90 degrees, and whether or not the new ball should be called for. A rhomboid ball, apart from being gratuitously alarming in aspect, might induce an even more oblique attitude to the game than that now complained of by our elders.

A right-angled triangular ball, however, escapes these objections. One would be constantly in the presence of the fact that the square on its hypotenuse equalled the sum of the squares on its other two sides; but we have faced worse things than that. What is important is that the prestige attaching to Pythagoras might engender a general re-examination of the true geometrical principles of the game.

Players might begin to remember that the shortest distance between two points is a straight line; that the circumference of an opponent is less important than the radius of his swerve; above all, as in Euclid's prescient postulate, that figures may be freely moved in space without change of shape or size. Which, give or take a cauliflower ear or two, is what this game is really all about.

*The Western Mail, February 15, 1964*

Sir David Llewellyn, brother of Olympic show-jumper Sir Harry Llewellyn, was educated at Eton and Trinity College, Cambridge, read for the Bar at the Inner Temple, served with the Welsh Guards in World War II, won the Cardiff North seat in 1950, and was appointed Under Secretary of State at the Home Department after the Conservatives were returned at the 1951 general election. But his great loves were journalism and horse-racing. He wrote regular columns for *The Western Mail* and its sister paper the *South Wales Echo*. And for 27 years before he died in 1992, he wrote the Jack Logan column in the *Sporting Life*, where he often took up the reins for the underdog, fighting the racing establishment in print.

# Selling a Lily to buy a Loaf

## By Sir David Llewellyn

I STARTED collecting china during the war at Oxford. My commanding officer, Col. Wilkinson, of Worcester College, had reached the time of life when porcelain fascinated him more than parades. And why should three officers stand around looking decorative when one at the most would do?

"I have a job for you," he would say.

"Sir," I would reply, stamping my feet as Guardsmen will, and trying to sound fierce and obedient at the same time.

Then we would go hunting among the antique shops for treasures. Twenty-odd years ago they were marvellously cheap.

I learned from my friend, long since dead, alas, only to buy the best. One good thing, he would say, however small, will increase in value far more than a dozen of the second best.

When I protested that I liked things for their beauty, he would protest that I was young, foolish and single, that my taste would change, but that the value of

110

the best of its kind would always rise. Buy nothing chipped, nothing marked, nothing whatever riveted.

And so I bought. My army pay was not much, but there was nothing to spend it on. I had worked out, in retrospect, that by converting money into porcelain I was getting a general's pay, tax-free.

Last Thursday at Sotheby's I sold my collection, mostly Swansea and Nantgarw. My motives were mixed. The fact that Welsh porcelain, like French furniture, has become a kind of bearer bond, easily convertible, is one factor. But greed did not move me along.

One day I decided to wash my collection (I have never so much as broken a kitchen plate all my life), when I suddenly realised that I did not want it.

Not to want the genius of William Pollard, Pardoe, Morris and Moses Webster! I could hardly believe it. It was true all the same. Their message was over.

What had been a passion had become a habit. A labour of love had become a chore. *Sic transit gloria mundi.*

I wondered if my wife would mind if I sold. She was, if anything, relieved. For long she had feared that our youngest child might take a fancy to the china cabinet, with foreseeable results. And her attitude to things whose value can disappear in the twinkling of a small boy's eye was rather like that of Mr Jorrocks to dogs – "Confound all presents wot eat!"

Besides, she has a better eye for a balance sheet than mine and dislikes intensely the colour of bankers' red. It only transpired later that she had one or two other uses for the proceeds of sale.

At any rate, before I had time to change my mind, each piece was being packed with exquisite skill. If any bachelor happens to be reading this, I beg of him to marry for love a girl who can pack parcels.

Next day, I delivered the cream of my collection at Sotheby's with no more compunction than a murderer leaves a trunk at a left-luggage office.

I did not go to the sale. My being there would not have added a penny to the price and there is something undignified about speculating, so to speak, about the contents of the will at the graveside. No, I let all my pieces be dispersed, on their merits, for what they were worth. And without any moaning at the bar and no calculation of profit.

Looking back, I see that my old Commanding Officer was right. Buy the best. Buy for posterity. Enjoy things while you will and then be done with them, and enjoy the proceeds.

I think it was William Morris who advised the owner of a shilling to buy a lily and a loaf. On Tuesday all my lilies were sold. The baker and the banker will make merry, and for the life of me, I cannot find it in my heart to be sad.

*The Western Mail,* July 11, 1964

Poet and novelist Robert Nye was born in London in 1939. He moved to North Wales in 1961, living in a remote cottage without electricity or running water, already determined to make his own way as a writer. When his first book of poems was favourably reviewed in *The Western Mail*, Nye wrote to the literary editor suggesting that he might write the occasional article for the paper. This is one of the pieces that resulted. Nye went on to write novels, including the best-selling *Falstaff*, winner of both the Hawthornden Prize and the *Guardian* Fiction Prize, but poetry remains his first calling.

# Let's take the Bull by the Horns

## By Robert Nye

A FRIEND pointed out to me recently that I had fallen into the awful habit of saying toilet when I meant lavatory. So insidious is the habit of euphemism, the language of cant, the use of disgusting and inelegant elegantese which afflicts us on all sides in these most unplainly spoken days. What next, I wonder? Posterior instead of backside? Coloured gentleman instead of negro? Underprivileged instead of poor? Fall asleep in the Lord instead of die?

These expressions are not only comic, pretentious and inaccurate, they embody and enact a complete misuse of language, by disguising and obscuring what they would convey. If we respect language as a means of communication we do not talk about the john, the w.c., the w., the loo, the bathroom, the convenience, the closet, the gents, when we mean the lavatory. (Even the word lavatory – literally "a place for washing" – began as a euphemism for the better Elizabethan words, the jakes or the privy.)

Nor do we refer to what we do in the lavatory as spending a penny, paying a visit, washing our hands, seeing our aunt, going to see a man about a dog, etc.

Such phrases arise, fairly obviously, because people fear to use language for its proper purpose – the giving of names to real things – and because they fear reality itself.

The fact of death, for instance, is apparently improved or smoothed over in some minds if thought of as something called passing over, and everywhere the honest undertaker is giving way to something filthy called a mortician. Even the dead are the Dear Departed. It seems time to point out that a spade is not only a spade but that it is actually the better for being called spade.

The word euphemism comes from a Greek word meaning "to speak favourably". The Greeks, indeed, were past masters of the art – witness their calling the Erinyes, the Furies, by the fate-averting name of the Eumenides, the Kindly Ones. The principle of euphemism is, then, quite simply, to blunt or diminish some fact which frightens, disgusts or otherwise daunts our normal speaking habits. It is the language of the squeamish, the embarrassed, the dishonest and the cowardly, at worst. At best, it is an affection of the excessively polite.

Once accepted in principle, there are fine shades of meaning to be conveyed in choice of euphemism. If I say, for instance, that Jones has gone west or kicked the bucket I imply that, while not being ungentlemanly enough to wish to mention in decent company that Jones has dared do anything so disgraceful as dying, I have no piety towards Jones as Jones.

Generally speaking, only cowboys and unpopular schoolteachers are said to go west or kick the bucket; while gangsters croak.

With a thin degree of greater respect I might say that old Jones has pegged out (a croquet term) or popped off. If I was employing euphemism because I liked old Jones and couldn't bear the thought of him being dead, I would more likely say that he had breathed his last, or departed this life, or closed his eyes, or yielded up the ghost, or paid his debt to nature, shuffled off this mortal coil, taken his last sleep, gone the way of all flesh, awoken to life immortal, crossed the Stygian ferry, been called Home, etc., all these expressions being what we might call shabby semi-literary religiosities.

If Jones and I had been big buddies and I wished to convey our mutual toughness I'd more likely say he'd bought it, handed in his chips, or gone for a Burton.

And so on and so on... anything but the excellent verb die, which describes what Jones has done without insulting his memory with periphrastic phrases expressive only of my own fear of death.

Imagine for a moment, if you doubt the dignity of the word death, that Donne had written not

*Death be not proud, though some have called thee*
*Mighty and dreadful...*

but

*Demise be not proud...*

Or that Thomas Nashe's magnificent stanza:

> *Beauty is but a flower*
> *Which wrinkles will devour;*
> *Brightness falls from the air,*
> *Queens have died young and fair,*
> *Dust hath clos'd Helen's eye.*
> *I am sick, I must die.*
> *Lord have mercy on us!*

had

> *I am sick, I will obtain Happy Release*

in place of its simple and moving penultimate line.

And it is not only death that your accomplished, smooth and half-literate euphemist is afraid of. He is afraid of life, too.

His autobiography might run like this: "I came into this world, attained my majority, sowed my wild oats, got spliced, perpetuated my kind, kept body and soul together by pursuing a gainful occupation, became a senior citizen, felt a bit under the weather and joined the great majority."

Anything rather than use such obscene English words as born, grew up, fornicated, married, had children, worked hard, aged, sickened, and died.

It ought to be said that euphemism is never pleasing and that the truth is always better for being plainly told rather than skated over or danced round. Without wishing to deny the importance and elegance of approaching some things obliquely (a crooked line may sometimes be the shortest distance between two points, at least in poetry) it is arguable whether a gain in irony compensates for a loss in forcefulness.

Here I recall the story of the Restoration parson who is supposed to have ended a sermon on the following rousing note: "If you do not live up to the precepts of the Gospel... you must expect to receive your reward in a certain place which 'tis not good manners to mention in church."

And talking of Hell let me now be a devil and suggest that in future men do up their fly-buttons instead of adjusting their dress before leaving, employ rat-catchers and dustmen rather than rodent operatives and refuse disposal officers, sin rather than commit psycho-neurotic errors of adjustment, have bastards instead of illegitimate infants or Little Mistakes, insist that they want a second-hand car and not a used one, get fat and not corpulent, drunk and not half-seas over, say they are sorry when they are sorry instead of tendering their heart-felt condolences, and refer to their wife as being pregnant if she is – anything rather than the absurd expecting, the hilarious in the family way, or the extraordinary in an interesting condition.

*The Western Mail, July 18, 1964*

Saunders Lewis – dramatist, poet, critic, literary historian and nationalist – is the foremost figure in Welsh literature of the 20th century. After studying English and French at Liverpool University, he served as an officer with the South Wales Borderers in France, Italy and Greece before becoming a lecturer at University College, Swansea in 1922. In 1925, he was one of the founders of the Welsh Nationalist Party, later Plaid Cymru, and became its president in 1926. In 1936, he was gaoled for arson at the RAF bombing school at Penyberth, Lleyn, and lost his job at Swansea. For five years from 1952, he was a lecturer in Welsh at University College, Cardiff before retiring to his home in Penarth to concentrate on his writing. His BBC Wales annual lecture in 1962 – Tynged yr Iaith – warned of the demise of the Welsh language by the end of the century and was a strong influence in the development of Cymdeithas yr Iaith Gymraeg. In the mid-60s, he contributed regularly to *The Western Mail's* Literary Review.

# A Renaissant Colossus

## By Saunders Lewis

A WEEK today, October 17, will be the centenary of the birth of John Morris-Jones. Very properly the Honourable Society of Cymmrodorion is meeting at the University College of North Wales, Bangor, where he was so long a supreme figure, to celebrate the birthday. This monthly bulletin, which aims at telling the worthy Welshless Welsh about Welsh literary developments, must speak as well as it can this time of John Morris-Jones.

We have no such figure today. Why, man, he did bestride the narrow world of

Wales like a Colossus. By no means merely the world of scholarship. He was also the unchaired, uncrowned, undisputed king of the National Eisteddfod. From its platform he taught the Welsh-speaking nation the rhythms and cadences of its ancient poets.

He seized that poor Cinderella, the written Welsh of the 19th century, stripped her in public of her anglicised rags of idiom and syntax, plunged her in a Palladian bath of Renaissance classics, frightened the very life out of her, but left her a seemly bride for the princely work of a T Gwynn Jones and a Williams-Parry.

Every Welsh poet and every memorable prose-writer from 1900 to 1940 were or are his disciples. The National Eisteddfod itself would have died in pitiful obloquy about the turn of the century had he not taken it in hand at Bangor in 1906 and turned it into an instrument of incredible poetic rebirth.

He was born in Anglesey, went to school at Brecon, graduated at Jesus College, Oxford, in 1887, in mathematics. He read Welsh manuscript and printed texts in the Bodleian with Gwynogvryn Evans and followed the lectures of Sir John Rhys in Celtic philology. He was a founder member of the Dafydd ap Gwilym Society, began writing verse, translated the lyrics of Heine, did propaganda and public speaking for Young Wales, and began the reform and standardisation of Welsh orthography.

It is important to appreciate that he came to linguistic and literary studies from a serious academic training in mathematics. Mathematical studies are especially an aesthetic discipline.

They aim at clarity and beauty of form: not merely at the right solution of a complex problem, but at the elegant, the Mozartian solution. Elegance is an essential, not an accidental, part of mathematical rightness.

That was the discipline that Morris-Jones transferred to the study of Welsh grammar, Welsh lyric verse, the shaping and spelling of the Welsh sentence, the prosody of the *cynghanedd* metres. Grammatical forms for him were not changeable, corruptible things, whose corruption eventually becomes the accepted, and therefore for its period the right form.

That is the relative, undogmatic, modernistic view of language; not Morris-Jones's. He placed himself completely and finally in a paragraph of his preface to his Welsh Grammar which was published at Oxford in 1913:

> Dr John Davies published his grammar in 1621, the year after the appearance of the revised Bible, which is believed to be chiefly his work. The grammar represents the result of a careful study of the works of the bards. It was the first Welsh grammar to be based on an examination of the actual facts of the language of standard authors...
> the author's analysis of the modern literary language is final; he has left to his successors only the correction and amplification of detail.

Grammarians and philologists today could only gasp in amazement at such a statement. It is a Renaissance, a Revival of Learning point of view, and John Morris-Jones is really the "successor", the peer and heir of John Davies of 1621.

It was in precisely the same spirit that he analysed the metres of the classical poets of the *cywydd* period and produced his marvellous standard work on them, *Cerdd Dafod*. For him, beauty in phrase and strophe is always a sculptured, frozen, marble thing, like Bramante's *Tempietto* in Rome. It has its laws; to deviate from them is to destroy the mould. It was thus Renaissance scholars thought of Latin, of the golden age. Thus Morris-Jones thought of Welsh metrics and of Welsh grammar. He was a Renaissance scholar born in Anglesey in 1864.

Let me venture a single example to illustrate what I consider the Aristotelian quality of his mind. There is a jumble of old Welsh bardic metres and strophes and verse-forms which are sometimes called the Twenty Four Measures. They vary from the sixth century to the 15th, old ones dropped, so-called new ones proposed. The poetic grammar books tried to put some order into the jumble by arranging them in three classes. John Morris-Jones takes the whole lot and in a single sentence produces a complete principle of classification:

> One can reduce all the old Welsh verse-forms to lines of four or of six stress-accents.

And he proceeds to classify accordingly – and finally. It is simple, but no one before him and no contemporary had seen it, and it produces order as beautifully as the first chapter of *Genesis*.

Now it was just this kind of mind that Welsh philology and Welsh literature needed at the beginning of this century. He gave Parnassian standards to Welsh poetry and prose. He edited a new quarterly, the *Beirniad*, and, short as its life was, to be accepted in its pages was as much distinction for Welsh poem or story or essay as, say, for an English writer to be made free of the *Criterion* when T S Eliot was editing that.

Later, of course, there has been a reaction against the standards of Morris-Jones. That was as inevitable as it was necessary. But his contribution remains and his figure becomes only larger and more significant as our century advances. We shall forget his lessons only at our dire peril.

*The Western Mail, October 10, 1964*

James Morris was the former name of the Anglo-Welsh writer Jan Morris, who underwent a change of sexual role in the early 1970s. She has written works of travel, history, biography and fiction, lives in Gwynedd, and has been especially preoccupied with Wales during the last 30 years. Her son is Twm Morys, the Welsh-language poet, who co-authored with her in 1994 *A Machynlleth Triad*, a fantasy concerning the future of Wales. An honorary D. Litt of the Universities of Wales and Glamorgan, she is a member of the Gorsedd of Bards and was made a CBE in the 1999 Birthday Honours. This article had a wider exposure in *Life* magazine.

# The Welshman

## By James Morris

WHEN Henry Morgan, the buccaneer, savaged the Spaniards of Porto Bello; when Richard Burton, the actor, swept off her stiletto heels the Cleopatra of our time; when H M Stanley mouthed the preposterous inquiry, "Dr Livingstone, I presume?"; when Ivor Novello set a nation mooning to Glamorous Nights; when Dylan Thomas soliloquised beneath Milk Wood; when Lloyd George billowed into Versailles in clouds of cloak and rhetoric; when Frank Lloyd Wright proposed to build, as a last glorious effrontery, a skyscraper a mile high – when all these famous men behaved in these memorably characteristic ways, they were honouring a common inheritance. The pirate, the poet, the explorer, the statesman, the architect, and two matinée idols all had their roots in one small and insignificant corner of Britain, a rain-swept, hilly little place, the very nook or alcove of an island: Wales.

They were men of disparate backgrounds and accomplishments, but to them all there was a flare of something dangerously close to romance. It was liable to degenerate into cruelty (Morgan was a horror), or mawkishness (Novello could make a spaniel squirm), or deceit (Lloyd George was not above selling honours for his party funds), or mere verbosity (Thomas's ungovernable weakness).

It was, however, in them all, a sign of virile originality. Wales has not been a sovereign entity for seven centuries, but the national ethos of the place has powerfully survived, and no blood strain is more resilient than the florid but energetic heritage of the Welsh.

One Welshman can usually tell another, and this is not necessarily because either looks Welsh, or acts Welsh, but simply because both ARE Welsh; the Welsh are one of those peoples, like the Jews, and the Venetians, who do not depend for their character upon language, culture, environment or religion, but only upon history and blood.

The Welshman has Celtic origins, and he often looks like the popular conception of the Celt – dark, dreamy, and aloof. He is seldom a patrician: if he is handsome, he is handsome in a rather coarse or blowsy way. His style is seldom authoritative – he has more often been a guerrilla than a divisional commander – and his demeanour is often diffident.

Watch him as he enters a bar, buys his pint of beer and settles alone in a corner. He is a smallish, stocky man, and beneath his trousers, which incline to bagginess, his legs are very likely bandy. The expression on his face, as he lifts his tankard, is one of self-conscious wariness, as though he not only expects some hostility, but is rather looking forward to it. He is not at all an elegant figure. His dark hair is tousled, his eyebrows are bushy, his prominent nose has tufts of hair in its nostrils. A handkerchief half-tumbles out of his breast pocket. His tie is askew. The evening paper under his arm is folded tattily at the racing results.

He emanates, all the same, an animal fascination – the kind of curious allure an elderly badger exerts, if ever you see his shaggy form plodding silently through the wood at daybreak. Though often sweaty and often plump, our Welshman is not a prosaic figure. He does not look a bore. He is not absorbed, blank and unprotesting, by his background. He looks like a man on his own. And when, a moment later, he catches sight of a friend the smile that illuminates his face is unexpectedly sweet, his eyes gleam with a promise of comedy, and in the gentlest of singsong lilts, like a Bengali politician, you hear him ask: "How are you then, boy? What d'you fancy, then?"

Welsh roots are very strong, and whether this archetypal figure is buying his beer in London, Sydney or Philadelphia, he is likely to feel a nagging attachment to his homeland – nothing so vulgar as the Scotsman's professional nostalgia, but still all too likely, at maudlin moments of reminder, to start him weeping in his cups.

Welsh songs, the principal expression of popular Welshness, are mostly concerned not with Welsh men, women or events, but with Wales itself – *Land Of My Fathers, We'll Keep A Welcome In The Hillsides,* and other such perennial

Sunday-evening tearjerkers. This is perhaps because it really is a very beautiful little country. And although Wales is a mere 200 miles from London, it feels physically separate from England, its great neighbour to the east – its grass a subtly different green, its moors wilder, its hills higher, and a sense of alien remoteness in its landscapes.

Its very smallness helps. If you squashed it in a bit at the sides you could get the whole of it into the State of Maryland and there are more people in Jakarta or Los Angeles than there are in the whole of Wales.

It is not, however, an easy country to get about.

A muddled mass of high ground – some impressive enough to be called mountainous – occupies most of it, its ribs running this way and that, criss-cross and diagonally, in such complicated patterns that there is scarcely a straight road in the country, and the traveller must often start his journey in the opposite direction to the one he eventually hopes to pursue. No direct railways run from north to south and few roads. The capital, Cardiff, is on the south coast, and if people from North Wales want to go there, they must travel via England – just as the most convenient centre for Welsh national conferences is the English city of Shrewsbury.

All this means that Wales remains a place of small and self-sufficient communities – or of no communities at all. In the south the great coalfields of the Rhondda feed the ports of Cardiff, Swansea and Newport; in all the rest of Wales there is not a proper city. The Welsh do not take easily to the hugger-mugger life, and their ideal is generally a farmhouse all alone, a pub within striking distance and nothing else but themselves.

This isolation, this ruggedness, this introspection and awkwardness – all make for evasive shades and ripples of character. The Welshman is a creature of moods. Across his face the suspicions, the scowls and the smiles pass precisely as the clouds dapple Welsh hill-sides – changing, incessantly, from gloom to sunshine. His is a high-flown country, and he himself has a weakness for the ornately mystical. Merlin was a Welshman, and the national emblem is a red dragon raising a sharp right claw and sticking out an elaborately heraldic tongue.

To the ironic English next door, so sceptical, so gimlet-eyed, Welshness has always looked a little absurd, and the Welshman has generally been a bit of a joke. Seen out of the splendours of English success, the very existence of Wales seems unnecessary, and the desire of Welshmen to remain Welsh looks just plain cranky.

Shakespeare's Hotspur spoke breezily for England, when he called Owen Glendower "tedious as a tired horse", with his skimble-skamble talk of dragons, moldwarps, griffins and finless fish. One of Shakespeare's most successful comic characters was Fluellen, the stout Welsh soldier, who talked in just the, same hilarious Welsh dialect that figures in a thousand funny stories to this day. The

Welshman has been guyed for centuries, rather as the American Negro used to be, in the days when he staggered on stage as a farcical domestic or buffoon.

But the laughter that habitually greets the Welshman is partly the nervous giggle that is a normal response to the unfamiliar – coupled in Shakespeare's case, perhaps, with dim memories of the days when the Welsh, not so far from Stratford, were lawless primitives out of the west. Wales is a strange sort of country. In its hills the moldwarp and the finless fish ring true. Its history is embedded in colourful myth and fancy – misty kingdoms of the sunset, lost cities of the sea, dragons in lakes and magical decisions on mountaintops.

The Romans never altogether subdued Wales, settling in many of its valleys, driving their roads westward to the Irish Sea, but leaving the hill people well alone.

The Saxons never got much further than the foothills, and from the struggle of these western Britons against them sprang the epic legend of King Arthur and his knights, recorded first in the Four Ancient Books of Wales – *The Book of Aneirin, The Book of Taliesin, The Black Book of Carmarthen* and *The Red Book of Hergest.* Heroes with outlandish names glorify the old Welsh chronicles – Gruffydd ap Llywelyn, or Hywel Dda, or Llywelyn the Last, whose decapitated head was set in silver and stuck on the Tower of London.

For the Welsh the centuries after the Norman Conquest of England were one intermittent war of survival, a dismal sequence of raids, rebellions and occupations, with the great castles of the English ominously rising from Montgomery to Harlech and the Welsh guerrillas operating from high moorland fastnesses. The Welsh never quite gave in; the hostilities ended only after two Welshmen, Henry V and Henry VII, had acceded to the throne of England.

Since then the Welshness of Wales has been constantly under pressure. Sometimes the English have deliberately tried to suppress it; sometimes the mere presence of England has threatened to obliterate it. Economics, politics, tourism, television, the movement of population, the decline of the old Welsh Methodist religion – all have hammered away at the personality of Wales, and tried to fuse the little country more thoroughly with the world outside.

Even so, Wales has managed to remain apart, and the Welshman preserves his reputation – part shady, part funny, part beguiling. The Welsh language fitfully survives, so that there are still odd corners of Wales where you will hear little else but its breathy *glissandos,* and its rhythms have sometimes influenced English poesy too; Dylan Thomas could read no Welsh, but his master Gerard Manley Hopkins could, and reproduced the magic of traditional Welsh euphony in lines like:

> *I caught this morning morning's minion, kingdom*
> *Of daylight's dauphin, dapple-dawn-drawn*
> *Falcon, in his riding*
> *Of the rolling level underneath him steady air…*

Weird but haunting phrases, lingering tales of ghosts and fairies, ridiculous place names like Llanfairpwllgwyngyllgogerychwyrndrobwllllantysiliogogogoch, fantasies of every kind, the tragic fascination of the Rhondda in the slump, the repeated emergence from Welsh poverty of men like Emlyn Williams and Aneurin Bevan, slag-heaps, slate quarries, sheep on bare hillsides, fiery Calvinism in grey chapels, inspired demagogues, dotty bards, the faint echo of harps and the open-throated fervour of male-voice choirs – all these things, supported always by the blue mystery of those western hills, have kept the idea of Wales a little mysterious still, although the Kings of Wales have long been laid beneath their cromlechs and even the wizards are hard to identify.

*The Western Mail, March 15, 1965*

Gwyn Alf Williams was born in Dowlais and educated at University College, Aberystwyth, where he was appointed lecturer in Welsh history in 1954. He became reader and then professor of history at York University in 1965, and in 1974 professor of history at University College, Cardiff. When he retired in 1983, he emerged from the cloisters of academe to write and present a number of historical television programmes. His work adds up to a major contribution to the history of Wales, and is characterised by his passion, erudition and colourful style. His books included *The Merthyr Rising* (1978), and *When was Wales?* (1985), and he based on the latter his part in the television series *The Dragon has Two Tongues*, which he co-presented with Wynford Vaughan-Thomas.

# In the Margins of Magna Carta

## By Gwyn A Williams

WHAT was Magna Carta to the Welsh? A clutch of clauses chopping out their staccato litany of captives, hostages and castles? To the Welshman of 1215, certainly, it was no palladium of liberty; his breed lay without that law. A peace settlement, then, wrested from King John by courtesy of the barons and bishops of England? Scarcely even that, for, within months, the sword again rang in the heads of mothers and the three Welsh clauses of the charter were one more broken treaty by the ford.

In England, too, war came hard on Runnymede; the death of John was its real ratification. Yet who would deny that Englishmen were right to call this baronial manifesto a Great Charter from the beginning? It may well have been the Puritan lawyers of the 17th century, seeking a warrant for their Great Rebellion, who made it the foundation text of English liberty. They were myth-makers. But a myth is not a lie.

From the moment of its sealing, some of its 63 jumbled clauses were timeless; there is a real continuity of spiritual commitment stretching back to that June day in 1215. They were right to venerate Runnymede as one of those moments of which Auden spoke when he wrote of:

> ...the dangerous flood
> Of history, that never sleeps or dies,
> And, held one moment, burns the hand.

But what Welsh hand is burned at Runnymede's touch? In 1215, to us as a people, or rather as a congeries of piratical little polities, Magna Carta was a truce in the seemingly endless battle for a Welshman's liberty and a Welshman's licence. Even in the 17th century, when English democracy went to war, with the charter for a flag, we turned out against it and died by the thousand to keep ourselves in chains.

As individuals, certainly, we shared the warmth of the Whig high noon, but not until we got our gentry off our backs could we talk in the style which the charter's myth made proper. Even then, the accent of many of us was that of those Levellers who found Magna Carta "a beggarly thing, containing many marks of intolerable bondage" and who considered the Glorious Revolution of 1688 to be "a coup d'état by landowning bandits". Towards traditional English liberty, as towards traditional English monarchy, not a few of us have been a shade reticent.

No, the Welsh peep out from the margins of Magna Carta like caricatures in Matthew Paris's chronicle. True, we also have our myth. It makes its appearance a trifle late, as befits the Highland Zone, in the December of 1215, a couple of months after the charter had been blown away in civil war.

In that month, Llywelyn ab Iorwerth, Prince of Gwynedd, came down to the South with an army drawn from every Welsh district which had kept its independence. For the first time the shadow of the new Gwynedd fell across the new Wales.

Early in 1216, royal power in the South crumbled and, at the celebrated assembly at Aberdovey, Llywelyn partitioned the land between the shrunken heirs of the old dynasty of Deheubarth.

To the charter of English liberties then, we oppose a Welsh Prince of Wales in embryo. Magna Carta emerges as a punctuation point in the title-deeds of the first Welsh Parliament.

These myths, like the peoples who generated them, are yoked together. The 13th century saw the making of the English community. Its continental empire lost, the cosmopolitan aristocracy sank its roots in English soil. English consciousness turned inward; this is the century of Magna Carta, of Simon de Montfort and Parliament, of the great statutes. In Wales, it is the century of the two Llywelyns, of the building of a miniature Welsh feudal state, with its focus in Gwynedd.

On the morrow of the English civil war over Magna Carta, Llywelyn ab Iorwerth established his claim to be *de facto* Prince of Wales. On the morrow of the English civil war over Simon de Montfort's Parliament (whose ambiguous anniversary we also celebrate this year) Llywelyn ap Gruffydd established himself as Prince of Wales *de jure*. The first Llywelyn married the daughter of John; the second married the daughter of "St Simon" himself. Both, allied with the baronial opposition, called upon foreign powers and the Papacy for help.

It was an age of state builders, in which Magna Carta and the assembly of Aberdovey seem to have their appointed place. As in England we can trace the unlikely origin of that splendid Whig myth of freedom broadening down from precedent to precedent, so in Wales we can pinpoint the ambivalent source of that Welsh Principality broadening down from the first Llywelyn to the last, prolonging itself, after the Conquest in an occult underworld which runs through Owain Glyndwr to our own day, when memorials are raised, myths rationalised and 20th century obsessions duly read back into 13th century minds. We merit, then, at least a footnote to Magna Carta.

But our myth does not enjoy the ultimate sanction of success. Macaulay's schoolboy felt no call to be shrill about Magna Carta – consider Owen M Edwards on Llywelyn the Great. "Where was power and which the road to it? It was no abstract question for us," writes another marginal Welshman of our own century. It was a question the Llywelyns failed to answer.

The first tried to anchor his power in the feudal system of England, to legalise it on his overlord's terms. He ploughed sand. Within a year of his death, his polity was in ruins. His grandson's desperate enterprise alienated half his own people. Welshmen staffed the armies which brought the Welsh Principality down.

In the last resort, both these crowned revolutionaries were broken by tradition, the rooted aristocratic particularism of Wales – a Welsh way of life far more ancient than their new-fangled principality. In the 13th century, the English aristocracy built a kingdom; the Welsh aristocracy destroyed one.

So, across 750 years, Magna Carta and Aberdovey, a melancholy couple, blink back at the Welsh like doleful beacons through a mist. In Welsh history, the tenses are always conditional, the mood inescapably subjunctive.

*The Western Mail, June 11, 1965*

Poet and journalist Harri Webb, born in Swansea and educated at Magdalen College, Oxford, where he read Romance languages, was a Royal Navy interpreter during World War II and then joined the Druid Press at Carmarthen. In 1954, he became a librarian at Dowlais, and from 1964 until 1974, when he retired, at Mountain Ash. A passionate nationalist, he was a member of the Welsh Republican Movement before helping Plaid Cymru. His output of poems, many of them about the history and social problems of Wales and showing his caustic and sarcastic wit, was prolific; in the 1970s he began writing a series of scripts for television, including *The Green Desert* and *How Green was my Father*. His adaptation for children of tales from the *Mabinogion* was published as *Tales from Wales* in 1984. He died in 1994.

# Babylon has the edge on Zion

## By Harri Webb

THE Mabinogi of Branwen, the daughter of Llyr, is a tale of Western seaboards and the Celtic Sea. The armies move between Wales and Ireland, the magic birds sing at Harlech, the seven knights ride down from Menai to Pembroke, and the door that must not be opened looks towards Cornwall. But the talisman head of Brân must be buried in London under the White Hill.

This break in the geographical unity of the story is not so much an artistic flaw as the entrance to one of the great enigmas of the Welsh mind, that ambivalent special relationship with our only neighbours, and the even more special role of London.

As soon as our history emerges from myth (if it ever has done) the chronicles echo the Mabinogi and speak not of the King of England, but the King of London.

English historians, dedicated to the concept of national homogeneity, minimise the particularism of their capital as of any other region. More detached and realistic, the Welsh knew better.

The nearer and more familiar English counties and towns have been to us mere market places. The great border cities and ports, for all their military and economic impact, have never been absorbed into the national imagination.

English, not Welsh, poetry familiarises us with Ludlow, Wenlock and Clun. The emigrants are either short-range, never really leaving home, or, in every sense, get lost.

Does anyone know or care how all those Welsh surnames came to be on the shop-fronts of Burford in the heart of the Cotswolds? Or what happened to "Banastre's Welshmen," a considerable medieval exodus to Lancashire?

True, the Welsh clergymen of the West Riding irrupt on to the scene with important educational proposals in the 19th century, but they seem visitants from a limbo of Saint David's Day dinners scattered to no purpose over the broad alien acres.

How otherwise with the Welsh of London! Their continuous history goes back far further than their most successful exemplar (Welshman for King. Pembroke boy makes good), back at least to the Petit Waleis that clustered around the Tower, that very White Hill of the Mabinogi, in the days when the Princes of Gwynedd were still defying its ruler.

By a weird appropriateness, the site is now a forum for those tame agitators beloved of our English friends.

Our best poets, the late medieval *cywyddwyr*, do not scruple to draw similes from London life. Dafydd ap Glyndwr is familiar with shops of Cheapside and the cloisters of Westminster, and unhesitatingly weaves them into his praise of a man hostile to the commercial and political policies they embodied.

And if the Act of Union had its genesis in a memorandum drawn up in Brecon, its genocidal intentions were largely nullified by the deliberations at Lambeth which sponsored Bishop Morgan's Bible. And for the next 300 years London was the only place where a sufficient number of influential Welshmen could gather to take important decisions.

The bijou societies of our market towns could not compete, could only breed imitative pretensions. And the first urban centre of any importance in Wales itself was the mining camp, Merthyr Tydfil, until Cardiff came up in the 1860s, one of the younger capitals therefore, and to be forgiven some of its youthful inadequacies.

London, the market of our herds, attracted not only drovers, but, as the Court, called to all those "impatient of labour and overmuch boasting of the Nobilitye of their stocke, applying themselves rather to the service of noblemen than giving themselves to the learning of handicraftes", as

Humphrey Lloyd put it in a comment which, *mutatis mutandis*, has an oddly contemporary ring.

The dichotomy of tribal, agrarian Wales is thus early established, part retreating ever deeper into defensive emphasis on everything that differentiated it from the outside world (eventually to nurture a cross-grained puritanism utterly at odds with every characteristic that made us a people) and part of it reaching out to embrace commercial and political advancement in a spirit of shallow and pliant opportunism which brought its own nemesis; so Sir Hugh Middleton sunk the fortune of his Cardiganshire mines in the New River scheme, which beggared him.

To this day, Ludgate Circus is cluttered with a paltry obelisk commemorating a Montgomeryshire worthy who had made his pile; offered in desperation by the City to his native place, it was refused.

But such acid anecdotes are not the whole story. The Cymmrodorion have, in their day, deserved well of Wales: the attorneys of Tavie's Inn, depicted by Hogarth, the radicals who foregathered with Glan-y-Gors and Iolo Morganwg, the drapers and milkmen, pillars of Jewin and King's Cross.

The recent death of Sir John Cecil-Williams brought to an end a recognisable period, and poses a fundamental question: Is there still a role for the London-based Cymmrodorion? Or should they now seek a home in the Welsh Capital?

It is a question of legitimate interest far outside the confines of the Honourable Society and of some historical significance.

But there has always been a wider spectrum of London-Welsh than the official and self-conscious element. The Depression may have filled the East End with blue-scarred postmen and chuckers-out, and the purlieus of Paddington with girls who never let on to mam, but this was no new thing.

> O na bawn i fel colomen
> Ar ben Saint Pauls ynghanol Llundain
> Er cael gweled merched Cymru
> Ar eu cluniau'n chwynnu'r gerddi

The country poet who wrote this pennill (still quoted in West Wales pubs) lusting for the pretty knees of the girls who had gone as migrant labour to weed the gardens of London, illuminates a whole unofficial history.

The existence of this great mart of opportunity on the doorstep of a conservative-minded hill country has had consequences which have never really been calculated.

Life in Wales is easy-going, democratic, neighbourly. Or it is slow, inefficient and claustrophobic. If the latter, the escape route is at hand.

Economic necessity, after all, cannot possibly account for the volume and character of our emigration, especially when you consider the number of English people who have to be brought in to keep the country going. The fact is that Babylon has always got the edge on Zion.

The Welsh (or ex-Welsh) community in London embraces a wider spectrum than anything in Wales itself, from Tony Armstrong-Jones, who married a princess, to Timothy Evans, who was hanged by mistake, from Bronwen Pugh who became Lady Astor to Betty Jones who became a gunman's moll.

It took an English writer whose sensibilities had been sharpened by living in Wales, Mr Kingsley Amis, to point out that the most tangible internal frontier in this island is the one surrounding London.

Now that the world no longer thinks tomorrow what Manchester thinks today, the great industrial centres of provincial England have lost their importance, like their predecessors the landed magnates of the shires. Of the old ruling class, only the Crown has retained any significance. And from the centuries of industrial growth, London has emerged as the only effective centre of influence.

It is not rash to prophesy that decentralisation and regional autonomy will offer very little corrective. If anything, London will expand at England's expense, and its ethos and standards will extend their frontiers over new territories of the land and of the mind.

Already its outposts are only a county away from Offa's Dyke. Bristol may lurk just over the Severn Bridge, but the launching-pad in respect of which the distant-early-warnings are already sounding is the Chiswick flyover.

The city that made its own treaty with the Conqueror, the wool wharf of the Hanse, almost as much a city state as any in the League, whose mobs survived policy and whose prentice bands brought down the monarchy, the northern Venice Canaletto saw, the foggy liberal refuge of expatriate visionaries, the hub of Empire, the front-line capital is facing change with a confidence not born of wealth alone.

Sprouting skyscrapers, marketing now not only its old wares, but the tertiary products of the contemporary scene – the fashions and the trends – it outlives its empire like Byzantium, to become one of only a few such centres in the world, cosmopolitan in the literal sense of the word, a market and a magnet for the increasing proportion of the world's population who have the means of mobility, the desire for diversion, the tastes to enjoy and the incomes to afford lavish amenities.

And, even by British Rail on a good day, less than three hours from a country where livestock roam in the streets, business never seems to get started before mid-morning, and any activity after 9 pm is regarded as night-life. No wonder there is so much out-way traffic.

Not all the emigrants are a loss to us. Mr Morgan buys a ticket at Swansea High Street, he disappears en route, and Mr Morton gets off the train at Paddington. We have more than our share of people who cannot live with their own identity.

Recently a Welsh lady beat with her umbrella an African speaker at Hyde Park Corner who suggested that people should stay in their own country, including the Welsh in Wales.

Not only was the unfortunate blackamoor belaboured with our dreaded national weapon, he was fined for a breach of the peace, for it is important to our expatriates and their hosts that this escape route be kept open.

It must often seem to be a delusive escape – into a dead-end ghetto which has been called "Tregaron-on-Thames," an incredibly old-fashioned community, walled in by the busy indifference of the great city to the private lives of individuals.

But even this tranquil back-water is feeling the wind of change. The once-a-year Welshman, the long-distance patriots of the Eisteddfod field and the capricious benefactions are greeted not with the respect of yore, but with something like contempt.

Elfed could achieve personal ascendancy in Wales, part of which was based on the very fact of his long years at King's Cross. Wales today would not accept as national patriarch one so largely representative of the diaspora.

The grotesque "new national flag," which was invented in London, has died the same death as the even more grotesque idea of staging the National Eisteddfod in the concrete and claustrophobic halls and galleries of Earl's Court.

The social bases in Wales, from which this retrovert colony is mostly recruited, are themselves either eroding or evolving.

The most aware members of it are consciously seeking a new formula for Welsh life in London.

One interesting by-product is the emergence of *The London Welshman*, under the editorship of Mr Tudor David, as an English-language monthly seriously commenting on Welsh affairs – currently the only such.

But it is the Welsh in Wales who must give the effective answer, if they can, to the dilemma of living in the same world with such formidable competition.

Whatever one's assortment of political nationalism, it is obviously only a partial contribution to the problem of maintaining the national identity of a country naturally conservative, whose most active elements have such an attractive alternative so easily available.

Paradoxically, the proximity of London has reinforced the conformism and suspicion of change which are both the strength and the weakness of highland zone societies, and a thorough-going revision of all our attitudes, in every sector of our national life, is the only hope for the survival of the nation.

Sentimental longing for a Wales which never was, or is deservedly dead, will not save us. The Mabinogi is over. The head of Brân is buried under the Tower Hill.

*The Western Mail, November 6, 1965*

Gordon Parry has written many articles for *The Western Mail*, many of them when he was chairman of the Wales Tourist Board from 1978 to 1984. He became a life peer, as Lord Parry, in 1976. A teacher by profession, he is keenly interested in educational matters, and rarely misses a major debate in the Lords. Here, he dissects the road crash in which he was severely injured in 1965 and tells of the lasting consequences. He was not to know then that he would have to have an operation in 1989 to immobilise his shattered ankle joint. When Barbara Castle, then Secretary of State for Transport, saw the article, she ordered that a version should be sent to other provincial newspapers.

# Hurled to the Edge of Life

## By Gordon Parry

IT WAS a Bank Holiday weekend in 1965. Do you remember what the weather was like? The Saturday had been light and soft. The breeze had been almost warm and very gentle.

We had had a good day and we were happy as we turned on to Arnold's Hill for the run down into Haverfordwest. There were three of us in our car.

A moment later, we all but died.

Nothing can be said about how we came to crash. What matters now is that we did. What matters now is that we were, in that moment, hurled to the very edge of life.

And what matters more than anything is that some of us who were broken in that moment are still – 17 months later – struggling painfully back towards health that may never, for some of us, be fully regained.

I can say here only that there was a second when I knew that we were going to crash. Sitting beside the driver, I reached out for something to hold me in my place. Then the grinding, the tearing, the crashing and the beating were all around me, and nothing could hold me still.

In that last split second I thought of no one and nothing but me and my own efforts to hold on to life.

The first strike hurled me from my place. My hands and arms have always served me well. They've always been able to cope with the strains that I've put upon them in a pretty active 40 years of living.

Suddenly, I was having to ask them to do too much for me. My left hand had anchored to the door grip. My right was flat against the dashboard with the elbow bracing it rigid for the shock.

Not only was I asking my hands and arms to do too much, I was making them do the wrong things. When we struck, the physics of the situation ruled. My arms and hands were as helpless to combat the forces let loose by collision as were the feet and legs which I was forcing down into the chassis.

On impact, I pivoted. My left arm twisted at the shoulder joint until the joint dislocated. It turned at the elbow until the elbow gave out. My right hand slipped from the facia and palmed a hole in the windscreen.

Under me, the seat was tearing from its moorings. Its leading under-edge was strip steel, and it bit into the bones and tendons of my straining left foot.

A reflex kicked my right foot up and out of the way and, as my body followed through, my knees impacted against the forward structure which was crumpling back into us.

My face followed my punching hand through the shattering glass, and the bench seat, following me, mercifully pinned me into the wreckage that I had been about to leave in a violent orbit of death.

My rib cage, breasting the dashboard, cracked and buckled and, as suddenly as it had begun, the noise and the mad movement ended. I had been beaten to the edge of life. I couldn't breathe. But I was alive! I was even conscious!

More than anything, I was conscious that if I didn't begin to breathe, I should die. This feeling of being outside oneself, waiting passively for something to happen that is without one's own control, has been written about.

I don't understand it, I merely confirm it. That's the way it was. I – whoever I am, and wherever I was in that instant – waited what seemed like a long while for my breath to run back into my twisted and busted body, knowing that if it didn't there would be no point in my going back into it.

However long in time it was that I waited, it was at least long enough for my wife, who had been battered senseless behind us, and was bleeding very badly, down there on the floor in darkness, to gain her wits and to think of me.

She said, "Are you all right, Love?"

Now, it seems funny to both of us. Now, it may seem trite to you. To me, in that moment, it really meant, "Are you going to live?"

It was probably in that very moment that I knew that I was. Certainly, I remember thinking very clearly, "I shall be all right, Love, as long as I can get my breath."

There were to be many bad moments in the months ahead before everyone else was convinced that I would live. For me, there was no doubt after I took that first breath of new life.

We were trapped for a time. A coachful of soccer players – the Milford United team – came racing to our aid. They didn't stop to measure the danger of fire.

They swarmed all over the wreckage. Others – people whom I've never adequately thanked, nor even properly identified – came, too.

My wife, who has a rare blood group, was lifted, treated, carded, so that there should be no mistake in transfusing, and carried gently to the players' coach, where she lay, with all her buffeting and bruising, worrying only about me and my injuries.

Our driver was conscious now, too, and he and I were even able to talk while we were freed, tended, left lying back in our places until the ambulances came.

We were able, then to think about the others. Were there others hurt? Were they hurt as badly as we were? Devoutly, we hoped that they were not, and, happily, only one other in the triple crash had been seriously injured.

The others involved were hurt, of course. They were badly shocked, but the injuries to three of us were so dramatic that others, like my own wife, found that their own were largely discounted as friends and relatives concentrated their interest on us.

For this, we, all three, have apologised many times since.

When my injuries came to be totalled, I had dislocated a shoulder and an elbow, received massive injury to the right ankle, broken and impacted my right femur so that the leg was shortened for a time by about five inches, broken a number of ribs down my left side, and spread my nose across my face.

In addition, the accident had set up processes which caused my lungs to collapse and took me back, on more then one occasion, into danger of death.

I was to be an in-patient of the orthopaedic ward at Glangwili Hospital for a very long time, a daily attendant of the physiotherapy department at Haverfordwest Hospital for even longer.

In a month or so, I have to return to Glangwili for further surgery, involving the removal of the ironmongery that served as a core to my femur while it was restructuring itself.

Even then, I still have to face further surgery to correct the collapse that is slowly taking place in my left ankle.

Incidentally, my suffering has been small compared with what happened to my father. You see, he was killed in another road accident while coming to visit me in hospital.

*The Western Mail, March 27, 1967*

Duncan Gardiner held a succession of senior editorial posts on *The Western Mail* in the 1960s before joining the *Sunday Times* as editorial manager. He returned to become editor of the *Mail* in 1973, and edited the paper for seven years. During his first spell in Cardiff, he wrote a regular Saturday column on food and wine.

# Vins d'Etergent
## By Duncan Gardiner

LESSER-KNOWN wines with unusual labels are always a challenge for the connoisseur; a look through some of the catalogues, the end of bin sales and so on can provide the enthusiast, not only the connoisseur, with enough food, rather drink, for much thought.

Then to track them down, to trace them. The results can be most gratifying.

The rather floury *Chateau d'Az (plus blanc que blanc)*, for instance, which has no particular bouquet. But the peasants of d'Az generally take it at slightly above room temperature with a little water. The result is pleasingly effervescent, providing a good clean after-taste.

In a similar field would be the slightly more expensive *Eau Meau* (slightly more expensive, yes; yet there is generally more in the bottle), which is treated in a similar way to the *d'Az*.

Certainly, it's a good clean wine, with just a hint of sparkle – ideal, perhaps, as a pick-me-up after a heavy weekend on that washday morning.

Basically, these two would come under the generic heading of Vins d'Etergent. Their peculiar value comes, without doubt, from the fact that they face the drying wind on the north bank of the Ergine River, particularly the Eau Meau which lies round the Ess bend.

*St Ergine*, a rosé, is another of the principal wines from this little-known area. Slightly more aromatic, it is also stronger: dilution is clearly necessary for the beginner.

I would not recommend that these Vins d'Etergent be used to flavour stock or as a basis for sauce: it is possible, nevertheless, that just a trace on the cooking utensils might add a certain soupçon.

Further south in one of the off-the-beaten-track areas of the Pyrenees, you find the *Pers Il (El Sinq)*. I'm told this wine is the result of a highly-kept secret but there are rumours in the trade that the shippers, Lever Frères, have spent a great amount in experimenting with a powdered version which would enable them to bring down the prices and perhaps offer something further with their packet deals.

You will rarely find any of these wines lying loose; much will be bonded, but no extra charges are generally made when they are offered "in original cases" nor for carriage. The usual seven days allowed from the date of sale to allow payment of duty and clearance from bond does not apply.

More rare still, from Germany, is one recently introduced to me by an antique acquaintance, Pierre Philpot. M Philpot (pronounced Philpeau) presented me with an intriguing little *Zurff*.

This *Zurff (mit Wasser getrunken am Hamburg, Reeperbahn '66)* has a magical formula, apparently, which cleanses as it soaks. It can, I'm told, sometimes be found at the end of bin.

Curiously, you probably can't find these wines. Nor can gourmets or connoisseurs often get the chance to discuss them or to write about them. The sad fact is that it is only before opening time on a morning like this that they can be found.

*The Western Mail, April 1, 1967*

Cefneithin-born Carwyn James was capped twice for Wales at fly-half before starting a coaching career with Llanelli in 1969. First he made the Scarlets the best side in Wales, then in 1971 he took the British Lions on a victorious tour of New Zealand. A passionate Welshman, he was admitted to the Gorsedd in 1972. He had earlier taught Welsh for two years at Carmarthen's Queen Elizabeth Grammar School for Boys and Llandovery College. He declined the post of national coach in 1974, and instead coached around the world and freelanced as a journalist. But he also had a lifelong love of cricket: as a vice-president of Glamorgan County Cricket Club he watched them play, at home or away, whenever he could. He died at 53, from a heart attack, in 1983.

# Bradman… lbw James

## By Carwyn James

O NE of the great thrills to me as a boy was to watch the County play; a greater thrill even was to anticipate the game and play in it. I would always put the Aussies in first, feed them with lots of runs, take the occasional wicket and then, moment of moments, he would come in, the great man himself.

How I used to hate him. I would attack his off peg, give the ball a lot of air and make it turn towards second and third slip, and I allowed him to thump the occasional one square and through the covers. But at the right psychological moment I always got him. With a straight, quick, low one, and I appealed arrogantly and confidently and he was out.

Bradman, D… lbw James C… 23.

His back on the long, lonely walk to the pavilion showed his anguish. I was sorry for him and I wasn't sorry for him.

It wasn't all fantasy. It isn't now.

As a small boy, and later, St Helen's was a "must" on August Bank Holiday Monday. Who cared about the noisy brass bands at the National, anyway. I would catch the early United Welsh, Sunday service, complete with sandwiches. I went early for one reason only, to bag the nearest seat to the sight-screen, and there I would sit and watch in admiration all day long, watching every ball from behind the bowler's arm, watching for turn and twist, length and lift, floater and full toss.

I noted how one batsman would flash and feel outside the off stick and how another, with a bat twice as broad, would half volley a good-length ball effortlessly along the ground to the ropes before cover point or extra moved one inch to its path. It was such an innings of rare quality that I was privileged to watch on one of these feast days.

The gentleman concerned was Weekes, Everton Weekes, one of the three W's of the West Indian side of the Walcott era. He had started his innings on Saturday evening, he resumed it at 11.30 on the Monday morning. Before lunch he had scored 100 delightful runs, the like of which I had never seen before. It was cricket with art. The bat seemed to belong to his person, a part of the man's anatomy. A bit of wood, gracious, elegant, cultured, producing shots of such quality that one looked to the arts, to music and poetry, even to ballet to try to express them, such was his artistry.

When he played back he seemed serious and contemplative and in the minor key; mostly, he was joyously playing his symphony in the major, the sadness of his very being giving way to an optimism which lives only for that moment in the present when the skies are blue and warm – rare moments to be savoured there and then and for all time, for they happen too seldom.

It was an impossible task to bowl at him. That morning he made a mockery of the art of bowling. His front foot dominated, and as it sprang to the pitch of the ball, in turn, cover, mid-off and fielders straight behind the hapless bowler could only applaud as they acknowledged a passing acquaintance with the ball. This was genius born of accurate, rangy technique. Craft covered by inspiration, the romantic in a rare creative mood. I saw it and I shall never forget it.

And then, in anger or in admiration, I shall never know, the heavens opened; it rained torrential West Indian rain and St Helen's in no time was like a lake. Everything that day was done on the grand scale. It was not a day for mortals.

I went home drenched to the skin but happy. In the bus I sheltered behind an old newspaper, read not a word, and recalled privately, greedily, every shot he had played. I played them all back slowly, over and over again in the mind's eye. Oh, for the power of total recall. I still play those shots in my day-dreams, imperfectly I'm afraid.

Cricket to me was never the same after that innings. I had witnessed a new dimension, the intensity of which was almost frightening. I now began to understand and believe in Neville Cardus. His poetic and musical images are right, not that I sit in judgment, to describe the heroic and romantic deeds of Fry, MacLaren, Ranji and Trumper. Genius describing genius. Listen to his description of Fry, the young man who walked about the field like a Greek god. In his description there is graciousness, charm, dignity.

"I once saw Walter Brearley, a fast bowler, hit Fry on the hand; and Fry walked almost to the fence on the square leg boundary shaking his bruised finger, with not a loss of dignity at all, not to announce his agony to the world; he was simply absorbed, like a student of metaphysics, in the problem of pain."

To me and my generation the savoury moments came from the likes of May, Cowdrey, Graveney, Lewis and many, many such moments from Majid. Majid, a rare soul, whose wavelength, as far as I can judge, is tuned to a higher pitch than anyone else I have seen in the game at the moment. How fortunate Glamorgan are to have him. How fortunate we are to have Glamorgan.

I have heard it said, too often, that cricket is not a game for Welshmen. They may be alluding to the birth of the game and its history, but the pedigree of rugby football is equally suspect, and we seem to be doing all right at that.

Is it temperament, then, that the game of cricket is too slow and ponderous for us? There is, I suppose, some truth in the belief that we lack stamina, that we start well and finish badly, and maintain our enthusiasm for short periods only. And then we think of Emrys Davies and Allan Jones: stayers, grafters, with the guts, the durability and the hardness of purpose to match even the Australians.

Craftsmen doing an honest day's work. Untypical, it could be said, the triumph of self-discipline over the Celtic temperament, in which, unquestionably, there is poetry, style and a spirit of adventure, but dampened too often by a climate too cold and wet to breed the cavalier-type batsmen who thrive on hard wickets on which shots can be played because the ball comes through true and fast.

Despite our weather, Glamorgan are an attractive side to follow. One supports them – support, incidentally, meaning membership and presence – not because of patriotism or duty but because one wants to. The enthusiasm of the side is infectious, the clash of temperaments challenging, and their generous spirit in defeat and victory manly. May each one of them, at some time during the season, in bowling, batting or in fielding, achieve such a moment of greatness as I saw in Weekes.

In Weekes's innings there was no winter; one felt the freshness of spring and the warmth of summer.

*The Western Mail, May 22, 1972*

Critic, poet and broadcaster Aneirin Talfan Davies started his career with the BBC in London during World War II, and moved to BBC Wales when it ended, becoming Head of Programmes in Cardiff in 1966. He started the publishing house Llyfrau'r Dryw (now Christopher Davies Ltd.) with his brother Alun, and wrote two books – on Carmarthen and Glamorgan – for a series published by the company. He died in 1980.

# The Fearless Knight

## By Aneirin Talfan Davies

I FIRST met Saunders Lewis at his father's home at Swansea. His father, the Rev. Lodwick Lewis, and my father were both Calvinistic Methodist ministers. It was at this time that I fell under the spell of the man who must be the most influential figure Wales has seen in this century. In those far-off days I used to accompany him to speak at meagrely attended meetings of the Blaid Genedlaethol, the Welsh Nationalist Party, the beginnings of what is now the more influential Plaid Cymru.

The thing I remember best from those days is Saunders Lewis's handling of his powerful car, which he drove with the panache of a medieval knight galloping to war. He was a fearless driver, a characteristic of his leadership in the realm of politics, religion and literature.

It was this fearless independence of mind which led him into the Roman Catholic Church in 1932, and in so doing shocked the whole of Nonconformist Wales; the same fearlessness led him and his two friends, the Rev. Lewis Valentine and the late D J Williams, to commit that symbolic act of arson on the beginnings of the RAF aerodrome on the Lleyn Peninsula, which landed them, after two trials, in Wormwood Scrubs for nine months.

It is this characteristic steady nerve, "keeping his cool" is the modern cliché, which made it possible for him to accept a commission to write a play for the BBC between the two trials. This was the beginning of his life as a playwright. He had written one or two plays before, one at least in English. It's worth remembering that as a grammar-school boy in Wallasey, Liverpool, he had written drama criticism for the *Wallasey Chronicle*.

A glimpse of the honesty of the man was seen some months ago, on the night when he was presented with the volume *Presenting Saunders Lewis*, published to mark his eightieth birthday, when he went out of the way to praise Sir Rhys Hopkin-Morris for what he called the most courageous act of the century, in commissioning a play when he was being reviled by obtuse critics throughout Wales, and when University College, Swansea, sacked him before he had even been tried.

This play was *Buchedd Garmon*, based on the 5th century saint who was called over to Wales to fight the Pelagian heresies. But the contemporary undertones are unmistakable, and the shadow of the Old Bailey plainly discerned.

I have always thought that his tactics at that trial were among his greatest mistakes.

I was present at the trial, and noted the well of the court overflowing with journalists from all over the world, with their pens at the ready to record the speech that never materialised. He refused to plead and refused to recognise the court. He had delivered his defence for his actions in the trial at Caernarvon, to the intense and undisguised annoyance of the judge.

It was a great defence of Christian morality and will remain, I think, one of the great documents produced in the annals of the courts in Wales. Even in reading it, one cannot help being moved by its majestic eloquence. It has all the marks of an honest, all too honest, politician.

There is not a facet of Welsh life where you fail to see the modifying influence of Saunders Lewis's hand, although as a politician he was a failure.

Years ago, when I interviewed him on television, I taxed him with this failure. With searing candour, he replied, "I was rejected by everybody; I was rejected in every election in which I stood as candidate; every one of my ideas – I started with the sociology of nationalism – all has been thrown aside. Therefore, there was nowhere else I could turn, but to speak of my vision by writing the history of Welsh literature, and by writing plays."

I think many people are thankful for his "failure" – for he has used this most terrifying of instruments, the creative word, in his plays and poetry to express his vision, which is only now bearing fruit.

From this recluse-like living in the suburbs of Penarth, he has dominated the literary and political scene in Wales. He is feared, rightly so, for as R S Thomas has written about him in one of his poems:

> *He kept his pen clean*
> *By burying it in their fat*
> *Flesh.*

Such a man cannot expect to be loved; but for those of us who know him he engenders a loyalty and a love which never falters or fails. I salute a brave man, a sensitive critic, a superb poet, an incisive, creative mind. He is slowly changing the face of Wales.

*The Western Mail, October 20, 1973*

Born in Swansea, distinguished poet and film-maker John Ormond began his career with *Picture Post* in 1945 after graduating from University College, Swansea. In 1949, he returned to Swansea to work as a sub-editor, then in 1957 moved to BBC Wales, where he established an international reputation for film-making and won many awards for his documentaries. He had his first poems published before he was 20, and continued to write throughout his life. In the mid-1970s he contributed a Personal Column, of which this is one, to *The Western Mail*. He died in 1990.

# The Land Remembers

## By John Ormond

GEOGRAPHY IS about maps and history is about chaps: E C Bentley said it first, and left little room for argument. But one summer morning a few years ago, when I was driving in the Prescelly Mountains in North Pembrokeshire, the two separate subjects got so close together that they virtually coincided.

As I drove through a maze of lanes, hedges and by-roads I had an Ordnance Survey map by my side. I was reaching nowhere fast.

Large as the scale is supposed to be on these ordnance sheets, the miniscule size of the actual type and the signs can be a strain on the eyes. A pair of crossed swords, indicating the site of some historic battle, I easily mistake for a small letter x strayed from who-knows-where; or for a crushed insect, or even one of its smaller offspring.

On this particular morning I was anxiously trying to locate a point on the map which said "Burial Chamber" in gothic letters that called for a microscope. It signified a grave of the Megalithic period. Now Megalithic simply means big stone;

and, somewhere or other off those serpentine lanes, that big grave-stone, which had been standing on its hillside for four or five thousands years, was very successfully eluding me.

A string of other cars and vans followed me as I went round in circles, for I was accompanied by a film crew and was supposed to be making a film. I wanted shots of the tomb to suggest the long history of Wales and the ancient settlers who had once lived in these hills.

Now I was lost; and film crews, like soldiers, are justifiably mutinous when their so-called leaders lose the way.

But finally, after parking and walking up an overgrown farm track for perhaps three-quarters of a mile, the film lads humping the camera gear behind me, I found what I was looking for. There it stood, the tombstone, the cromlech; a still island of stones in the middle of a field of barley which hissed and swayed and cavorted like a yellow sea lapping the grey, lichened monument.

It was a magnificent sight. We did our filming, and got what turned out to be very beautiful pictures. As we worked I sensed that we stood inside the time of the windy, sunny morning; and that somehow, too, we stood outside time.

A few years later I began to write a poem about the experience of seeing that ancient tomb, and about the emotions and thoughts aroused by the sight of it. And very soon I got stuck for the want of different words for stone. Once you've said slab and pillar and rock, there aren't many words for stone around.

Seeking help, I telephoned my oldest friend, a geologist; and when I'd told him my problem, and described what part of Pembrokeshire I'd been in, he said, "Oh, that cromlech could have been dolerite, porphyry or gabbro, for instance."

The marvellous, sonorous words were incorporated in my poem immediately. But, over months, as the poem grew, I again ran out of words for stone. Writing a poem isn't all wine and roses.

In Cardiff Central Library I found a book called *Megalithic Sites in Britain*, by Alexander Thom. Although not an archaeologist by profession, Professor Thom had spent many years of his long life surveying the stone rings of Britain, the druids' circles, as they are sometimes called; the originals of the fake circles the Gorsedd of Bards assemble at during the National Eisteddfod each year.

From Professor Thom's list of sites I lifted some of the evocative names by which, in various parts of Britain, the standing stones are known: Long Meg, Three Kings, Nine Maidens, Twelve Apostles.

In due course the poem was completed. By now I had become so interested in the theories put forward in Alexander Thom's book about the origins and functions of the stone circles that I resolved to persuade the BBC to allow me to make a film, with Professor Thom in it, explaining the mathematics upon which the layout of some of these ancient monuments was based.

For now I was learning that the people who had set up the cromlechau, the stone tombs, were also responsible for the circles, many of which were engineered, in pre-history, as lunar and solar observatories.

Soon afterwards I began work on the film, and got Professor Gwyn Williams to talk with Alexander Thom on the top of a mountain in the Berwyns, at the site of a tomb known as Moel Ty Ucha.

A little later I was reproaching myself for how little I knew of the landmarks of history that came in later periods. With Gwyn Williams I invented the title *The Land Remembers* and proceeded to make a series of six films, tracing the development of Welsh history from earliest times up to the 13th century. The story took us all over the country, dutifully followed by long-suffering technicians.

We saw strange and wonderful things. Apart from the films, we could have written a book about some of our encounters. Indeed, Gwyn is including some of the material in a volume he's actually writing at the moment.

I remember our astonishment when we found quern-stones, which the Celts used for grinding flour from grain, in the heather at the top of Tre'r Ceiri, in Caernarvonshire. They had lain in the heather on the mountain top, near the Celtic stone huts, for thousands of years.

Some time after the first films were shown on television we decided that the land did not stop remembering in the 13th century. We planned another six films with the same title, taking up the story of Welsh history in the time of Owain Glyndwr, and going on until the Industrial Revolution.

We visited and filmed at such places as Sycharth, where Owain Glyndwr was born about 1354. The mound on which one of his halls once stood is still to be seen there; and we went to Monnington Court, in a remote corner of Hereford-shire, where there is some evidence for believing the great Welsh leader lies buried near the farmyard.

I don't know how many miles we travelled and how many places we visited in making the six new films for *The Land Remembers*. For example, we spent days following the route that Henry VII took on his march from Pembrokeshire to Bosworth Field.

The series ends as we visit Llangeinor and the birthplace of Dr Richard Price; in the old farmhouse, where no plaque marks the fame of one who was the first in Britain to speak out in favour of the French Revolution and who advised in the drafting of the American Declaration of Independence, all our journeyings seemed to have taken me so far away in time from that windy hill and the barley field in North Pembrokeshire.

But as I've been typing these words I have set the completed sheets under a paperweight on my desk. It's a stone axe-head, found on a hill above Penmaen-mawr. Continually it reminds me of all the miles and of all the many centuries.

*The Western Mail, March 4, 1974*

Broadcaster, journalist and musician Chris Stuart has been a member of the comedy band Baby Grand since he left *The Western Mail* in 1976. A busy presenter of programmes in many guises (mainly for the BBC), he is also a composer of music for television and film. In addition, he runs his own production company. Doing a Toscanini was one of a series of articles in which *Western Mail* writers lived out the secret ambitions which all of us have, but few of us ever fulfil.

# Doing a Toscanini

## By Chris Stuart

I THOUGHT I detected a gleam of wicked triumph in the eyes of Welsh National Opera musical director Richard Armstrong as he formally placed the Welsh Philharmonia into my temporary care.

"Ladies and gentlemen," he announced with a knowing grin, "I would now like to hand you over to your distinguished guest conductor, Mr. Chris Stuart."

I was slipping nimbly into my starched waistcoat and bow-tie at the time and my only response was an embarrassed nod. The orchestra, for their part, mustered an ironic cheer and treated me to a selection of mock-welcome sounds that thoroughly tested the range of their instruments. It sounded like a crowd scene from Tarzan. Help.

"I'm sorry, I can't stay," said the still-smiling Mr Armstrong, as he shook my moist, trembling hand. "I've got to dash off to another engagement."

I see. The cruel, heartless torture that this wizard of the baton has persuaded his cohorts to mete out is going to be too painful to watch. He's leaving me to my doom.

Confucius he say man faced by 500 marauding warriors got nothing to fear compared with man faced by 50 professional musicians.

Certainly there are some pretty tough-looking nuts among the Welsh Philharmonia. I recall with particular trepidation a trumpeter who looked as if he could teach Attila the Hun a thing or two about unarmed combat. What would he do to little me?

If ever there was a time to back down and salvage a few scraps of jaded honour this was the time. I went on. Plucky, that's me.

As I mounted the rostrum it was like leaving the world behind. I had visions of them having to carry me off. My attire – full evening tails, minus the winged collar which I felt might impede stern ripostes in the direction of the 'cello section – prompted a barrage of cat-calls and wolf-whistles. Still, I thought, it's the music that matters. Face the music.

The chosen work for my epoch-making, 30-minute session was Rossini's overture *The Thieving Magpie*.

Now contrary to what some ill-informed musical socialites might try to tell you, this is one of the trickiest works in the entire orchestral repertoire. Despite its four-square appearance there lurks beneath its polished surface a multitude of hidden pitfalls for even the most experienced conductor.

I had expressed a desire, in the first flush of enthusiasm, to have a stab at Mahler's Eighth, but Mr Armstrong persuaded me against it – purely the time factor, you, understand, and the non-availability of a massed choir.

*The Thieving Magpie*, a shorter work, was my second choice, but I felt it was suitably rousing for this debut occasion.

I have always had this theory that in a previous but not too remote incarnation I was the great Arturo Toscanini. I wake up at night thinking I'm in La Scala, and bowing ostentatiously to the bookcases. A Rossini overture seemed to do justice to this fantasy.

"Silence," I whispered, with absolutely, no effect. Try again. "Er… do you think we could perhaps make a start possibly, if it's all right with you, please? Say if it's not, and I'll go away and think of some other long-held ambition, like breaking up pianos or taking stones out of horses' hooves. Something like that."

Perhaps they felt sorry for me, but order was by now more or less restored. I could tell they thought I looked pretty ridiculous. They said so. Well, they were wearing jeans and tee-shirts and things, and here was I looking like a well-pressed extra from Jeeves. What would Arturo have done at a time like this?

"Right, let's start and see what happens," I ventured – not inspired, I agree, but practical.

I looked at the side-drummer, a lovely girl at whom in any other circumstances I would have been delighted to look. Right now I wasn't so sure.

A cursory flick of my newly-acquired baton, 42p and a snip at the price, and the drum rolled. A second flick. Silence. Exactly like it said in the score. This is easy. Why didn't I invite the agents?

Yet again a flick, but with a finger raised pleadingly to my lips and a Hoffnung-ish expression etched timelessly on to my face. "Softly this time," it said. And it worked, it worked. Flick and off. Silence. Not Toscanini, I thought. Liszt, Beethoven, Mozart, for heaven's sake. The latest in a line of all-time greats.

Disillusionment arrived in bar three, the point at which everybody joins the solo drummer. A good, steady march tempo I had suggested, but although my baton was beating the air frantically the music moved off like a Centurion tank tackling a one-in-four incline.

"Looka 'ere," I said, settling for Toscanini, "When I say pleeza to play da piece lika da march, I donna mean lika da bloody funeral march. Fromma da topa, pleez."

Second attempt, and a slight increase in tempo, but not so as you would notice. This was clearly a deliberate pIoy, part of a well-plotted humiliation process. I could see them glancing at me from the corners of their eyes. Looking to see whether 1 was crumbling.

It was at this point that I played my master-stroke.

"Look," I said, keeping a perfectly straight face, "I don't want the fact that I'm going to be reviewing your next opera season to affect in the slightest the way you choose to play for me. Just play as you normally would."

Not for nothing am I known as the demon of the veiled threat. The result was miraculous. The clouds of torment lifted.

Making every conceivable allowance for the fact that my baton was waving about with the glorious unpredictability of a weather vane on a gusty day, they played like the skilful professionals I always knew they were, and even obeyed my modestly-proffered suggestions.

They must have been inspired by the smug expression on my face. Now at last I was truly happy. "Right," I said, bringing things to a halt, "Now let's try it with the instruments." And we played the whole work through from beginning to end.

Apart from one or two unscripted solos from the wags in the brass section – and I want them to know that I've made a note of their names – the only major problem in an otherwise memorable account of this epic work came when WNO Press officer Chris Senior decided to take over on fourth horn.

I'm not sure what devil-may-care Mr Senior was playing, but it certainly wasn't *The Thieving Magpie.* In fact, it sounded more like *Goodbye Dolly I Must Leave You,* but I may have been mistaken.

It is a tribute to this superb orchestra's gritty dedication and, I like to think, an indication of the esteem in which they by now held their conductor, that they played on regardless, ignoring Mr Senior's pathetic attempts to raise a cheap laugh.

So far I've not been invited to conduct anybody else, but I'm open to offers. In the meantime I can live with the office jokers who greet my arrival each morning with, "Oh no, here's Andre Previn."

I bet Andre, like me, had his problems, making it into the big time.

*The Western Mail, August 18, 1975*

John Billot, who joined *The Western Mail* in 1946, spent a remarkable 44 years with the paper, the last eight as sports editor and chief rugby and cricket writer in succession to the legendary J B G Thomas. His pre-match sketch tracing Scotland's rugby forays into Wales appeared on the morning of the international at Cardiff Arms Park in February, 1976. Wales won, of course, by 28 points to 6, and Gareth Edwards scored his 17th try for his country, the then record.

# Edwards the 43rd

## By John Billot

SCOTTISH victories at Cardiff Arms Park are as difficult to come by as copies of *Inside Linda Lovelace*. In 90 years the raiders from the north have gone home with so little plunder that their journeys have hardly been worth the trouble.

Just five successes spanning all but a century and only one of those since 1927. It is enough to make a thistle wilt and a kilt curl with humiliation. And no one thinks the pattern is going to change today.

History has it that Edward the First earned the title of Hammer of the Scots after his victory at Dunbar at the end of the 13th century. Now, in the 20th century, we have with us a modern "Hammer" in Edwards the 43rd; or to be more exact, Gareth Edwards with his 43rd cap today.

Edward was the greatest English king, next to Alfred, and a soldier of considerable fame. He promised to give the conquered Welsh a prince born in Wales who could speak no English; and legend has it that he presented his baby son, born at Caernarfon, who was too young to speak, to become their champion.

Well, Edwards the 43rd didn't make any promises. Welsh-born, Welsh-speaking and our greatest rugby champion, he simply presented his clansmen and women with a gift that money can't buy – an overwhelming superiority complex on the rugby field.

He did not confine it to Scotland, of course. Edwards – or Gareth the Great, as some prefer to call him – dispenses his talents impartially, as his try-scoring record reveals.

No scrum half anywhere in world rugby has come remotely within range of the Gwaun-cae-Gurwen Guru's record of 16 tries for his country, and that purely in full international matches.

Another one try puts him alongside Wales's record-holding trio of pre-World War I wings Reggie Gibbs and Johnnie Williams and post-World War II wing Ken Jones. That try could be coming Gareth's way this afternoon, because he looks a wee bit overdue for another one against the Scots.

I considered giving him a ring and asking at which end of the ground he was thinking of scoring it, and then remembered that the Big Five had gagged the entire team – possibly in case they inadvertently gave away some of coach John Dawes's secrets to probing Pressmen.

Scotland would love to have Edwards bound as well as gagged when they meet today. Short of an assassination squad, there seems no way to keep the scrum half genie corked up in his bottle.

He scored at Murrayfield in 1969 and 1971 and had the rugby world agog with his super-try against the Scots at Cardiff in 1972. Actually, he scored two tries during a three-minute spell in that match, but it was the second one that was something else. Of all the tries he has scored this is the big one; the super-duper mind-boggler.

Yet if Rodger Arneil's arm had been an inch longer we would never have witnessed that astonishing scoring run. The thought of being deprived of that magic moment is horrific; more dreadful than the price of potatoes or Mr Wilson's missing personal papers. Arneil flung an arm at Edwards as the scrum half came around a scrum in the Welsh 25 (the old designation for the 22 metre zone) and for a split-second it looked as if the Welsh wonder boy would be clobbered.

But Edwards ghosted past and set off on the sort of charge that Edward the First would have led at Dunbar. The defence closed, so Edwards kicked on. Then it was a chase with every heart aflutter.

Scottish wing Lewis Dick ran menacingly at his shoulder; a dark blue presence with equally dark intentions. But Edwards went down that South Stand touchline, heading for the Westgate Street end, as if there were a million pounds in a bucket all ready for him to collect.

Again the scrum half hacked the ball on. Then there was the final desperate sprint; forcing his legs to greater efforts before catapulting over the goal-line and on to the ball, face first in the red mud of the greyhound track.

*Western Mail* photographer Clive Lewis took a famous photograph of Edwards, the mud-plastered hero, as he walked back, and copies can be seen hanging in high places in the rooms of the top brass in the *Western Mail* offices… they are the only pin-ups permitted.

Wales that day ran up a record score against Scotland; prancing away for five tries in a 35-12 victory that had all the hallmarks of the Hammer of the Scots about it. Not just the hammer – the anvil as well that day.

But for a moment let's dwell on another day at Cardiff – the only occasion since 1927 that Scotland have looked up at the scoreboard when the final whistle sounded and seen, almost unbelievingly, that they were winners.

We can be generous in permitting our young folk a peep into the past at this single skeleton in the cupboard of Wales-Scotland matches at the Arms Park during the last 49 years. If there were any doubt about the outcome of today's tussle, of course, we would not dream of drawing back the curtain of time and looking, even briefly, at the events of 1962.

The truth, if it must be dragged out, is that 1962 was as black a year as Welsh rugby wants to forget. We went to Twickenham and drew, no-score. Such an arid situation is unthinkable in today's modern concept of rugby as an attacking game—and with penalty goals still ten-a-penny.

The season ended without Wales scoring a single try in the International Championship. Plague and pestilence could be endured, but not to score a try…

We beat France by a penalty goal to nil, which even to Welsh rugby beggars was no source of comfort, and lost 8-3 to Scotland and drew three-all with Ireland. But it is with Scotland we are concerned.

They had some pretty good players such as Ken Scotland, Gordon Waddell, Hughie McLeod and Dave Rollo. They may not have got into Aberavon Green Stars' first team, but Welshmen said they were not bad. However, one player in Scottish ranks definitely was a first-teamer – Arthur Smith, that lovely, gliding wing of everlasting memory. He had scored some sparkling tries against Wales, but was not needed for such activity this day. A couple of Scots' forwards did the work for him, and Kennie Scotland converted one. We had a dropped goal by Glamorgan batsman Alan Rees, the Maesteg fly half, to show for 80 minutes of uninspired effort.

What could we say? The weather was atrocious. It was Cardiff Arms Park at its most muddy and miserable. But it was the same for both teams. Kilted fans danced in the mud and chaired McLeod off to mark his record 38 caps. But away with such mournful memories. We have Edwards the 43rd out there today; the champion of Welsh rugby; one try short of his country's record. Somewhere, I suppose, Rodger Arneil will be remembering…

*The Western Mail, February 7, 1976*

Ryan Davies was one of Wales' most versatile performers. After National Service in the RAF he went to Bangor Normal College and then to the Central School of Speech and Drama in London. In 1960 he began teaching in Croydon, but left the profession to become a full-time entertainer in 1966, when he signed a contract with BBC Wales. He starred with Ronnie Williams in the popular BBC Wales series *Ryan and Ronnie*, as Twm Twm in the Welsh-language series *Fo a Fe*, and with Max Boyce was one of the anchormen in the *Poems and Pints* series. A talented musician, he accompanied himself on the harp, made records, and won acclaim as a cabaret artiste. He also enjoyed acting, and starred with Richard Burton in the film version of Dylan Thomas's *Under Milk Wood*. He died, at 40, from an asthma attack in New York in 1977. Here, he indicates that he wasn't particularly amused by an intellectual laugh-in in Cardiff.

# Thanks, Dai and Will!

## By Ryan Davies

DID you hear the one about Dai and Will going up to the international at Twickenham? Well that night Dai and Will went down to Soho, and...

It could be the beginning of any one of a hundred gags – though in Wales we prefer to call them stories – that you have heard so many times before. Where would we be without Dai and Will? They have been to Twickenham together ever since we allowed the English the fixture: they have attended every National Eisteddfod ever since Hywel Dda realised he was on to a good thing: they went over the top together at the Somme and Vimy Ridge and plucked the Zulus' feathers at Rorke's Drift, and still they go marching on.

"Aye, well, they're part of Welsh Humour, see."

Welsh Humour. Now there's a phrase for you. There's one for all the pundits to conjure with. Can't you just see them in the bars and pubs, in the cottages and the mansions, discussing and thrashing out important issues on Welsh Humour?

Pretty soon now our educationists will have it included in the O-level syllabus. There will be another three "Rs" for us to worry our children with. Religion, Rugby and Rollick, without which conversation in Wales would be limited to the weather and... Well, there you are.

And, who knows, one day the students in our universities will be allowed to read "Welsh Humour" and graduation day will be an even bigger laugh. "Gaudeamus Igitur" will be replaced by a rousing chorus of "I Wanna Be Happy," and they will walk to the podium in a yellow gown, with a purple tie which lights up, and receive their scrolls.

B.A. Dip. Hum. (Aber). The board of examiners will consist of the entire panel of *New Faces*, ychafi, who would then be sentenced to a never-ending summer season at the Palladium, Rhos y Bol (Oh yes, it does exist. It's in Anglesey. Maybe I lied about the Palladium – it's the Coliseum).

But hold on, dear readers. This humour business is a serious business. So serious, in fact, that there is to be a symposium on humour in Cardiff soon. It's a fact. A number of eminent psychologists and psychiatrists are getting together to find out what makes the nation laugh, and this couch of psychiatrists, or whatever the collective term is for them, perhaps suite of psychiatrists would be suitable, anyway all of these eminent men are to be addressed by none other than Professor Ken Dodd, from the Department of Giggleology, University of Knotty Ash.

Now whether you agree with this kind of laugh-in is neither here nor there. Personally, I've got about as much interest in it as I have for the effect of the Gulf Stream on the mating habits of a Peruvian yak. I suppose, being a professional comic, I should try to find out what makes us laugh, but I'm one of those people who say and do something which I think is funny and thankfully, my audience laugh, bless them.

My type of humour is, of course, Welsh, and that poses the 64,000-dollar question. What is Welsh Humour? Where do we find it? Does it in fact exist? Surely we do not have exclusive rights on the Dai and Will situation. I'm sure there must be a Russian comic somewhere at this moment telling the story about Yuri and Ivan going to see the Dynamos, and finding themselves in the Red district, if you'll pardon the pun.

"But Yuri knew what she wanted, aye."

"His photo of Barrislov Johnsky."

This must surely be true of them also. So what is Welsh Humour? I'm not completely sure that I know what it is. I can tell you what it is not. It is not the slick, so-called sophisticated humour that some Americans throw at us on our TV screens. Neither is it that infantile, giggly rubbish that Donny and Marie Osmond give us, oh so thinly disguised as comedy.

I don't think we go for the satirical humour of some English comics either, and most certainly not for the blue stand-up comic. So what do we go for? If we have to define it, and I think it's a shame that we do, I would say that the humour of Wales is to do with her people, with her "characters". "He's a character, aye," and "Duw, he's a card when he gets going," are phrases we have all heard many times, and it is an extension of the "characters and cards" which makes us Welsh laugh.

Remember Mam and Will? There are thousands of them up and down the country, our versions were only slightly larger than life, or were they? And we laughed at them, indeed at ourselves.

I was once told by a comic that the Welsh cannot laugh at themselves, and that he had proved that theory time and time again. His big problem is that he is English, and his "look you, indeed to goodness" quips were going down with his audiences like lead balloons. Oh, yes, we'll laugh at ourselves all right, as long as we are doing the ribbing. Mind you, I was once accused of taking the mickey out of the Welsh. I ask you. Me? Who was weaned on laverbread and Welsh cakes – together. Well if I and my Welsh colleagues can't do it, who can?

Whereas I am not entirely convinced that there is such a thing as Welsh Humour, I am convinced there are traits of humour which belong exclusively to us, one of them being our insistence on giving everyone nicknames. In this we resemble the Red Indians, who called their warriors Running Bear, Crazy Horse or Swift Arrow, although I must admit that Evans the Death, Bessie the Milk and Dai Bread do sound a little less lyrical that Shining Water and Little Red Deer of the Forest.

The practice of naming a son or daughter after the parent is a commonplace one and a very old one. Sion ap Sion means John the son of John, Dafydd ap Dafydd is a perfectly respectable, aye, e'en honourable name. Dai ap Dai smacks a little of disrespect, while Dai Dai, which means exactly the same, is very basic indeed. Occupations also provide us with fodder for nick-names. I once met a chemist who was known as Wil Pilsen (William the Pill), though I suspect that in this permissive age this would be more apt for the head of a family planning clinic.

Sir David Maxwell Fyfe, when he was Minister for Welsh Affairs, was known as Dai Bananas, for obvious reasons. Her Royal Highness Princess Margaret, on her marriage to Lord Snowdon, who had family connections in Bontnewydd, Gwynedd, was known as Maggie Bont. We respect no one.

I suppose the cleverest one of all was the name given to the man who had but one tooth in the middle top of his mouth. He was promptly named Dai Central 'Eating. A classic one that. And no doubt you have your favourite, and each town and village boasts of many such affectionate nicknames. The strange and wonderful thing is – although they sound insulting, mocking and often downright cruel, there is no malice in them at all.

There are many who believe that humour should be barbed and cutting, and no doubt such humour has its place, but Welsh Humour is never cruel. Sometimes uncomfortable, yes, but never cruel.

I cannot hope to cover all those aspects of our varied society which provide us with a laugh or two, You have your own views on this. You could argue that the Humour of Wales is to be found in the mines of the Rhondda, in the slate quarries of Gwynedd, in the farming communities of Powys and Dyfed, in the industrial parts of Glamorgan and Clwyd, in the chapels, on the rugby fields, in the choirs and in the schools, and you would have a strong argument. If I may misquote Dylan Thomas, and why not, everyone else does: "Praise the Lord, we are a humorous nation," and leave it at that.

If you have your ideas of Welsh Humour, don't write to me, send them to that learned symposium in Cardiff. All I ask of you is – that if you think what I say and do is funny, just laugh and I promise not to ask you why.

PS. Thank you, Dai and Will, for everything.

*The Western Mail, July 10, 1976*

Miner's son Richard Burton, born Richard Walter Jenkins in Pontrhydyfen in 1925, was befriended and later adopted by his English teacher, Philip H Burton, who encouraged his acting and study of English. He changed his name to Burton in 1943, and made his London stage debut in Emlyn Williams' *The Druids' Rest* in 1944. His first film, *The Last Days of Dolwyn*, in 1948, followed RAF service and a six-month course at Oxford. In 1954, he was the narrator in the famous radio production of Dylan Thomas's *Under Milk Wood*. Burton went on to win international stardom on stage and screen, and, married five times – twice to Elizabeth Taylor. When his great friend Stanley Baker died in 1976, Burton was in Los Angeles. His anguish – and his undoubted skill as a writer – show in this article.

# Lament for a dead Welshman

## By Richard Burton

THERE are so few of us, and God knows we can't afford to give many of us away; for I mean you can take a lot of the Irish and the Scots and the Jews, and the French and all those others, including the Russians and about a billion Chinese and all those people who live in the United States, but there are so few of us and so many of the others. And I mean it's not fair to take away from me and mine a rough and terrifying old boot like Stanley Baker.

There are the English in their millions too, and the Irish with their poetry, and the Scots with their carefully controlled romanticism (there's a lot of them about), and the English forever carrying on from Italy how much they would love to be in England now that April's there, except that it is June in Los Angeles and I have just heard that my beloved Stanley Baker is dead.

Now let me tell you about him and you may accept it as a murderous love-letter if you like, but stand by for the kind of thing that he would like to hear if he could hear, which he can't. Though I'm not sure he would even if he could. He was tallish, thickish, with a face like a determined fist prepared to take the first blow but not the second and if, for Christ's sake, you hurt certain aspects of his situation, like his wife or his children, or even me, you were certain to be savagely destroyed. And he is dead. And did you know the funny little poem that Stanley loved and which he pretended he didn't, which went:

*He had the plowman's strength in the grasp of his hand,*
*He could see a crow three miles away.*
*He could hear the green oats growing*
*And the southwest wind making rain,*
*And the trout beneath the stone,*
*And he's dead.*

Let me tell you how rough and strange a life he had with a father who fell down a pit cage when he was fourteen years old and lost a leg (I mean the father was fourteen, not Stanley) and about Stanley and his adorable family who found the world as bizarre as any invention I could make, and of course he's dead. It is not fair!

He was the authentic dark voice of the Rhondda Valley. He was the first man who skidded with exaltation under the Co-op stallion and pelted the privileged as they came out of the grammar school because he was disallowed entry, and all the street-corner poets stood on his massive shoulders and tried to dwarf him, and of course the cosmic bastards killed him behind my back, and I'll have a word or two to say to them one of these days because somebody has been mucking around, otherwise he wouldn't be dead, would he, and whose tears are burning my cheeks and whose heart is shifting uneasily in mine and why is he dead?

Who arranged it? Tears, idle bloody tears, tears from the depth of some divine despair on the edge of a cowing swimming pool in Los Angeles, and there's a girl playing the piano and it's the Sonata Pathetique and she's playing the bit that's called *allegro molto e con brio* and we should do all that, shouldn't we? If we could. Not that my Stanley liked pianos. He used them as footstools. In fact the lovely old Stanley wasn't exactly cultured. He read minds not books, he was harshly unpoetic, he didn't like people very much and made it clear, sometimes painfully, and he hated to lose at anything and rarely did, but what the hell can you do if you come from such a murderous background?

Those low hills, those lowering valleys, the Rhondda Fawr, the Rhondda Fach, and their concomitant buses and grey roofs and pitheads and dead grass and crippled miners and cages endlessly falling with your father inside and smashed to bits, and since with a convulsive heave Stanley shrugged off the mighty mountains and strode across Europe, who or what the devil killed him?

It couldn't be his heart because mine is still going. Not his brain because mine is still weeping, and for Christ's sake he is not allowed to be organically dead because I am alive and we are the same.

What strange fury burned his bones? What malevolent God knocked him off behind my back? How dare the swine shift him and not some bloody Indian or Chinaman or German or Frenchman or any bastard or me. They can afford a death or two. We can't. I mean we cannot, and especially people like Stanley. I mean there are very few around. People, I mean. Like Stanley.

I saw him act in a church once in New York. It was incongruous. The clashing of two alien eternities. He knelt before the altar and stared at it. The altar gave in and has never been the same since. I got him a part in a play once, and if you like the authenticity of inconsequential detail it was called *Adventure Story* and was about Alexander the Great, and anyway I was playing Hephaestion and Paul Scofield was Alexander the Great and, would you believe it, Stanley went on to splendid things and I was fired on the third day.

Stanley was the one who took the razor from my throat and sharpened it. Before handing it back. And he was the chap I kept for about ten weeks when he was broke and indeed-to-god I gave him two pounds sterling every pay-day and when he was successful later he paid me back – with interest. He's one of the only two men who paid me back, out of hundreds, and the only one with interest. And he is dead. Well now, what can you do in the middle of the night beside a swimming pool in Beverly Hills except to call up that girl and ask her to play an impromptu of Chopin's *allegro assai, quasi presto,* and shouldn't we all if we knew what it meant, and it is as impromptued as a careful step? What thieves these dead men are, because what do they do except steal your soul away with memories or hex you with iambic, and who am I to forget Stanley's bitter humour and the look from the eyes when somebody was boring the marrow out of him?

There is a class of Welshmen, original and unique to themselves, powerful and loud and dangerous and clever, and they are almost all South Welshmen and almost all from the Rhondda Valley, and there are not very many of them, but even in London you can find them if you search a bit.

There are the Donald Houstons and the Gwyn Thomases (if you've never read him you must in order to understand us) and the Cliff Morganses and short, obese, slightly-bowlegged Bleddyn Williamses, and they are as charming as daggers. Others are deferential to the point of sycophancy and you must watch out in case they turn to murder. In fact they are an alien race and nobody knows where they come from or what they are.

If you move about forty miles west you will find the relatively exotic other Welsh people like Dylan Thomas and Daniel Jones (I believe that Jones is the only man who has written seven symphonies and speaks Chinese), and Harry Secombe and the mad woman who said to me one day, "I'd love to be your mother," and I said with brilliant dispatch, "You are." And she said, "Lucky boy."

But Stanley was inwrought with his valley and so am I with the *idea* of the valley, that incomparable valley, burned and black, and how curious it was that it took a total foreigner to show me how lovely it was in its brutal way.

"Stop the car," she said, a Californian no less, and indeed there was that valley, and I stood beside the Californian lady and she pointed out as the winds howled around our ears like dementia how perversely magical it was. And she said, "Aren't you ashamed that you don't recognise your own country?" And I said, "It's Stanley's." And it is.

It took me years and years to understand the line *"After the first death there is no other."* What, I said to myself about this otherwise admirable poet, does he mean? And what he meant was that after Abel was killed under the green tree by Cain, mortality had invested our lives. And, of course, you can't shrug the thing off. You can dance and laugh and giggle, but it takes a direct intelligence – not a woolly mind like mine – to understand the most obvious things.

And now we get back to Stanley again because I said to him one day with some condescension, because I knew he didn't read poetry or anything much except scripts and books that could be made into scripts, "What the 'ell," I said, "does this mean?" "What?" he said. "This bloody thing," I said. "What bloody thing?" he said. "It has been tormenting me all my life." "How does it go?" he said. And I said, "Well now, Stanley, it's from the Bible and it goes, if you want to see it going: 'In the beginning was the Word, and the Word was with God, etc.' What," I said, "does it mean?" And little Stanley, though he was a big fellow, you know, said, "Well it's obvious isn't it? It's a mistranslation. The Greeks probably don't have a word for it." "Word for what?" I said. "Idea", he said. "Change the word 'word' to 'idea' and the whole thing makes sense." And, of course, the clever reader will know immediately that I am not merely writing about Stanley but about all of us. And about me.

Brothers are chauvinistic about their kind. Nobody knows us except us. Nobody knew Stanley except us and we can only talk about him to foreigners with a kind of desperation because they couldn't possibly understand him, except for one exquisite alien called Ellen, his wife, and it took her a bit of time too, I bet.

And, of course, I moved around the periphery, occasionally setting a careful foot inside the ice-cold circle and being dismissed or thrown out. And we fought. Physically, I mean.

We smashed windows and broke trains and lusted after the same women and drove through the continent together, pustular and acne'd and angry and madly in love with the earth and all its riches, and we met unforgettable people in forgotten bars, and once we were in a bar in Biarritz and there was this impossibly drunken American sunk in a reef of Scotch whisky, blind as an eyeless bull, muttering inanities to himself, and we tried to prop the poor bastard up but he was unsavable and finally I got bored and said, "Let's go. He's a useless son of a bitch." And Stanley said, "Good God, Rich, we can't leave him to the French, he's William Faulkner." And he was. And immediately my intellectual snobbery surfaced like a dead fish and Faulkner has never been so fêted, Nobel Prize and all, as he was for the next three days. But, of course, it took Stanley to recognise him.

Stanley's death reminds me so acutely of other South Walians who are dead, like a brother of mine and a brother-in-law called Mogs, and the more notorious like Dylan Thomas, and what really disturbs me about their respective deaths is that I took them all for granted.

I didn't realise until the men had gone how much I loved them and how careful I have to be to nurture those alive, the remaining ones, with all the amiable eccentricity emblematic to that strange race, and my brothers and sisters, and, indeed to God, you can shift down the great valley for a second and you'll find one of the greatest living writers of the English language, yclept Gwyn Thomas, lauded but unread, except of course by us.

What fascinates me and excites me is not the word, but the idea, of race. You can shift a little west and north and you will find the most remote man you've ever met, a man who makes an iceberg look inviting, a priest with a face that's never allowed itself to smile, but Christ, and I use the word very carefully, how passionately he writes. Nobody has insulted the people and the bare hills as violently as he has and I hope does. And his name is Thomas too, R S of that ilk.

And Stanley was a little bit the same as R S Thomas. Not that he ever wrote poetry, God knows, but his whole life was an examination of the people surrounding him, suspicious to the point of paranoia, especially with foreigners. And now I am forced to have a look at them all, the Welsh I mean, and worry about them and try to understand them. But nobody understands the tremendous thrill of vitality that runs through the lot of them, and their humour, as black as the bowels of the earth. What the devil, we can't help where we were brought up, and those of us who could swim a couple of thousand years ago got to Ireland and found the land so soft and smooth and zoetic that we can't stop killing each other to this day. A terrible fury, one might say, was born, and all this because a Welshman that I loved is dead.

This elegy is done in a hurry and I could quite easily write a staid and unpublishable exequy, but I know the way we talk and sometimes think and I remember Stanley taking my breath away by quoting lines written by Emlyn Williams. I knew the lines and knew they were beautiful but had not understood with such intensity the true accent of the aspiring and doomed collier:

"*When I walk through… the shaft in the dark I can touch with my hands the leaves on the trees and underneath where the corn is green.*"

I stood there, we were in Madrid, and shook like a wet dog. And everybody has his curse to carry, of course, but those funny lines of Williams's came home to me like a stab under the heart, and I had no idea that Stanley knew the words, and indeed I played the man who says the lines – and as far as I know Stanley had never played it – but those stupendous words are true of all of us.

Stanley's father went down the mines when he was a little boy. So did my father, but it took a genius to understand what happened down there and express it so perfectly. "There is nobody like us," as the Scotsman once said. "Damn few," was the reply, "and they're all dead."

And as I hover over this old typewriter like a bird of prey, silly and ridiculous, a dreadful Welsh judge, you might as well wrap it up and I, of course, misquote, but it has to have an end. And this is it.

*The Western Mail, July 12, 1976*

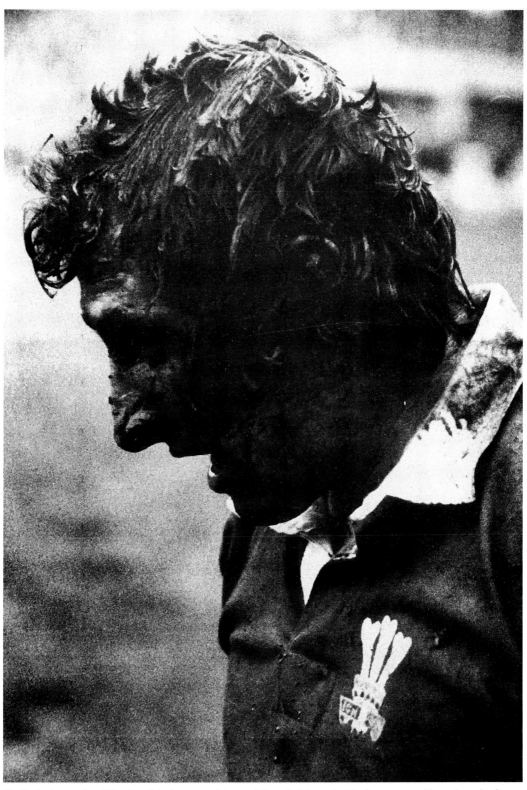

**Staff photographer Clive Lewis's famous picture of Gareth Edwards, his face covered in red mud, after his super-try against Scotland at the Arms Park in 1972.**

The Prince of Wales (later Edward VIII and Duke of Windsor) is presented to the Welsh people by King George V at Queen Eleanor's Gate at Caernarfon Castle in 1911. With them is Queen Mary.
*(Press Association picture)*

A PRESENT TO WALES.

In days of yore a Warrior-King presented,
Borne on his shield, in brave time-honoured fashion,
His infant son to the assembled chieftains,
Saying to them, 'mid roars of glad approval,
"Here is your Prince, born in your Cymric stronghold.—
     Eich Dyn!"

Far is that age, its pageant past for ever,
Tumult and warfare vanished into silence.
Gone are the Romans, Saxons, Danes, and Normans.
But still our Wales lives on with mightier vigour;
And once again a King makes presentation—
     " Eich Dyn!"

Ye warriors of old time, ye bards and Druids,
Could ye with all your lore unveil the future—
Our Wales to-day part of a world-wide Empire,
Keeping her pride of place and adding to it,
So that the world can say of the true Welshman,
     " Eich Dyn!"

Science and Faith and Industry and Learning,
These are the glories of the day we live in.
We are a Nation, copying no other,
Anxious to be ourselves—no imitation ;
Looking towards the Highest, Purest, Noblest—
     " Eich Dyn!"

'Tis the King speaks, our own most honoured Monarch,
Him we revere, and his most gracious Consort,
And the young Prince of a stout oak the sapling,
Pride of his parents, joy of a gallant people,
King of our own to be (in course of nature)—
     " Eich Dyn!"

Take him to thine own heart, dear mother Cymru.
He is most worthy of thy best affection,
Binding the Throne to our most ancient nation,
Worthy to stand with Anglia, Scotia, Erin,
In the great fourfold bond that none may shatter—
     " Eich Dyn!"

           IDRIS.

The cartoon by Staniforth which accompanied Owen Rhoscomyl's report of the investiture. Beneath it, a poem written by Idris (Arthur Mee).

Daniel Lewis, Arsenal's Welsh goalkeeper in the 1927 F A Cup Final, watches despairingly as the ball rolls over the line after he had fumbled Ferguson's shot. The only goal of the match, it gave Cardiff City the Cup.

The wreck of the cargo-ship *Samtampa* on the rocks at Sker Point, near Porthcawl, after being driven ashore in a storm in 1947. Her crew of 40 died — and so did the eight-man crew of the Mumbles lifeboat. *Below*: the shattered lifeboat becomes a funeral pyre after being set alight where she was found not far from the *Samtampa*.

# Western Mail.

No. 1.     THE WESTERN MAIL, SATURDAY, MAY 1, 1869.     ONE PENNY.

WESTERN MAIL & SOUTH WALES NEWS, WEDNESDAY, MAY 1, 1940.



Western Mail and South Wales News

FOURTH EDITION.

THE NATIONAL DAILY OF WALES AND MONMOUTHSHIRE

No. 22,096. Estab. 71 Years. WEDNESDAY, MAY 1, 1940. ONE PENNY.



# GERMAN LOSSES IN GUDBRANDS VALLEY

## British Fighting With "Indomitable Courage"

## NAZI DOMBAAS CLAIMS UNCONFIRMED

**AFTER repelling with heavy losses strong German attacks, supported by tanks and low-flying aeroplanes, Allied troops in the Gudbrands Valley on Sunday withdrew to a position covering Dombaas, it was announced by the War Office yesterday. Three Nazi tanks were destroyed in the engagement.**

It was claimed by the German High Command yesterday that Nazi troops had reached the railway junction of Dombaas and Storen, and the line linking Oslo and Trondheim was in their hands.

In well informed circles in London there was no confirmation of the German claims, and the War Office, in a second announcement just before midnight, stated:—

**In the Dombaas area the British, fighting with indomitable courage, have resisted any further advances by the enemy.**

**North of Stenkier the British troops again proved their superiority in patrol work, inflicting heavy casualties on the enemy.**

**Fresh landings have taken place along the coast of Norway.**

## THREE GERMAN TANKS DESTROYED

The War Office last night issued the following communiqué:—

"In Sunday's fighting in the Gudbrands Valley the enemy attacked strongly with the support of tanks and low flying aircraft.

**"All attacks were repulsed with heavy losses, including the destruction of three medium tanks.**

"During the night our troops made a short withdrawal to a position covering Dombaas.

"Air attacks on Aandalsnes and Molde continued during the day.

"In the Namsos and Narvik areas the situation remains unchanged."

It is understood that the reference to "during the night" applies to Sunday night.

### *Namsos Alive With Guns*

FORMOFOSS (Norway), Tuesday.

British and French anti-aircraft batteries have virtually silenced German air attacks in the entire Namsos area during the past 24 hours.

At five o'clock yesterday morning a German airman on the usual early morning patrol flight flew over Namsos just as if it were a private Nazi aerodrome.

**He dropped a single bomb and then the British batteries opened up and blasted the surprised German into the upper air.**

A few moments later he turned the nose of his machine for home.

Since then his comrades have kept clear of Namsos or flown extremely high.

One enemy machine was shot down yesterday.

**The air defences have only just been established, but when the sun set yesterday the Namsos hills were alive with guns, each manned by specially selected crack crews.**

Seasoned British troops and not raw recruits are holding most of the front.

Namsos itself is in ruins. Great yawning craters and blackened buildings show the fury of the German attack.

### *Nazi Guns Silenced*

Under the protection of British guns, however, the inhabitants have resumed a normal life amid the ruins of their town.—Associated Press.

**Reports received at Stockholm last night from Riksgraensen, on the Swedish frontier, indicate that the British forces have succeeded in silencing the German artillery at Narvik with several direct hits, states an Associated Press message.**

The Germans have abandoned their positions in the mountains and are now entrenched on the shore, which they are defending with machine-gun nests which the Allies are also bombarding.

### *Reinforcements Arrive*

STOCKHOLM, Tuesday.

While the latest German claims have not so far been confirmed by independent Swedish dispatches, it is known that contact between Allied and German forces has been made at various points along the Dombaas-Storen railway.

**The Allies are strongly reinforcing their troops both along the railway and south of Dombaas.**

These reinforcements are believed to have been brought up from fresh landing points on the coast between Trondheim and Bergen.

One landing is said to have been made in Sunndals Fiord, 30 miles north-east of Aandalsnes, which is connected by a direct road to Opdal, on the Dombaas-Storen railway, 40 miles north of Dombaas.

The second landing is reported in Nord Fiord, 60 miles south-west of Aandalsnes.

A German detachment which left Tynset, in the valley by the mountain road to Ulsberg, north of Opdal, was reported to be still held by Norwegian troops at Kvikne.

### *Skagerrak Naval Action*

A big naval action is believed to have taken place in the Skagerrak yesterday, according to to-day's "Gothenburg Post."

**From three p.m. onwards,** it says, **flashes of heavy gunfire were seen south of Lysekil. Towards 10 p.m. the firing increased and the fighting appeared to be moving southwards.**

Naval activity has been frequently observed from Lysekil. Two nights ago a convoy of 12 vessels suddenly scattered, but owing to the distance it was impossible to distinguish whether submarines or mines were responsible.—Press Association War Special.

### *New British Positions*

PARIS, Tuesday.

The new positions which the British forces have taken up in the Gudbrands Valley are at Brennhaug, about 12 miles south of Dombaas, according to reports received here.—Press Association War Special.

## NAZI COMMANDER'S IRON CROSS

BERLIN, Tuesday.

The German High Command claimed to-night that the main railway line linking Oslo and Trondheim was in German hands.

Troops advancing up the Gudbrands Valley, it was stated, had reached the railway junction of Dombaas, and other forces had captured the town of Opdal to the north-east.

Earlier the High Command had reported that German forces, advancing north from Oslo by way of Tynset and others advancing south from Trondheim, had made contact near Trondheim on the railway south-west of Storen.

The German High Command's claim is hailed in Berlin as news of exceptional military importance.

The German troops in Trondheim, states the official Nazi news agency, are now no longer dependent on air and sea communication with Germany, but are linked by land with Oslo, where "reinforcements are continually arriving."

Hitler in an order of the day congratulating German troops on securing a "land link from Oslo to Trondheim," says the army, navy, and air force accomplished "the mighty task which I had to impose upon you," and announces the award of Knights Insignia of the Iron Cross to Gen. von Falkenhorst, Commander-in-chief in Norway.—Press Association War Special.

### *Sweden's Precautions*

Further districts in Sweden are to be closed to foreigners as from Friday under a Royal Decree broadcast from Stockholm yesterday.

The ban is extended to the island of Gotland, certain parts of Stockholm province, the Gothenburg and Bohus province with the exception of Gothenburg town, and the area opposite the Trondheim fighting zone.—Press Association War Special.

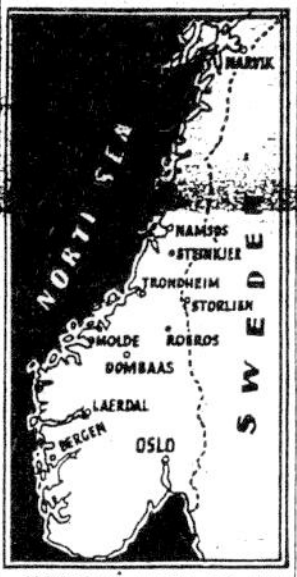


**STOCKHOLM reports state that British forces have silenced the German artillery at Narvik, where the Nazis are now entrenched on the shore.**

## ITALY ALARMS YUGOSLAVIA

ZAGREB, Tuesday.

Reports of intensive Italian military activity near the Yugoslav frontier to-night alarmed the Croatian regions of Slovenia and the Dalmatian coastal districts.

The Prime Minister (M. Cvetkovic), arriving in Zagreb from Dalmatia, issued a reassuring statement, however, asserting that the country's internal situation was good and expressing confidence that Yugoslavia could preserve her neutrality.

Railway workers returning from Italy told of seeing a train-load of tanks being moved up.

Others crossing the frontier said that new A.R.P. shelters were being erected at Fiume and Trieste, with many persons in those cities expecting war.

A virtual suspension of Italian coal shipments from Germany via Slovenia was attributed here to heavy military traffic on the Italian lines leading to the Yugoslav frontier.

Large German concentrations were reported in the Klegenfurt area near the frontier.—Associated Press.

### Italian Cabinet Meeting

ROME, Tuesday.

Signor Mussolini will preside over a Cabinet meeting to-morrow morning.

Political circles believe the meeting will deal at length with the negotiations, diplomatic and economic, now in progress between Britain and Soviet Russia and between Yugoslavia and Russia, and the tentative trade talks between Britain and Italy.

The Italian Press devotes much space to quotations from the newspapers of London and Paris regarding the attitude of Italy in the present conflict, the correspondents being at pains to suggest that both capitals realise Italy holds the scales. — Press Association Foreign Special.

## Britain's Mediterranean Shipping Precautions

It was learnt in authoritative circles in London on Tuesday that pronouncements by Italians in responsible positions and the attitude of the Italian Press have been recently of such a character as to make it necessary for the Government to take certain precautions as regards British shipping which would normally pass through the Mediterranean.

They do not intend, however, to continue these precautions any longer than is necessary, and they hope that circumstances will permit their cancellation in the near future.

It is understood that the precautionary measures include the diversion of all merchant vessels round the Cape.

## French Overtures Rejected?

PARIS, Tuesday.

"From statements published in the 'Popolo d'Italia,' it follows that the Fascist Government is completely opposed to any idea of Franco-Italian conversations," says the well-informed Rome correspondent of the "Temps" this afternoon, commenting on the aggressive attitude adopted towards France by the Italian Press.

"This attitude is all the more striking," the correspondent continues, "since up till now the usual reproach made against France has been that she did not wish to enter into negotiations regarding Italy's 'natural aspirations.'

"To-day, at the moment when France declares officially she is ready to discuss matters, the 'Popolo d'Italia' takes up an outraged attitude."

The "Popolo d'Italia" is the Mussolini family journal.—Reuter.

## NAZI MOVE ON DANUBE EXPECTED

A new attempt by the Reich to create a pretext for the dispatch of gunboats to strategic points on the Yugoslav and Rumanian reaches of the Danube is expected shortly by French diplomatic circles.

The first attempt to attain this object was foiled when Hungary, Yugoslavia, Rumania and Bulgaria rejected an "international police" scheme inspired by Berlin. Instead, on April 17, these Powers signed a Four-Power Agreement which provides that each State will be responsible for policing its own part of the Danube.

The hand of Germany is seen in Paris in the new Hungarian proposal to the three other countries that the policing of the sector comprising the Iron Gate Narrows shall be entrusted to an international river squadron composed of ships belonging to all the Danubian States. This definition would include Germany.

Hungary's proposal has already been turned down categorically by Rumania and Yugoslavia, while Bulgaria's reply has not yet been received.—Reuter.

## Allies "Capture" 300 River Craft

BUCHAREST, Tuesday.

The Allies' campaign to cripple Germany's Danube trade scored again to-day when 27 French-owned barges and tugs left this river for Istanbul.

Other river craft under Allied control are moored at Sulina, ready to leave the Danube at a moment's notice.

Over 300 barges and tugs now on a mysterious voyage across the Black Sea towards Istanbul are regarded here as symbol of an Allied victory in the bloodless war of the Danube.

The Allies look upon these river craft as valuable prizes of war, the loss of which, they hope, will have a crippling effect on Germany's Danube trade.

As soon as the Danube froze this winter Allied agents went among the idle neutral boatmen offering to hire their craft at good rentals, payable in gold, if they would sign up for a year or two.

Though the agents have by no means signed up all the river craft, they think they have put enough boats out of commission to cripple Germany's transport.

Fleets of new river craft, most of them oil tankers, have now appeared on the river. All of them fly the Nazi flag and have been built during the winter in Austrian shipyards.—Associated Press.

## £45,000,000 Spent on Defence Last Week

Revenue last week dropped to £10,553,000, against expenditure totalling £46,440,000, of which £43,561,000 was for defence. Total expenditure between April 1 and April 27 was £180,958,000, which is almost exactly double the figure for the corresponding period of last year. The revenue total is £62,173,000, compared with £55,029,000.

Last week £144,000 was issued under the Anglo-Turkish "Armaments Credit" Agreement. Receipts included £5,711,000 from Customs and £1,960,000 from death duties.

Floating debt increased by £33,015,000, but is still £93,975,000 lower than at March 31.

## Anglo-Eireann Trade Talks Begin

The British Ministers of Supply, Agriculture, Food, and Shipping took part in the Anglo-Eireann trade talks in London on Tuesday.

Further discussions are to be held in the next few days with Mr. Sean Lemass and Dr. J. Ryan, respectively Ministers of Supply and Agriculture, who are Eire's representatives. The negotiations have added importance now that the Danish food supplies are in German hands.

The first meeting was held at the Dominions Office, Mr. Anthony Eden (Dominions Secretary) presiding.

The visiting Ministers were the guests of the British Government at lunch.

Births, Marriages and Deaths ............... Page 6

Public Notices, Legal Notices, Sales by Auction, Classified Advertisements ... Page 2

## STOP PRESS

**IT'S NO PLEASURE TRIP.—But the boys of the North Western Expeditionary Force, en route for Norway, relax just as if it were Bank Holiday.**

## MIDNIGHT ATTACK ON OSLO AIRPORT

For over an hour shortly after midnight on Monday R.A.F. aeroplanes heavily bombed Fornebu, Oslo's principal airport.

Details of the raid—the fourth on this aerodrome—were made known in London on Tuesday.

The attack was carried out by the Bomber Command and was in the form of a series of raids.

**Attacking singly and in succession, our aircraft dropped a large number of high explosive bombs and bursts were seen spreading in a line across the landing ground from north-west to south-east. In the absence of a moon, parachute flares were dropped to assist observation.**

Strong opposition from gun batteries and searchlights increased in intensity as the raid developed, but all attacks were pressed home and considerable damage is believed to have been done to the airport and aircraft dispersed around it.

One of our aircraft failed to return.

### Seven Encounters

Seven Nazi aeroplanes have been harassed by R.A.F. Coastal Command aircraft off the Norwegian coast within the past 24 hours.

One small flight of Blenheims over Aandalsnes gave chase to a Junkers 88 which accelerated to top speed and took refuge in cloud.

A Messerschmitt 110 was given a rough encounter and was last seen spiralling down in distress.

**Two other Coastal Command aircraft attacked another Junkers 88 effectively from quarter and rear. Its tail gun was put out of action, and as it fled great plumes of black smoke came from both its engines. The German was losing height rapidly as it made off.**

Four other enemy machines were chased out of sight.

## Heroes of Norway Air-Raids Decorated

A wing-commander who led two air-raids on Stavanger aerodrome and seaplane base in three days and a flying-officer who flew through a snowstorm and attacked the base in the face of heavy anti-aircraft fire have been decorated.

Tuesday night's "London Gazette" announced that Wing-commander Basil Edward Embry, D.S.O., A.F.C., has been awarded a bar to the D.S.O., and that Flying-officer William Henry Edwards receives the D.F.C.

**Describing Wing-commander Embry's action, the official account states that in the first raid he returned to his base with the whole squadron, despite the failure of one of his engines before he reached his objective. On the second valuable photographs were taken. During this flight he suffered from frost-bite.**

Flying-officer Edwards piloted his aircraft to Stavanger, although the weather was so bad that five aircraft were compelled to abandon the task. On another day he attacked a Dornier seaplane with his guns and scored hits.

The Distinguished Flying Cross is awarded to Flight-lieut. Peter Wooldridge Townsend, who whilst on patrol over the North Sea intercepted and attacked an enemy aircraft at dusk, and after a running fight he shot it down. This was his third success.

## Italy's New 35,000 Ton Battleship

ROME, Tuesday.

Italian naval authorities announced to-day that the Vittorio Veneto, first of four new battleships, has been put into active service. Her sister ship, the Littorio, is expected to enter service soon.

The Vittorio Veneto and her sister ships are 35,000 tons.

The Impero and the Roma are expected to be commissioned about January, 1942.

## French Take Prisoners

PARIS, Tuesday.

To-night's war communique states:—

"Local activity of the contact units. Our patrols have taken a few prisoners.

"Two local attacks by enemy detachments have been repulsed."—Press Association War Special.

## Hungary's Warning To Slovakia

BUDAPEST, Tuesday.

A warning to Slovakia that Hungary would "not hesitate to act in defence of her national honour" if the rights of the Hungarian minority in Slovakia were not respected was given to-day by Count Stephen Csaky (Hungarian Minister of Foreign Affairs).

Speaking in the Upper House of the Hungarian Parliament, Count Csaky warned Slovakia against "hiding behind the German guarantee" of her independence "because we fully believe in the stability of Hungarian-German friendship."

### SLOVAKS' DENIAL

Count Csaky's allusion to "the stability of Hungarian-German friendship" was interpreted here as meaning that the Government has reason to feel assured the Reich would not insist upon her guarantee of Slovak independence in case the Magyars found it necessary to take up arms to defend their minority there.

Diplomats in Budapest and officials at Bratislava (the Slovakian capital), however, called the declaration "a piece of nonsense" and insisted that the Nazis would back Slovakia.

These Slovaks denied that the Hungarians living in their country were badly treated "in comparison with the Slovaks living in Hungary."—Associated Press.

## NAZI PLANE CRASH ON S.E. COAST

## Forty Persons Injured

**The Air Ministry and Ministry for Home Security announced this morning:**

**"Late last night enemy aircraft approached the East Coast at several points.**

**"A.A. guns went into action and one enemy aircraft crashed in a coastal town in Essex and burst into flames.**

**"Houses in the vicinity were damaged and some occupants were injured."**

**About 40 casualties were taken to hospital.**

A *Western Mail* correspondent reports that following the crash an "alarm" message was circulated and the town's services mobilised. A.R.P. men, rescue and demolition squads, police, and the fire brigade were rushed to the scene and the area was cordoned off. Soldiers turned out to help.

Demolition and rescue parties worked feverishly practically in darkness, and a rescue party official said, "We can only be guided by such lights as are deemed safe."

Several houses were completely demolished.

The aeroplane which crashed was a Heinkel bomber. Its five occupants were killed.

Several smaller explosions followed the major one and incendiary bombs blazed out.

Military were assisted by airmen in the rescue work.

A resident told a *Western Mail* reporter: "The heavy Nazi bomber ploughed its way through six or seven houses and burst into flames."

Rescue work was made difficult by the black-out. It is thought that some people are still buried under the debris.

Just before the crash the aeroplane dropped a Verey light to try to find a landing space.

It is believed that another Nazi aeroplane was following in the wake of the crashed machine.

### Explosions at Sea

Two heavy explosions were heard off the Yorkshire coast on Tuesday night and there were several bursts of machine-gun fire.

Anti-aircraft batteries were in action on the North-East Coast shortly after 11.30 on Tuesday night.

# NEWS ON THE FRONT

The "Western Mail" was founded on this day, May 1st, 1869. From that day to yesterday the Front Page has been occupied by advertisements. But to-day, owing to the importance of the war news, a change has been made necessary and it has been decided to put the latest news on the Front Page.

Readers will appreciate the alteration as it will enable them to learn the latest news every morning without a moment's delay and advertisers, we feel sure, will fall in with the natural anxiety of the public to have the news of the day quickly. The rest of the paper will remain as little changed as possible. The identity and policy of the "Western Mail" as the National Daily of Wales will not be affected and the characteristic features of the paper will be preserved.

One great benefit will be that, during the paper famine caused through the invasion of Norway by the Germans, readers will be given an extra news page — the Front Page — and all advertisers' announcements will have the advantage of being placed next to reading matter.

*Have you placed a definite order for the*

**WESTERN MAIL**

**AND SOUTH WALES NEWS**

**It was not until its 71st birthday, on May 1, 1940, that *The Western Mail* put news on the front page for the first time. The lead story reported German advances in Norway, and war news dominated the paper.**

# CHILDREN SUFFER FOR WAN OF TRANSPORT.

## FIRM ACTION AT CARDIFF.

## MAILS AND SUPPLIES CONVEYED BY AEROPLANE.

The first day of the general strike in Wales passed off without any untoward incident.

"In the mining valleys of Glamorgan," stated a police report, "the men are behaving splendidly."

Lack of tram and 'bus services caused great inconvenience in the towns. Chief among the sufferers in this connection were the children, many thousands of whom depend on these facilities to get to and from school. Men engaged on essential duties suffered in the same way.

Determined efforts are being made by the local authorities to ensure the restoration of these services. Cardiff City Council are calling their tramway employes back to work on pain virtually of dismissal, a decision adopted by an overwhelming majority of the Council.

Meantime motorists are urged to do all they can, more especially to convey children to and from distant schools, and men employed on essential work.

Notable among the incidents of the day was the introduction of aeroplanes, which, for the first time, conveyed mails and certain supplies to Cardiff, whence they were distributed to Newport and other centres.

---

## SOUTH WALES NEWS.

James Farrel (34), seaman, was sent to prison for two months' hard labour at Cardiff on Tuesday for having stolen a suit of clothes.

George Fry (27), Mynachdy-road, Cardiff, was committed to the assizes on Tuesday on a charge of bigamy.

Cardiff Finance Committee decided to defer the expenditure of £23,000 on the erection of temporary buildings for small-pox hospital purposes at Caerau.

Mr. T. J. Euryn Hopkins, B.A., of the Presbyterian College, Carmarthen, eldest son of Mr. and Mrs. Joseph Hopkins, Gibson-terrace, Bynea, near Llanelly, has accepted the pastorate of Nebo Welsh Congregational Church, Hirwain.

Mr. T. R. Davies, M.A., has been elected president of the 1920 Club of the University of Wales (Bangor).

Sergeant P. D. Keep has been appointed chief constable.

---

## UNITY OF CHURCHES.

### BAPTIST UNION'S REPLY TO LAMBETH APPEALS.

The following reply of the Baptist churches to the appeal for unity by the Lambeth Conference was unanimously agreed to by the conference of the Baptist Union at Leeds on Thursday:—

"Union of such a kind as the bishops have contemplated is not possible for us. We say this with the assurance of our regret that the way the bishops would have us go with them is not open.

"Further progress in the direction of Christian unity can be secured, we are convinced, only by unreserved mutual recognition. The mutual recognition of the Anglican and Baptist ministries is significant and full of hope.

"We are prepared to join the Church of England in exploring the possibility of a federation ...of equal and autonomo

---

present in a
ons when the
esday. There
embers.
Secretary for
reports were
Servicemen's
at the death
n the Army
House of
of men had
ch re-imposi-

said his atten-
such report,
misleading.

ny founda-
think-
ched

RS.
ing to Mr.
as proposed,
regulations
Act. If any
sed besides
have to be
ssed by the

ONS.
udget resolu-
ated that the
te the reso-
deplorable

e attitude

would be
ll matters

n the reso-

hequer then
which was

*The Western Mail* was published throughout the nine-day General Strike of 1926. When the printers walked out, women typists quickly learned to handle the Linotype machines, and some of the pages carried reports which had been produced on typewriters and then photographed and reproduced as line or half-tone blocks.

Pontypridd-born Alun Richards has recorded many aspects of South Wales life in his various roles as short-story writer, playwright, novelist and scriptwriter. He writes with particular enthusiasm about rugby, and following the publication of this article in *The Western Mail,* he wrote the script for the WRU centenary film *A Touch of Glory,* which Richard Burton narrated, and was asked by his publisher to produce a book under the same title. Here, he remembers the greatest Welsh outside halves and, in particular, his hero Glyn Davies, of Pontypridd, the matador of the sidestep, who waited in the wings for "Billy Kick" Cleaver to stand down.

# Salute the Prince!

## By Alun Richards

I F EVER there is a row about Welsh outside halves, unreason is never very far away. There is something about the position which feeds our secret thoughts. We identify with this player more than any other.

The bigger we are, the more ungainly, the fatter, the paunchier, the more out of puff – the more do we pull on the three feathers ourselves and go off fleet-footed in our dreams, darting this way and that, and always scoring alone, not a forward up with us, naturally.

"Look, no hands!" we say. We are the Welsh outside half. We are underneath the posts. We have done it again. Ich Dien! There's even a job in the brewery going if we want it, the BBC is easy meat: the House of Commons is not out of the question.

I have never myself been entirely free of this dream or the unreason which surrounds it, and not long ago I stood by the Social and Political in Port Talbot. I had made two new friends, Ludo and Waldo, and we soon found we had common ground elsewhere.

"Yes," Ludo said. "I remember that night well. We had a meeting."

"Quite so," Waldo said. "We felt it wasn't right."

Dangerous South Wales words.

You know what Port Talbot is like in the winter. The ill-tempered wind comes up off the sea in vicious personal bursts as if it is looking for the sand the steelworks confiscated years ago. High above us on the bare mountain a convoy of tipper lorries like five hearses appeared on the skyline. It was funeral weather. Conversations were going on in my mind, conversations about old wounds and dark deeds of long ago. Oh, the unfairness of it all!

"Is that the Big Five they're burying up there? I didn't know they were dead?"

"If they're not, someone's playing a very dirty trick on them."

"Serve 'em right anyway. I got no sympathy whatsoever. Not insured, I hope, trouble with the wills, and all their houses in other people's names."

It's a long time since the Big Five had to hide on a Monday morning, but when Waldo and Ludo said they'd had a meeting, it brought it all back to me, a vituperative argument of long ago.

We were referring to an outside half such as we had not seen the like of before or since. More important, he was an outside half with whom I had grown up, and that is quite another matter, for I had that inside knowledge that leads to pronouncements.

A sidestep, like a wart, I can tell you, does not just appear on one day, it grows pore by pore, layer by layer. It is tried out, improved upon, first one foot, then the other, first this way, then that. It is perfected, then it is kept ready, locked away and waiting, part of the armoury.

I should say that only two men have I ever seen with perfect sidesteps. They did not just beat men, they humiliated them. There was no thief-in-the-night stuff about it, none of your contemporary shoplifting. And, moreover, your sidestep proper – in the vintage years of real centres and wing forwards who were never selected without previous convictions – your sidestep proper then was to *either* side, off *either* foot, in *any* conditions, and, what is more, it looked good.

This is the very essence of the matter. They do not still sing about Belmonte the bullfighter simply because he killed the bulls.

He had to kill with grace, with style, to expose himself to maximum risk, and then bring the exhausted animal to its knees, by wit alone. What the butterfly movement of sword and cape is to the bullfighter so is the sidestep to the duel of the outside halves. It is the style that matters, the sheer grace.

Waldo, Ludo and myself had already agreed that Glyn Davies of Pontypridd had this last matador's attribute more than any other fly half we had seen. The only other player in the *corrida* was Bleddyn Williams, but he was neither from Pontypridd nor Port Talbot. It is a pity, but there it is.

He also succeeded for a longer period of time, making a business out of it, whereas the essence of any art is that it is short-lived.

In the case of Glyn Davies, his light was never truly appreciated except by real aficionados and when he was spurned for another, this is what Waldo and Ludo had a meeting about all those years ago.

You will gather that this fly half was different, but I will go further and say that he was perhaps alone among all the post-war halves since his style of play at its best had a purity about it, an absolute purity, like a white shape under a halo, a crystal-wrought template by which to measure all other halves ever since.

Never a worker, he was an artist, and, like all artists, things had to go right for him. He had an air, too, a manner. Give him a bad pass or a slow heel, or mutter at the stick you were getting up front, and it was like belching in the presence of royalty.

He could, as I say, sidestep off either foot, but what sped him on was a wicked acceleration over 20 yards, and the capacity of all great players to stand out over their fellows to such an extent that other positions did not seem to carry quite the same importance.

After watching him beat five or six men, you felt that forwards should not perhaps receive a whole jersey. When he really went, he made even Tanner, the original blind-side bullet, look like a grumbling plumber in dungarees. This, I am telling you, was a Prince.

And what got him in the end, of course, was democracy.

Unfortunately, outside halves, then as now, come in pairs. Then, as now, there is the sitting tenant, maybe a good, dependable trier with connections down the road, and usually, somewhere up the valleys, there is a lesser-known flame that burns and burns and waits for its chance.

Just after the war the sitting tenant was W B Cleaver, of Cardiff, rightly known as Billy Kick, and I must now come down from the Bench, remove my wig and gown, and pick up a long-bloodied shovel, for even after all this time I cannot look back at these two halves dispassionately. To me, the debate was never a debate. There was our boy – grace, art, poetry, romance, risk, danger – and there was that cipher down in Cardiff.

To be fair (!) Billy Kick always seemed to me to be more of an accountant than an outside half, and I studied him closely as official spy, often fixing him with the evil eye, wishing black juju magic or even 'flu upon him – anything that might infect his already antiseptic play.

It was as if I had left d'Artagnan behind me to inspect this office worker, for he filed forwards with either boot – one, two, three! – pinning them back down the touchline so that they were forever jogging like muttering policemen sent on fruitless errands.

Each kick was like an income-tax demand upon the other side, with VAT to follow. When he found touch, as he always did, he was like a man filling in forms, contriving at the same time never to look ruffled behind his WRU desk.

I do not deny that his own forwards worshipped him, that his centres became legends, that he was the most unselfish of players (which the Prince was not). The point is – I said it then and I say it now – the Welsh outside half should not be a kicking cipher, nor a staff man, nor so obviously on the side of the bulls.

Otherwise it is not art, nor can it ever be art; it is bash-bash, Canterbury beef on the hoof, aided and abetted by the officials and the committee salivating in the slaughterhouse, the only profit accruing to the Red Cross.

I said all this to Ludo.

"You, are not exaggerating one little bit, boy!"

But one day there came hope and light and vision – and one of the Big Five from Ponty! Half backs: Glyn and Wynford Davies. Schoolboys! Oh, you can imagine the rumpus, but it was a return to the past and to the glories of the past. They did it before with Willie Davies, there was the first golden Cliff, and now suddenly the war was over and austerity was beat.

I myself stole the school bell "to put behind my ear for after." Tickets there were a-plenty. We went *en masse* – everybody. These were the days of long macs, cronchie haircuts, jam and gibbon sandwiches and a real pair of fly bags was as rare as a mink stole.

I will not describe that day, but a later one when the Prince ascended his throne and had his coronation. The first day was my day in a sense, for I had been working the 'fluence on Billy Kick for weeks. The real day was several years later, England v Wales, 1949 and the poetical accolade *Gains preference over W B Cleaver* appeared once more.

I have the report in front of me now. The average age of the English side was 24. It not only looked like an English side, it sounded like one: B Braithwaite-Exley, D'Arcy Hosking, along with Meinheer Van Ryneveld thrown in to represent the Home and Colonial.

The Welsh pack was led by the superb Bunner Travers, getting his ninth cap after an interval of 10 years! In one sense, the geriatric brigade was out again, but I do not have to tell you that the Prince came into his own.

First the sidestep, then the swerve, then this way, then that… bamboozling is the word, and in retrospect, although the score 9-3 does not look much, the Prince had also triumphed in accountancy, for he handed two tries on a silver salver to Les Williams, of Llanelli and Cardiff, who went North for £3,000 after the game.

"Set him up for a good while," I said to Ludo. "Tidy," Ludo said.

There were other days: there was death in the afternoon for the Irish full back in Swansea when he was foxed on to the wrong foot, standing there snorting and pawing and mesmerised so that it was a mystery that they did not remove his ear and dedicate it to the president.

Even the hand that held the only tuba in the Gwaun-cae-Gurwen Silver Band was sticking wantonly in the air in orgiastic salute. He scored himself that day, under the Mumbles posts.

Well, they dropped him in the end, of course – prematurely. They played safe. They brought back Billy Kick, and that was why Waldo and Ludo held a meeting. Cliff Morgan was already waiting in the wings, and he brought to the game a mixture of both their talents, including a range of facial expressions that would have done credit to an opera singer in La Scala, especially when he was late tackled.

But he was a little champion in another mould. From the Prince in all his grace, we had come to the untiring workman: mercurial, dogged, brilliant on his day, but ever haunted, it seemed to me, by the solemnity of the great occasion.

He looked as if he worried; he was a chapel outside half. The Prince was High Church and did greater things – less often, it was true – but with a cool, insouciant insolence that said, "Lay not your hand upon me, felon!" and when it came off, it was the high life; it was ecstasy; it was poetry in motion, and it was cool, cool and effortless, and oh, it looked easy. It had, in short, style.

"Yes," Ludo said. "I agree with everything you say. When they dropped him, I felt like they was dropping our kid, I did. And I didn't even know him."

I heard the other day that he was dead. I couldn't believe it. A friend rang me up and I just stared and stared. Perhaps there comes a moment in all our lives when the future can only be tinged with grey, for the brilliance of the past is so fierce it burns.

Or maybe it is that we can never truly savour those who are not our immediate contemporaries? I do not know, but I salute him on this day. Let other legends be made and let others praise their own. For me – and the really informed and knowing ones in Port Talbot, Madrid, Rhondda and elsewhere – he was on his day *the* matador, His Excellency, El Supremo, the most graceful and elegant of them all.

*The Western Mail, March 5, 1977*

David Rosser, former political editor of *The Western Mail*, covered many momentous stories in his career. But the first, and the one he remembers most keenly, was the Sker Point disaster of 1947, when the Liberty ship *Samtampa* was wrecked with the loss of 40 lives and the eight-man crew of the Mumbles lifeboat also died. No one survived. His exclusive reports from the scene led to a national journalism award and a presentation from Lord Kemsley – and they also clinched his appointment as the *Mail's* lobby correspondent at Westminster, where he covered all the great Parliamentary stories for four decades. On the 30th anniversary of the disaster, he recalled the…

# Nightmare at Sker Point

## By David Rosser

IT HAPPENED on a Wednesday, 30 years ago today. Forty-eight lives were lost in what must be the worst-ever disaster off the Welsh coast… and I was there. It seems incredible that already 30 years have passed since that gruesome night when 40 seamen, the entire crew of the Liberty ship *Samtampa*, perished on the notorious Sker Point off Porthcawl, and the full crew of the Mumbles lifeboat, the 14-ton Edward, Prince of Wales, eight brave men doing a voluntary job, went to their deaths.

There are some things in a person's life which will remain forever vivid. For me, the *Samtampa* is one of those things. Recollections of that nightmare 10 hours are almost as fresh today as they were less than 24 hours afterwards, when the grim tally of 48 was completed.

Chronologically it developed from late-afternoon reports that a ship in ballast was battling its way through the channel towards Newport against heavy seas and high winds. By teatime its engines had broken down and it was drifting. An SOS was sent for tugs from Swansea, but conditions prevented any leaving port. No one at that time considered what the dangers were and what the night would bring.

I had just arrived home in Bridgend for tea when a friendly police call from Porthcawl informed me a ship was drifting near Sker. I would be kept informed. It was a bit of a nuisance, I recall, because this was to be my evening off. Uneasy, I checked back with Porthcawl. It was about 6.30pm.

The officer concerned had gone off to Sker, I was told. Less than half-an-hour later, I was standing alongside him in terrible conditions. As winds of cyclonic proportions whipped waves crazily to 20 and 30 feet, there, on the grim Sker rocks in the fading light, was the outline of a ship firmly skewered and swinging in two. Spray and spume mingled with crude oil from the punctured tanks. And all this was happening not more than 300 yards away. But there was nothing anyone could do for the hapless crew. For within minutes of striking the rocks about 7 o'clock, when the alert was given by a 10-year-old boy, the process of destruction was well underway.

I've heard it said so often, "What was the matter that the coastguards had not rescued anyone?" And I say now, as I said then, that they worked as hard as their limited force could at the time. They tried everything, short of committing themselves to the merciless waves. But conditions were worse than anything one could remember. Repeated attempts to fire a line across the battered vessel were unavailing. The rockets were blown back like spent match-sticks.

We watched, helpless, and as the evening turned to night all that those on the foreshore could do was to pick up the corpses as the cruel sea gave up its victims.

At that time no one knew anything about the Mumbles lifeboat. That second tragedy was to be revealed some hours later.

The last I saw of the *Samtampa* before darkness fell – not even the headlights of cars drawn up on the sand dunes could pierce the gloom – was when the buffeting waves had torn it apart and about half-a-dozen of the crew were seen huddled on the aft part. I thought I saw one of them try to jump the few yards which separated the two parts and disappear. It could have been done, I think.

I still feel that had the others made the effort they might have survived. As it was, the aft part took the heaviest pounding, and they must all have been dragged down without any hope of surviving.

A couple of hours later, with an eerie suddenness, the wind dropped. The tide had receded and a sickly moon appeared behind scudding clouds. Was there anyone alive out there? I remember Police Inspector Bill Jones leading a dangerous trip to the twin hulks. We jumped from rock to rock in the ghostly, dim moonlight. Everything was slippery with crude oil. There was the danger of sliding into pools of oil and water. Everyone was in a mess. I slipped and landed on something soft which ejected a spout of oily water. It was one of the dead crew.

Then we reached the side of the fore part, towering 50 feet above the grim, debris-strewn, oil-drenched rocks. Inspector Jones stooped, picked up a stone, and banged on the hulk. It sounded like a great bass bell... it was a death knell. Then silence. Not a sound penetrated the grim darkness.

"Well, boys, I fear we must abandon all hope of finding anyone alive," was his terse comment. We turned and made our hazardous way back, me to file what I thought was my final story of the night, and they to comb the tide line for victims. But little did we know...

It was about 2 am, and I was at the Sker farmhouse which had been my contact point with the Cardiff office, when the first mention reached us of concern about the safety of the Mumbles lifeboat. It had been launched about 6.30 the previous evening, had turned back a short time later when it failed to find the distressed ship, and then set out again under Coxswain William Gammon. It might have been the car headlights that attracted it to Sker; or it might have caught sight of the ship before the light went entirely. No one knows. We who were on the spot saw and knew nothing of the proximity of the lifeboat.

At first light, as police and coastguards went about their grim task of raking in the *Samtampa* bodies, Police Sergeant Austin and Inspector Jones walked along the foreshore towards Porthcawl. I followed. Suddenly, as we turned a sandy bluff, there were two groups of huddled bodies. One lot, five of them together, could be distinguished by their oilskins and cork lifebelts. We had found the Mumbles crew – as the sun rose they looked like ebony statues glistening in the all-encasing oil.

Less than 100 yards away, on an outcrop of rock, was the lifeboat, upturned and with its gunwales smashed in and mast ripped off. For a moment the ghastly significance did not penetrate.

When the police officers telephoned Mumbles a few minutes later (and I contrived to get the news into the last editions of *The Western Mail*) it was the first hint that disaster had befallen the lifeboat. It was the bitter finale to the worst night of tragedy ever experienced on the Welsh coast.

The Mumbles crew had shown the utmost bravery in their bid to rescue the *Samtampa's* crew. I shall always believe so. I cannot accept the suggestion that had been made that Coxswain Gammon had been foolhardy in creeping to windward of the stricken vessel without regard for the notorious Sker Rocks. But there seems little doubt that the force of waves and wind had carried the lifeboat either into the wreck or on to the razor-sharp rocks, hurling the crew to their deaths.

April 23, 1947, will ever be a day to remember. I wish it hadn't been—but I was there.

*The Western Mail, April 23, 1977*

Playwright and author Elaine Morgan has written a series of major television serials and documentaries for BBC Wales, and her books include *The Descent of Woman* (1972), a feminist view of evolution, and *The Aquatic Ape* (1982), a theory of human evolution. When she wrote a series of articles entitled *My Wales* for *The Western Mail* in 1978, she looked first at the town of Mountain Ash, where she still lives.

# Don't Weep for the Good Old Days

## By Elaine Morgan

I T'S A well-known fact that short descriptive pieces about the South Wales Valleys are meant to be full of anecdotes about rugby football and male voice choirs and grim slag heaps and chapel pulpits and tough, hard-bitten miners with blue scars.

There will probably be a lot of consumer dissatisfaction if these features are not given their full weight, but there's not much I can do about this since I can't sing, I don't go to chapel, I can't tell a scrum half from an up-and-under, and I don't even know the surname of the hero Max Boyce keeps celebrating when he waves his leek and shouts, "Oggie! Oggie!"

It is easier than you might imagine to live all your life in the Valleys and never see a rugger match – almost as easy as living in London and never running into a Beefeater. As long as I can remember the game has been present as a kind of background noise – a thing you hear men arguing about in trains and women complaining about in cafes.

But I've never witnessed the game, I've never understood why the ball is long and thin, though I've heard some pretty wild theories about it, and I've never grasped why a pastime invented by the alumni of a pukka Eton-and-Harrow type English public school should go down like a bomb in places like Dowlais and Tonypandy.

In fact, if you ask me when was the last time I watched people around here engaging in a sporting activity, I can't remember whether it was four people playing squash in the Abercynon Sports Centre, or a bunch of huntsmen in pink coats assembling outside the Jeffrey Arms in Mountain Ash. But I can tell you this: when people come here with cameras hoping to record What Life in the Valleys is Really Like, the last thing they want to go home with is a picture of people playing squash.

One thing I can always offer them, here at the posh end of Mountain Ash, is a shot of a pit wheel. They find that very reassuring and characteristic, though it's not really characteristic at all. Indeed, if we hadn't moved from Aberdare, I couldn't have obliged them in this way, because Sweet 'Berdâr, like a lot of other Valley towns, lost the last of its 30 pits some years ago.

One of these documentary-minded visitors was so enthused by the pit gear that he made a point of hanging around one of the collieries when the shift was ending in order to take a picture of a typical rugged Welsh miner. The first one to emerge had a cheerful, chubby face, a mass of frizzy blond hair flowing down on to his shoulders and a badge in his jacket saying "Sex Pistols". The best of British luck to him, was my own reaction.

I see no reason why our teenagers, any more than anyone else's, should be expected to adhere to the folkways of their grandparents, like flies preserved in amber. But as "Portrait of a Miner" he was felt to be a let-down, and that was one camera that never went click.

And now, as to the obligatory item about the tips – for I have never heard anyone native to the Valleys use the word "slag heaps" unless incited to by a BBC interviewer – the most recent development is that over the last few years some of the older tips have spontaneously, and over a wide area, turned as purple as Ben Lomond.

I'd be the last one to minimise the crassness and vandalism that inflicted those black scars on a once beautiful landscape and I'm happy to see that some of them are being shifted and the land reclaimed for constructive purposes. But it makes me uneasy when I hear economic "realists" computing the total acreage of spoil involved and deciding that the cost of removing all the tips would be prohibitive. Because they then privately go on to conclude that the visual aspect of the Valleys must remain forever obscene, and that investment in them would therefore be money thrown away.

The fact is that a disused tip, like any other ecological niche, doesn't remain empty for long. If it's left alone it grows grass; it grows gorse and brambles. If it's in a sheltered place it sprouts birch saplings and covers itself with woodland, or if it is an exposed one it covers itself with heather.

It's happening more readily today because the decline of the older, more polluting industries has meant that in most of the Valleys the air is now demonstrably cleaner and sweeter than down by the coast. We are beginning to feel the benefit of a piece of good fortune for which town planners in any industrial area of comparable size would have thanked Heaven – the fact that every little Valley town, because of the mountain terrain on each side of it, is surrounded inviolably by its own private green belt.

But if the Valleys have made a distinctive mark on the history of Wales and, indeed, of Great Britain, it's not of course because of the landscape or the vegetation – it's because of the people, and the great legend of their courage and passion and endurance and sense of community. "And where has all *that* gone to?" people ask. "It's not the same there any more, is it?"

Well no, it's not the same here – it's not the same anywhere – and there are some among the older generation who look back with nostalgia, just as Londoners look back to the Blitz, to a time when ideals were high and all men were brothers. To my mind though, a city in flames is a high price to pay for a communal knees-up; and anyone who feels sentimental about the Thirties because they heightened our sense of solidarity has forgotten what those years were really like.

For myself, I derive intense pleasure from sitting in a ladies' hairdressers and hearing the contented chatter of a couple of old-age pensioners in pastel-coloured cardigans who are splurging on a not-infrequent shampoo and set and a touch of the blue rinse because they are going out somewhere that will make it worth their while to dress up, and I think of their grandmothers at the same age, shrivelled and broken with toil, clad in shabby black and waiting to die – don't ask me to weep for the good old days.

Yet, there remains an atmosphere and a friendliness that, in my experience, no other place quite matches. People in the Valleys are urban enough to be witty, rural enough to be relaxed; urban enough to be tolerant, not metropolitan enough to be pretentious.

Of all the people born and bred here who have moved out and sometimes attained fame and fortune, I have never heard of any who named their birthplace with anything other than pride.

*The Western Mail, August 5, 1978*

John Greally, born in Belfast and brought up in Cardiff, joined *The Western Mail* in 1950 to train as a journalist. After National Service in the RAF he returned to the *Mail* to work as a reporter and sub-editor before becoming a student in the Jesuit order for nine years, three of which he spent teaching. More journalism followed, with stints at the *Catholic Herald, Daily Telegraph, The Sun*, the *Financial Times*, and the editorship of the weekly *Cardiff Journal*. He has published a novel, *Dante Comes to Town*, a comedy set in the London of the swinging Sixties. He is also a composer, his first work to be professionally performed being a piano sonata premiered in Cardiff in 1987 and since broadcast on Radio 3.

# The Literary World Must Judge

## By John Greally

THAT does it. I am going to publish, and be damned. Reproduced for the first time in this column is a newly-discovered 11-line fragment by Dylan Thomas.

I have been nerved to it, despite my professional scepticism, by Oxford don Gary Taylor. Gary has gone into print with his historic discovery of a lost 99-line poem by Shakespeare.

Like the Shakespeare verses, the Dylan fragment might seem, to the untutored eye and ear, just a cack-handed spoof of the poet's work. But like Gary, I have put my Dylan fragment through every test known to man and to modern technology.

I discovered the fragment – hand-written on the inside of a torn Capstan packet – tucked into a road drain not far from Mumbles Head. Now the literary world must judge:

*But me no butts of bow-tied export ale*
*This bubble-winking night,*
*As I play with my beads*
*Of sweat.*
*In waking, or in Felinfoel-dark sleep,*
*I keep*
*A leaf-of-grass-sharp lookout*
*Over my time-hunted shoulder,*
*And always I feel*
*The hot-blowing breath of bottleflies*
*On my delirium-tremendous neck.*

That, I would hazard, is about as tragico-lyric as poems come. But if you think it's a staggering turn-up for the world of culture, hold on to your hat.

A few days ago I was browsing in *The Western Mail* cuttings library. What do you think I turned up? Mysteriously stuck to the inside of a file of newspaper stories on *Agriculture: Beet Crops* was a fascinating scrap of paper, covered with six lines of script in the late Middle English style.

Carbon dating and ion tests have proved the stanza to be from the pen of noted bard Geoffrey Chaucer. It goes:

*O swete, o tendre sugar bete,*
*Myn herte doth sighe, and dye —*
*E'en as thou, milch cow,*
*Dost dye thy lovely lokkes*
*Now grene as any yaffle,*
*Now piebald yellow and rede, me for to baffle.*

No question, that's vintage Geoff, if ever I saw it. But what was my amazement last weekend, when I was idly poking around the Roman foundations of Cardiff Castle.

You've guessed. There, on a flaking patch of parchment, was a missing hexameter from the fifth book of Virgil's *Aeneid.*

That immortal line, written in haste during a tour of the war-torn Middle East, now sees the light of day for the first time in 2,000 years:

*Genio mi Iacobe indulgeo bumpety tum-tum.*

My classicist colleagues are cock-a-hoop about it. One believes it may be the long-hidden basis for the popular modern apostrophe: "I'm all right, Jack."

Another, intrigued by the phrase *bumpety tum-tum*, considers the line definitely late Virgil. He has yet to determine whether the poet was moving into a satirico-comic phase or simply beginning to fail in his powers of invention.

Never mind. Back in Wales, about 600 years ago, best-selling bard Dafydd ap Gwilym was penning the following fragment, which was unknown to literature until I fished it out of a rock pool near Aberystwyth the other day:

*Adwaen forwyn leddf, a cuwchau du,*
*Ni ffraethach yw – rhy ofer hi*
*Mawr ei deudroed ar aelwyd goch,*
*Yn lloft ei chwyrnu rhu yw'r moch.*

Welsh scholars tell me it contains romantic paradoxes – typical of Dafydd's love poems – such as the juxtaposition of maidenly gentleness with a habit of thunderous snoring.

But now for my most truly important find of recent weeks. The following stanza was conceived by the most sublime of Tudor England's poets, the quite peerless Anon.

Those who today demand that the artistic works of former ages should be "relevant" will be gratified by the caustic sentiments of Anon. His is very much a "modern" message:

*Come merie punkes! That bene so coy of gere,*
*Your haires y-spiked high in egge yolk.*
*Come merie punkes! Raise your quartes of bere,*
*Sing: Deeth to olden folk!*

That's all for now. If I find any more gems germinating in the mind of genius, I'll let you know.

*The Western Mail, November 27, 1985*

Terry Campbell started his journalistic career on the *Abertillery Gazette* before joining the *South Wales Echo* as a district reporter in Merthyr. He later moved to Cardiff as a feature writer on the *Echo* before joining *The Western Mail* in a similar role. His individual style and sense of humour quickly became popular with readers, and his Monday-morning column *Now Look Here* ran for five years in the mid-1980s. Forced to retire early through ill-health, he died in 1995.

# Now Look Here

## By Terry Campbell

IT'S FUNNY how you get things mixed up. To this day I can't think of the Communist Party without haddock crossing my mind. And the Revolution is forever associated with hake.

It's all the fault of the town crier, an estimable gentleman who used to stop opposite our house when I was a kid and deliver his announcements.

He was regular in his visits to the spot, and at the first sound of his handbell I'd go racing out of the house and stand open-mouthed waiting to hear what the great man had to tell us.

Watching Mr Thomas prepare to make his delivery was more exciting than viewing the preliminaries of any TV news bulletin. He would take deep breaths, draw himself up to his full height and look across imperiously at the bunch of kids who formed his audience. Then he would get on with the news.

To me it was always of massive importance. Why else would Mr Thomas leave his house and go around the streets, stopping at key points to inform the public of what was happening?

Mr Thomas was a highly-respected coloured man and was known without the slightest disrespect, in fact you never gave it a second thought, as Mr Thomas the Darky. The description was purely functional, to distinguish him from Thomas the Milk, Thomas the Undertaker, Thomas the Builder and Thomas the Hernia.

To me, Mr Thomas had more impact than any other newsreader I've ever seen or heard. After all, they have disasters and other such events to whet their audience's appetites, whereas Mr Thomas's supply of news was strictly limited.

In fact, I only remember two items. But to me they took on an aura of world significance, simply because Mr Thomas announced them. As I write I can still hear Mr Thomas's voice echoing down the corridor of the years, as he declaimed them in stentorian voice to us wide-eyed kids.

They weren't wrapped up in verbiage, but were brief and to the point, for Mr Thomas was fully aware that the crowd around him had a short attention span. In 30 seconds the bulletin would be over. And we would have learned that (1) Mrs Cammerman had had a delivery of fish and (2) the local Communist Party would hold a meeting on the Square on Sunday.

Week after week Mr Thomas pumped the news into the community.

Mrs Cammerman, a splendid woman, was, of course, a local fishmonger. A refugee from a pogrom, she had no connection whatsoever with the Communist Party, and there was no link at all between the two items. But for years I associated the arrival of the fish at her shop with the Communist Party meeting.

I thought that the Communist Party members had caught the fish, and now they were back home they wanted to tell everyone how they had done it; or else I imagined that now Mrs Cammerman had had her delivery of fish the Communists would have the necessary protein to give them the stamina to hold their meeting on the Square.

Once, for light relief, I suppose, Mr Thomas shook his bell and announced that a carnival was to be held. His audience were shocked. There wasn't a mention of Mrs Cammerman or the Reds.

We regular listeners at once protested and told Mr Thomas to watch it or we'd boycott him. The next week life returned to normal. Mrs Cammerman had had her delivery of fish and the Communist Party were holding their meeting on the Square.

*The Western Mail, July 7, 1986*

# The Real Goronwy Rees

## By John Morgan

WHAT FOLLY it is to think that there are no new experiences left. One thing I never dreamed possible was that one day I would see two close friends depicted on television, played by an actor and actress.

Yet, so it was the other night when Goronwy Rees and his wife Margie were represented as key figures in a drama about Marxist Russian spies Sir Anthony Blunt, Guy Burgess and Donald Maclean.

How they would have fallen about at the film as, I hope, their children will when they have overcome their proper anger. Goronwy and Margie were given to laughter: it was one of their many charms, even when they had a lot not to laugh about.

It was inevitable that the actor and actress in the BBC film would not look like Goronwy and Margie, nor talk like them, or behave like them; but not that they should be so unlike. Margie was one of the most attractive women I ever met, her voice as distinctive – even rather of the style – as Lauren Bacall's.

She was highly intelligent. In the film she seemed a pea-brained sweetie. In the film Goronwy was a plump man who seemed unsure, even frightened. In life he was, to his cost, slim, elegant, charming and brilliant, a man of reckless courage.

Of all the eminent Welshmen I've known, he was the most fascinating and, in terms of the conflicts of our century, the most important in his interests. Many maintain that he threw his great talents away: he didn't and I don't.

Since some will not know of him, his career, briefly, was this. He was born in Aberystwyth in 1909, son of a famous Welsh preacher. He was Welsh-speaking, which became important later on. He went to school in Cardiff, played rugby and then became the outstanding scholar of his time at Oxford.

He was a Socialist who lived in Berlin, came home to be an editor at the *Spectator*, where be wrote possibly the best, certainly the earliest, anti-Nazi journalism. Friendly with Guy Burgess and many of the rest of the Communist crowd – since they were mostly homosexual they were known as the Homintern – but volunteered for the Royal Welsh Fusiliers when war broke out.

His Marxist pals were against fighting since their hero Stalin had signed a pact with Hitler. When Hitler invaded Russia it became a different war. All this he had described in his two majestic volumes of autobiography. The BBC film suggested he was a Communist Party member and had been briefly a Soviet spy: neither claim is true.

As far as Wales went, in the 'Fifties he was persuaded by that Welsh *eminence gris* Dr Tom Jones to become principal of the University College, Aberystwyth. He fell out with the Establishment. He offended them as, for different reasons, he did the London Establishment, by publishing anonymously in *The People* an account of his friendship with Guy Burgess.

In this he was aided by Keidrych Rhys, the editor of *Wales*. Guy Burgess had by now gone to Moscow, telephoning Goronwy and Margie en route.

In London several were afraid of what Goronwy might write next and about whom? After all, hadn't Colonel Rees been General Montgomery's side-kick, been a senior Intelligence figure himself? In passing, almost, he had written the first and best novel on the matter of brainwashing – *Where No Wounds Were*.

He told me how his anonymity in *The People* had been unmasked. In the 'Thirties, before he married Margie, he had abandoned one affair with a famous woman novelist – he is the central figure in her best novel – for her friend, another writer. The latter, 20 years later, was to shop him because he had abandoned her. Time is surely long in affairs of the heart.

I came to know the Rees family after I had supported his Aberystwyth cause in 1956 in *The Observer*. In London in the 'Sixties, when I worked at the *New Statesman* and *Panorama*, we enjoyed ourselves in their company with their friends Richard Hughes, Arthur Koestler, A J Ayer and so many others.

Since I was often working in Central and Eastern Europe, their experience of the Nazi and Stalinist tyrannies was as illuminating as any on offer. (Sir Freddy Ayer has written in protest at inaccuracies in the BBC film.)

In the late 'Seventies, just before he died and just after Margie had, Goronwy and myself went on a journey to Berlin, Vienna and his old haunts. We were making a film for HTV Wales which Aled Vaughan had proposed in the teeth of the opposition from two members of the Aberystwyth Establishment on the company's board.

In Vienna we saw a performance of the Brecht-Weill *Mahagonny*. Goronwy was moved, since he had seen the premiere so many turbulent decades earlier. He had known Bertolt Brecht and translated his poems. That night he told me that Anthony Blunt had been the Fourth Man, and named a Fifth.

He talked about the Communists he had known. His view was that anyone who remained in the Communist party, or even as a Marxist, after the Soviet putsch in Prague in 1948, let alone after the Hungarian uprising of 1956, no longer qualified as a human being.

The next day, in Geneva, he swore me to secrecy about Blunt. We were on our way to hear Margaret Price, Ryland Davies and Anne Howells sing in Mozart's *Cosi Fan Tutte*. An unusual couple of Welsh days, we agreed: a long way from Aberystwyth, would you say?

By that time Goronwy had become unpopular in certain Welsh circles. He was hostile to political nationalism. In his view also, Wales would be a healthier place if the language died, even though it was his first language. It was one of the few subjects on which we differed.

He was scornful of people who made a cause of the language when it wasn't their first language. This he saw at best neurotic, at worst opportunism. I think his vehemence was partly due to irritation with some troglodytes at Aberystwyth, but also because the language cause had not then become a non-political affair.

He used to maintain that Saunders Lewis had once said that it wouldn't be all bad if Hitler won if that meant the Welsh language surviving. In Goronwy's view the battle must always be against the totalitarian, whether Fascist or Marxist. His insights had certainly been learned the hard way.

One of the pleasures, away from his company, of meeting Goronwy's contemporaries at Oxford, where he was a Fellow as well as bursar of All Souls and generous with his hospitality there, was their jealousy of him. Two Labour Cabinet Ministers could scarcely speak of him, so sharp was their envy of his mind and style.

There was puzzlement at his lack of ambition, since he probably had the sharpest intelligence of any Welshman since David Lloyd George.

He's described his view of himself as a "bundle of sensations" in the philosopher Hume's terms. His curiosity and fastidious, private integrity baffled a lot of people. The BBC play exhibited surprise that Margie called him "Rees". This is a common trait among West Wales's women, yet Margie was English.

His five children also called him Rees, still do. I always found it curiously charming and characteristic, a trait of warm, affectionate distance, a signal of healthy independence; and independent he certainly was. He could look on tempests and not be shaken, even if they were often of his own making. He was as indifferent to the might of English Establishment pursuing him as the Welsh; and amusing about both.

His final derisive view about the row at Aberystwyth was that it was due not to his *People* articles, nor his drinking with students, nor his bills at the off-licence, nor local wives' hostility to Margie being English, but to something fundamental.

When he sold off some property in the interests of the college, he called in neutral, alien, estate-agents and solicitors to deal with the sale, rather than locals. That was too much for the Cardigan Welsh. At least, that was what he told me, laughing.

*The Western Mail, January 20, 1987*

Poet, editor, translator and literary journalist Meic Stephens founded *Poetry Wales* and edited it from 1965 until 1973. Within a year of joining the editorial staff of *The Western Mail* in 1966, he was appointed Literature Director of the Welsh Arts Council, a post he held until 1990. As the compiler, editor and translator of many books, he has made an important contribution to Anglo-Welsh literature. A lecturer in journalism at the University of Glamorgan, he was awarded an Honorary M. A. by the University of Wales in 1999. *The Oxford Companion to the Literature of Wales*, which he edited in 1986, was published in a revised and expanded form as *The New Companion to the Literature of Wales* in 1998. He writes a regular book column for *The Western Mail.*

# Spade Money

## By Meic Stephens

THE HEALTHIEST work I ever did was the digging of graves. During my college days I had a variety of jobs to fill in the holidays and earn a little money. Every Christmas I used to work as a postman, delivering letters around Pontypridd. At Easter I would work in the bakery of Hopkin Morgan or in one of the factories on the Treforest Industrial Estate.

This kind of work was tough and boring, but it was the way most students paid for their university education in the 'Fifties. There was no dole for students on holiday in those days.

The £100 we received from the county council each year was hardly enough to pay for our books, our lodging and our food.

It was possible to earn as much as £12 a week during the holidays – if you were willing to sweat for it. This was the equivalent of what my father earned. I was glad that I could at last contribute to my family's finances – and keep something for my own use.

As I said, of all the holiday jobs I did, the most pleasant was in Glyntâf

Cemetery, across the river from my home in Treforest. I went there every summer for five years, digging graves and labouring with a gang of men who were old hands at the job.

A grave had to be cut in a day – and no longer. Usually, this was work for two men, with one working in the narrow ditch at a time.

Down we went, then, lifting the earth with a broad spade at first. Then the sides of the hole had to be straightened with a special tool and the oblong cut to the correct size – 9ft by long by 4ft across – to hold three coffins.

It became more difficult as we went down through a layer of wet clay, but as a rule I left this part of the job to Reg.

Reg was a great hulk of a man and a champion gravedigger. His secret, I think, was to spit on his hands before starting like a ferocious terrier to throw the earth up and place it in a neat pile on the edge of the grave.

Then we took a break, lying under "the patient yew" and slaking our thirst with a mug of cider or cold tea. It was good to feel the sun on my back and arms.

I spent every dinner hour, after eating my sandwiches, trying to teach Reg to read out of the *Daily Mirror*, without much success, I fear. There was not much point quoting "Alas, poor Yorick" to the likes of him.

Nevertheless, he was a cheerful and likeable chap. He used to say, "This is the dead centre of the universe," and "There's no slump in our trade," time and time again.

Back to work then, to finish the job by the end of the afternoon. From time to time we ran into difficulties while opening old graves. The feat was to dig down as far as the coffin without breaking through the rotten lid. Whenever that wasn't done successfully, we had to call the superintendent, Mr Burt.

Next day, we had to stand off a little during the interment ceremony. But when the mourners had gone our task was to fill in the hole once more.

Only on one occasion did we receive a tip for our labour. Yes, I saw the custom of offering "spade money" to gravediggers in Glyntâf Cemetery.

When I listen to people discussing the choice between burying and cremating the dead, I can speak out of my own experience. For I also worked quite a few shifts in the crematorium in Glyntâf, behind the curtains as it were, escorting the coffins to the furnaces.

My opinion is that there isn't much difference in the end. It is out of admiration for Dr William Price, the pioneer of the custom, that I tend to favour cremation.

Be that as it may, the memories I have of Glyntâf by now are much sweeter.

In 1961, for example, I had the privilege of witnessing the funeral of the poet Huw Menai. I remember the occasion mainly because I saw my English Professor, Gwyn Jones, walking with his usual dignity behind the hearse, together with two other writers who are among the literary giants of Wales – Jack Jones and Glyn

Jones. One of them, I recall, was wearing a bright yellow pullover under his funeral suit.

I am grateful to Glyntâf for another reason. There, each long and hot summer, I had a chance to read the gravestones and thus to nurture my growing interest in the Welsh language.

Words like *Er cof am* (In memory of), *yr hwn a fu farw* (who passed away), *gynt o'r plwyf hwn* (formerly of this parish), *hefyd ei annwyl briod* (also his beloved wife), *hedd, perffaith hedd* (peace, perfect peace)… these were among the first Welsh words I understood outside school and Sunday School. Yes, the well-known line *Iaith garreg fy aelwyd, iaith garreg fy medd* (The language of my hearthstone and the language of my gravestone) has a special meaning for me.

Black, on the whole, are a man's thoughts in a place like Glyntâf, I know. But as I look back at the summers I spent there, it is the sunshine and the greenness and the skylarks and the blue sky that I remember most.

Among the dead a young lad knew for certain that he was alive.

*The Western Mail, May 4, 1991*

Gethyn Stoodley Thomas was one of Wales's best-known television film-makers, and produced a string of documentaries and profiles of famous Welshmen such as Augustus John, Sir Clough Williams-Ellis and the architect William Burges. His much-praised series on the history of Rhondda, *The Long Street*, is an important record of industrial South Wales. The brother of J B G Thomas, former sports editor of *The Western Mail*, he taught in Cardiff schools for several years before joining the Royal Navy at the outbreak of World War II. He joined the BBC in 1950, and worked on the famous *Tonight* programme with Cliff Michelmore and Kenneth Allsop. One of his inspirations, *Songs of Praise*, still draws a faithful BBC 1 audience. He became *The Western Mail's* television critic when he retired from the BBC. He died in 1997.

# The Day We Rowed Churchill Ashore

## By Gethyn Stoodley Thomas

*"— who hast compassed the waters with bounds until day and night come to an end: be pleased to receive into Thy almighty protection the persons of us, thy servants and the Fleet in which we serve..."*

THE SOLEMN cadences of the familiar naval prayer had died away over the waters of Little Placentia Bay; the ships' companies of *HMS Prince of Wales* and *USS Augusta* had dispersed; the President of Great Britain had joined the officers for luncheon in the wardroom and the crew of Britain's latest battleship had eaten their dinner and settled to an afternoon of "make and mend".

It was Sunday afternoon, August 10, 1941, after the voyage that had brought Winston Churchill across the ocean to this lonely coast of Newfoundland, to meet Franklin Delano Roosevelt and to jointly declare the Four Freedoms to be enshrined in the Atlantic Character.

Down in the for'ard starboard messdeck, we slumbered on mess tables or hammock nettings in the comparative calm of a harbour watch.

The tannoy suddenly blared: "Away, first whaler's crew; lay aft to the quarter deck."

Thus rudely disturbed and still heavy with plum-duff and the rum ration, we staggered aft to the quarter-deck gangway.

There were five of us, all candidates for RNVR Commissions, serving our obligatory sea time as seamen ratings. We were as new as the ship and, in fact, had never rowed the whaler to which we'd been allocated.

This long, narrow craft, a relic of the days of whale hunting by sail, is rowed by five oars, three to starboard, two to port, or the other way round, and not the easiest for amateurs to manage.

Our unease at the prospect was made doubly so when our passengers assembled at the gangway. The Prime Minister had decided on "a run ashore"; he was dressed in his blue siren suit and yachting cap, the inevitable cigar well alight, and a stout stick in hand.

With him were two very large men, in dark suits and bowlers; his minders, you'd call them now, and patently security in every watchful glance.

By the time they and the midshipmen in charge had filled the stern of the whaler, we the oarsmen were crowded into the bows. Our rowing, already of dubious character, would be even more cramped, and the coast of Placentia Bay looked very distant indeed.

Happily, it was decided that a motor launch would tow us as close inshore as possible and off we set, hoping that we looked reasonably seamanlike.

Casting off the tow, we rowed the last few yards to the beach, A more ragged affair had not been seen since *Three Men in a Boat*.

We were, as the Ancient Mariner would have said, a ghastly crew. But somehow the boat was beached, and the PM disembarked.

"Let the men have a run ashore," cried that well-known voice. And ashore we duly scrambled.

It was an empty landscape with only a distant plume of cottage smoke to denote habitation. Far off, two tiny children watched us for a while, then ran off as we approached.

The PM and his party set off briskly along the coast, while we remained near our beached craft.

After half an hour came the order to row around to some rocks at the bottom of a steeply sloping shale bluff.

At the top of this cliff, we saw the great man standing. Then he sat down and with stick cheerfully waving, slid down on his bottom to the rock ledge where we waited.

As he careered down like any naughty schoolboy, I thought: "There goes the fate of Empire, and victory or defeat. If he breaks his neck…"

But he didn't; he stepped aboard the whaler, thanking us "for rescuing the marooned mariner!"

Once again we were taken in tow. And all the way back to *Prince of Wales*, Mr Churchill was looking about him and talking of a sudden plan to change the face of this deserted strand.

"You see, gentlemen, the thing to do would be to buy up all this land – cheaply – build hotels and suchlike upon it, attract hordes of American tourists here and then sell out at a handsome profit."

In the midst of war, and at one of our darker hours, the entrepreneurial spirit still bubbled to the surface. It may have been a mad idea, climatically as well as economically, but that didn't deter that maker of plans, both good and ill.

Six days after his return home, the PM broadcast to the nation, ending with the words:

*"This was a meeting which marks forever in the pages of history the taking of the English-speaking nations amid all this peril… back to the broad high road of freedom and justice."*

But there was no mention of the scheme for turning Little Placentia Bay into an international tourist trap!

*The Western Mail, August 10, 1991*

Patrick Hannan, educated at Cowbridge Grammar School and University College, Aberystwyth, was industrial editor of *The Western Mail* for two years before moving in 1970 to BBC Wales, where he was industrial and political correspondent for 13 years and, from 1983 to 1989, produced features and documentaries. Since then he has been a freelance writer, broadcaster and television producer, making documentaries for BBC 2, BBC Wales and HTV, presenting radio programmes for Radio Wales and Radio 4, and writing for *The Western Mail* and *Wales on Sunday* and other publications. The author of two books on broadcasting, he was awarded the MBE for his services to broadcasting and television in Wales in 1994. He is married to Menna Richards, managing director, HTV Wales. This is one of his light-hearted Friday columns.

# As the Bishop said to the Bishop

## By Patrick Hannan

IS THERE, I wonder, a more chilling phrase in the English language than "Christmas special"? It is particularly popular in broadcasting, where it generally means even worse than usual editions of programmes that are pretty uninspiring at the best of times. Psychologists now agree that this is one of the important factors in making Christmas the most popular time of the year for people to think of divorce – when they can get their minds off murder, that is.

There are other things, of course, including drink and an unusually prolonged exposure to members of your family, but there's no doubt that when it comes to rows it's hard to beat Christmas.

That's why it's good to see the Church of England leading the way in this festive tradition. And doing so in a manner that points up the ancient custom of making sure that the argument is entirely trivial, the sort of thing you would have shrugged your shoulders at if you hadn't started on the third bottle of Tescbury's claret.

I refer, of course, to the furore begun by David Jenkins, the Bishop of Durham, over whether some of the most cherished stories of Christian tradition are fact or myth.

Now I must admit that the Bishop of Durham is the kind of person who would get up your nose at any time of the year, never mind Christmas. He is a lethal combination of the smart, the smug and the prissy, which drives many of his co-religionists to view him with the same warmth as a Muslim does Salman Rushdie.

But the entertaining and interesting thing about Dr Jenkins is that he gets people to denounce him in terms reminiscent of the Inquisition, not by spouting heresy, but by endorsing orthodox thinking.

His views on various events in the New Testament do not, in general, bring him into serious conflict with most theologians. The Archbishop of Canterbury knows that better than anybody, but even so he has rebuked Dr Jenkins. Why he should do so, we'll come to in a moment.

The point the Bishop is making, it seems to me, is that the so-called facts of Christianity often gets in the way of what might or might not be its truths.

Is the whole faith diminished, for example, by the suggestion that there might have been up to a dozen wise men? Even Mr Gummer, who has set himself as more episcopal than most bishops, would have trouble creating a fuss about that one.

But what is interesting about all this is not who is right and who is wrong, but why we are having a row at all.

And here, it seems to me, Dr Jenkins's transgression is not theological, but political. It's not what he says, but the fact that he says it at all.

The Archbishop of Canterbury regretted that the Bishop should have "reopened these divisive issues at a time when most Christians would prefer to remember all that unites them in wonder at the incarnation of our Lord."

Well, you don't have to be a theologian to realise that really means: "Anything for a quiet life." This is hardly surprising since, as a rule, people who run churches prefer such things to be left for discussion between their own experts.

In churches, as in some forms of politics, it doesn't really do to have people going round thinking for themselves. The members – or the voters, come to that – must recognise the authority of the Institution and not cause trouble going on about things that don't really concern them.

Having seen the trouble the Church of England has got into over women priests, you can appreciate that point of view, but those who believe that public debate on all matters can only be of benefit think that Dr Jenkins must rank as something of a national treasure.

*The Western Mail, December 24, 1993*

Merthyr-born Alun Rees started his journalistic career on the *Walthamstow Guardian* in the early 1960s before moving on to Fleet Street, where he worked on the sports desk of the *Sunday Telegraph.* He later edited a weekly newspaper called *Inside Football.* In 1978 he joined the *South Wales Echo* as rugby writer, moving to *The Western Mail* a few years later. He has written his twice-weekly column since 1995. He has also had poetry published, and in 1996 won the Harri Webb Prize for political poetry.

# They don't make 'em like Willie any more

## By Alun Rees

THEY don't make 'em like Willie Jones any more. They can't. The left-hander from Carmarthen, who died last week, played his cricket not only in a different era but in a different world, in which players could be gentlemen and gentlemen could be players and agents hadn't been invented.

It was a tougher world for the professional; the life was not well rewarded and insecurity was a constant shadow. Jones himself waited a long time before going full-time with Glamorgan. He had a steady job as a county council road maintenance man; why take chances?

Different now. Even players of modest ability can enjoy bumper benefit years. The more famous gather loads of boodle, then flock off to media jobs, driving out the literate. Need at least three guys to assist them: one to write the stuff, one to fetch the champagne and one to fan their feet.

Of course, these gents – in between blasting the technical inadequacies and strategic idiocy of those still active – will assure you at every opportunity that cricket these days is far better than it was back in the Stone Age, when men like Jones had to wash off the woad before donning their whites.

Well, as the immortal Mandy Rice-Davies might have put it, they would, wouldn't they? It's tosh. Also bunkum, cobblers and codswallop. Yesterday's men might not win too many foot races against today's generation, but they were tougher, more diligent and certainly more rounded personalities.

There are always exceptions. Steve Watkin, with a battling spirit to match his mighty feet, is a throwback. If ever I need a heart transplant, I want his. Though if he's using it in one of those unflagging spells I'll let him keep it and slide smiling through the dark gates to start annoying the Devil.

Think I'm exaggerating? Consider all-rounders, who must have a real appetite for the game. The 1948 Glamorgan championship side had three genuine all-rounders – Wilf Wooller, Allan Watkins and Len Muncer; one very close (Jones); and one who had been and would be again briefly (Emrys Davies).

Now, if you can bear to do so, look at the current England team. Not a true all-rounder in sight. Hasn't been one since Ian Botham. They have to make do with batsmen who can bowl a bit and bowlers who can bat a bit.

Actually, that's a bit too kind. Some of the batsmen can't bat at all. And some of the bowlers need telling that talent is more important than posturing. Alan Mullally may have a bouncer's haircut and a reasonable line in glares, but there are more frightening creatures fighting for crumbs in my garden. Probably bowl better, too.

This is not mere nostalgia. This is also anger. Nothing infuriates me more than the patronising attitude towards cricketers of the past; dim-witted claims that, a few stars apart, they were a bunch of overweight layabouts who spent all their time down the pub and couldn't field to save their lives.

Just pop back with me to 1948 again. Four of the top seven in the batting averages were Cyril Washbrook, Len Hutton, Denis Compton and Bill Edrich. Reckon they'd get a Test cap today? The England attack in the first Test included Alec Bedser, Jack Young and Jim Laker. Would they? I should cocoa.

As for fielding, the overall standard is certainly higher now. The close catching is no better – it couldn't be – but there are few passengers in the deep. Still, you couldn't find a better outfit than Glamorgan's class of '48, or the Surrey sides of the 1950s.

I am not sighing for a return to the old days; not in their entirety, anyway. Professionals were often shockingly treated, and if they can get a decent deal and secure their futures I'm all for it. But I regret the passing of the genuine all-round cricketer. He still emerges in other lands. Rarely here. Very odd.

I also regret (and this is nostalgia) the passing of the all-round sportsman, the man who excelled at more than one game. The remorseless expansion of the seasons has rendered such characters all but extinct.

Jones was a fine example; a cricketer good enough to play in the 1949 Test trial, along with Glamorgan team-mates Watkins and Norman Hever, and a rugby outside half with Neath, Gloucester and Gloucestershire, who was called up for wartime international duty.

Watkins, Glamorgan's most successful Test cricketer, was another, a soccer professional until injury intervened. County skipper Wooller was a rugby union international, wicket-keeper Haydn Davies a leading squash player. And there were plenty of others, before and after.

Can't be done now. Current Glamorgan stalwart Tony Cottey had to choose between soccer and cricket. And while it is understandable, it is sad that we shall never again see the like of C B Fry, a triple blue at Oxford in cricket, soccer and athletics.

He went on to play in 26 Tests, won a soccer cap, appeared in an FA Cup final for Southampton, set a world long-jump record that stood for 21 years, acted as India's representative at the League of Nations and was even offered the throne of Albania. Now that's what I call an all-rounder.

Then there was J W H T Douglas, acronymically nicknamed Johnny Won't Hit Today because of his defensive batting.

He did hit some days, though, as when he won the 1908 Olympic middleweight boxing gold. He played in 23 Tests and won an England amateur soccer cap.

Jim Thorpe was an American football legend, a baseball star, a wizard at basketball, lacrosse and wrestling, and an athlete who won the pentathlon and decathlon at the 1912 Olympics only to be robbed of his medals by the pious prats who then ran athletics.

Maybe, though, even against this level of opposition the palm of outstanding all-round sports performer of the century belongs to a woman from Port Arthur, Texas – Mildred "Babe" Didrikson, better known after her marriage as Babe Zaharias.

As a one-woman track and field squad she single-handedly won the American team title for the Employers Casualty Company of Dallas in 1932. The same year she won Olympic golds in the javelin and the 80m hurdles. She was all of 18 years of age.

She was outstanding at swimming, diving, basketball and baseball, and even gave exhibitions in billiards, needlework and typing. And she was almost certainly the greatest woman golfer who ever drew breath, sweeping the amateur board and then dazzling as a professional.

No, they don't make 'em like that any more. Pity.

*The Western Mail, August 2, 1996*

Patrick Fletcher joined *The Western Mail* in 1987 as a senior reporter after working for the *Kent Messenger* group in Maidstone, where he was born in 1961. In 1990, he joined the *Western Mail's* sister paper *Wales on Sunday* for a four-year stint, and became acting news editor. He then returned to *the Mail* as chief investigative reporter. In 1996, he joined the *Mail's* news desk, where his responsibilities now include the content of the *Saturday Magazine.*

# Double Bluff

## By Patrick Fletcher

MY MISSION, as I've been volunteered to accept it, is one of infiltration. It is something of a challenge, as the organisation in which I've been asked to become a mole is the Security Service.

Well, all right, since the Security Service was advertising jobs in the *Sunday Times* at the weekend as well as the *Guardian* yesterday, it's probably worth a try.

It's worth making the distinction straight away that the Security Service which is asking for staff is not the James Bond gang over at MI6.

The Security Service we're talking about here is MI5, to whom foreign travel means a trip outside the ring of the M25.

"Intelligence," the advert headline says, "Use it to create waves and prevent repercussions."

I assume that means they want sneaky people who can do naughty things provided they can also get away with them. An interesting moral position.

In my interview I will therefore definitely mention that time I went scrumping in the field of Cox's Orange Pippins at West Farleigh. A week's supply of apples for school was gathered.

This operation certainly created waves after my co-conspirator got caught with an apple in the house and decided to turn Gran's evidence.

My brother claimed I'd pinched it and given it to him. However, I also used my intelligence to prevent the inevitable repercussions of my cover being blown by deciding to hide in the woods for three hours and eat all the evidence.

A clear demonstration of initiative under pressure, I think. Which would have been utterly successful had I a stronger stomach and not been quite so sick come teatime.

The advert also says that the Security Service offers a career like no other, but is one that requires qualities which a lot of people in fact possess.

What they are saying there is that they don't want people applying who fear they might get killed in the rush of applications. I know of at least three people in my office who reckon they are cut out for the spying game. At my interview I shall name each and everyone of my workmates and, indeed, anyone else whom I vaguely suspect might have seen the advert.

This will do three things. First of all it will demonstrate that I have a prodigious memory, surely a class-one requirement for any Security Service operative who must not get caught carrying documents he has no right to handle. Secondly, and rather neatly I think, it will kill off the chances of all those whom I have named by sowing seeds of doubt about their ability to keep a secret.

And finally it will show that even though I have a huge and eclectic circle of acquaintances, there is no one I will not betray on behalf of my country.

Unscrupulous is my middle name. Check my birth certificate (the forged one) if you don't believe me.

The secrete squirrels of Whitehall are offering two levels of entry into the shadowy world of espionage, lies and videotape (more of the first two and less of being caught on the latter, they hope.) Sex in the line of duty, I am reliably informed, is a serious no-no. No self-respecting spy ever did any good by playing away from home. Look at what happened to Mata Hari.

The advert does not mention the s-word anywhere; nevertheless, I shall be announcing in my interview that I am very happily in a relationship, we have one child and another is pending.

And, judging by the sexual enthusiasms of the more famous of the intelligence services' traitors, I would suggest every other applicant do the same. Fabricate if necessary.

Anyway, the first level of entry is for the young, upwardly mobile sort of spy.

For level one, the advert says, "Your starting point is three-four years of work experience and a good honours degree, or the intellectual clout with which you could have gained one had you so chosen." A clear invitation to people who planned to go to university, but could not be bothered. In short – drop-outs.

Nor does the advert say how I should have come by a good honours degree. So I shall buy mine from the University of Calcutta. Alternatively I shall claim that I made a conscious decision instead to spend three years yak breeding in Tibet at that well-known institution, the University of Life. It won't fail.

On second thoughts, given Britain's somewhat precarious relationship with China at the moment, English-speaking yak breeders living in what is a disputed

Chinese territory are probably already working on behalf of MI6 and would therefore be able to blow my cover.

Level two in the Ministry of Spies (home rather than abroad) requires some serious talent, apparently. The advert says, "Exceptional powers of communication and persuasion will make you adept at talking your way into situations with the opportunity for gathering useful information, as well as the resourcefulness to extract yourself from less promising circumstances."

If charming is what they want, charming is what they get. But, as I shall explain in my interview, you can get more with a kind word and a gun than you can with just a kind word.

The advert goes on to say that security threats never conform to a neat routine and neither will the work, so flexibility is also essential.

So what I reckon is that if I want a night out with the lads, I can. And plead, when I roll in at 3 am, that I can't say I've been in Sam's Bar since six because then I'll be in breach of the Official Secrets Act. And tomorrow night? Sorry dear, that's classified, too. MI5 is a job for the boys, or what?

All in all, I think I've got a pretty good chance of getting a job in the Security Service. I'm intelligent (well I'm not going to say I'm not, am I?), resourceful, I'm a terrific judge of human nature and I'd be quite happy to take a pay cut if I could serve my country.

But there is a conundrum in all of this. And it's this: Surely the people with all the initiative don't wait for an advert to apply to be a spy, they just go and ask for the job. If that is so, then those who do respond to the advert are obviously not of the calibre required. But, then, if one does not respond to the advert, then one definitely cannot get a job.

And, if both these contentions are true, it must mean that neither those who would have applied anyway nor those who are responding to the advert have any chance of success because it will be impossible for the people in grey suits to discriminate between the one kind of candidate and the other.

Hmm. Can I suggest this should be a set question in the MI5 entrance exam?

Another thing that might tell against me is the part where the advert says applicants should avoid telling friends that they're going for it, because discretion is a serious part of the Security Service.

I mean I'm not exactly playing my poker cards close to my chest by setting out my intention in 1,261 words and having it printed in 10-point Times type in 60,000 copies of *The Western Mail*.

Unless I can convince MI5 it is a terrific bluff. After all, who in their right mind is going to believe that I'm going to write all this and then actually make an application?

*The Western Mail, May 22, 1997*

Mario Basini's parents, both from the little Italian mountain town of Bardi, ran a café in Merthyr, where he was born. From Cyfarthfa Grammar School he went to University College, Aberystwyth, where he read English and history. Since joining *The Western Mail* in 1967, he has handled most writing jobs on the paper, including a long stint as Westgate, the diary columnist, and he is a former Welsh Feature Writer of the Year. He speaks Italian and a little Welsh. Three months after this article was published, the people of Wales voted – albeit by a tiny margin – for a National Assembly for Wales.

# Time to Stand and be Counted

## By Mario Basini

IF A WEEK is a long time in politics, then a fortnight can seem the gap separating eras. When I went on holiday, devolution simmered on the back burner, slowly maturing like a good saucepan of cawl.

Now it is boiling away merrily, spilling all over our front pages and scalding those, like me, who were complacent enough to believe the result of the debate was a foregone conclusion. It is time to stand up and be counted.

Let me say immediately that in this case at least, I am proud to be labelled a "Yes man".

All of us are fond of calling Wales a nation, even if it is only at international rugby matches when we take on "old enemies" like England.

The word implies that because of its shared history and literature, its mutual cultural and ethical values, Wales is a community strong enough and aware enough to exist apart from other nations in Europe or America or Asia or the British Isles.

But it seems to me that for the term to have any meaning beyond the sentimental lip service paid by well-oiled rugby fans or by pious politicians fishing for popularity, then the citizens who make up the nation should have the right to exercise an effective measure of self-government. Indeed, the ability to use that right with maturity and responsibility should be a measure of a community's fitness to call itself a nation.

Among the more depressing aspects of an increasingly strident "no" campaign as we approach the September referendum is that much of it seems based on those atavistic fears, misconceptions and divisions that have plagued Welsh life for decades.

Many in my own non-Welsh-speaking community in the South Wales Valleys seem to believe that an Assembly will automatically give Welsh-speakers the power to impose their attitudes and views on the rest of Wales. The argument appears to me to be nonsense.

In a democratically elected body how will it be possible for a minority making up only 20 per cent of the nation to dominate the majority? The very existence of the Assembly should guarantee that majority democratic control. Indeed, it seems to me that it could well be the Welsh-speaking minority who will have a powerful argument for assurances to be built into the new system to safeguard their position.

Ultimately, the Assembly will be the forum in which the English-language and the Welsh-language traditions – both vital to the future of Wales – will be able to thrash out their differences and eventually arrive at a position of mutual trust and support.

My arguments so far should have made it clear that I believe what is on offer under the Labour Government's proposals falls far short of what I consider a proper measure of self-government for Wales. I find it gratuitously insulting that Wales, with its own language, a history stretching back thousands of years and a highly-regarded literature, should not be considered worthy of the same degree of self-determination as Scotland.

But there is one overriding reason why you should say "Yes" to the present proposals, whatever your doubts about their adequacy.

After the black farce of the vote in the 1979 referendum, we are lucky we are being given a second chance to assert our own political identity.

This is the last opportunity we are ever likely to receive.

If the vote in September is "No", it will mean that we do not believe Wales has any more right to a separate existence than does Surbiton or East Cheam.

All those anodyne cliches about the Welsh nation will sound as hollow as a cracked bell.

The pride felt by those representing their country on the sports field or in the concert hall will become as meaningless as the emotions stirred by a Sunday morning kick-a-bout or a singsong in the bar on Saturday nights.

The chances are that the English regions will jump at the chance of a little self-government when it is offered to them.

If that happens and Wales has said no to devolution, we will be exposed as what we are: the remnants of a once-proud nation grown too timid to take our place in the world.

*The Western Mail, June 21, 1997*

Carolyn Hitt has been writing a weekly humorous column for *The Western Mail* since 1993. Born in Llwynypia, Rhondda, she read English at Oxford and began her journalistic career on the *Merthyr Express*. During her five-year stint with the *Mail*, she became features editor and won the Welsh Feature Writer of the Year Award in 1998. She now works as a broadcaster with the Cardiff-based independent television and radio company Presentable Productions.

# Blue-collar Blokes

## By Carolyn Hitt

ACCORDING to some American chap who wrote a best-selling tome on the subject, in verbal communication terms, men are from Mars and women are from Venus.

Taking this linguistic planetary analogy a little further, I would like to add a third category. Men are from Mars, women are from Venus... and workmen you allow into your home when you are a lone female are from the bottom of a Black Hole.

In fact, the same goes for most blue-collar blokes when you're a woman seeking their help on a practical matter. Basically, you are Penelope Pitstop with a frontal lobotomy and they are the fount of all knowledge with a nice line in withering sarcasm.

You may have a Ph.D. in Critical Theory, be fluent in seven minor European languages, and balance motherhood with a managing directorship but to Blue-collar Bloke coming to fix your fan belt, deliver your appliances or unblock your drains, you are just one thing. You are "Luv".

This all-purpose moniker will usually be paired with a number of stock phrases, such as:

"It'll costya, Luv." (Particularly common in the realms of motor mechanics and usually preceded by a whistling intake of breath.)

"Sorry, Luv, company policy." (A catch-all excuse for the near-legendary inflexibility of the average British service industry.)

"Is your husband around, Luv?" (Because only someone with testosterone will know where the boiler is.)

I hit a veritable asteroid belt of Blue-collar Bloke communication breakdown recently when I become embroiled in the trauma that was ordering a pine dining table from a well-known Welsh furniture and knick-knack shop.

It was all so exciting at the start, choosing my first real dining table amid the wafting fragrance of pot pourri and surrounded by aesthetically-pleasing household ephemera.

"It will be delivered in two to eight weeks." I could barely contain my thrilldom. But nine weeks later, the nightmare began. First there were the dealings with the man who organised the deliveries, who became affectionately known as Grumpy Drawers in our household. "We can't deliver this Saturday because you didn't confirm in time," said Grumpy Drawers.

I'd told the shop any Saturday was absolutely fine. So when can we have it, I demanded, awash with disappointment.

"Next Saturday."

"Great, that's confirmed then."

"Er, no. You'll have to confirm on Wednesday," said Grumpy Drawers.

"But I'm telling you, I'll be in next Saturday."

Be in? Blimey, I was organising a Welcome Reception for my first piece of real furniture. But Grumpy Drawers was having none of it, company policy and all that. Saturday arrived, as did the table and three delivery men. One look at the front door prompted three simultaneous whistling intakes of breath.

"It's not going to get through there, Luv. If we take the door off, have you got someone who will put it back on?" (i.e. someone male in possession of a power tool).

They then went into a conspiratorial huddle and I was able to glean all sorts of interesting consumer facts which no one had mentioned in the fragrant furniture shop.

"See, the contract says only deliver to the door."

Great, lads, just leave it in my front garden in the middle of a monsoon; we could protect it with my disconnected front door.

Much huffing and puffing later, and minus its top, the table was in the living room and the furniture-delivery world's answer to the Marx brothers were becoming increasingly amused at "Luv's" anxiety.

Harpo was on my phone to Grumpy Drawers.

"See, we gottit in one room, but the lady wants it in another room," he chirped, exuding mirth and incredulity in equal measures. Actually, the lady wanted the dining table in the dining room, not dismantled in the middle of her lounge.

Harpo suddenly guffawed, "I won't tell you what he just said," he chortled. Even better. There's a strange man in the middle of my house on my phone talking to another strange man who is making jokes about me.

It was time to tackle Grumpy Drawers. I told him I'd like to swop the dining table for one that fitted. The mother of all Company Policy speeches ensued.

It's up to customers to check their dimensions (Should've told me before I bought it, Grumpy – I thought the legs came off); the table couldn't be swopped unless someone else wanted it, and that couldn't be guaranteed; it couldn't be taken away because the Marx brothers had to finish their day with an empty van, but if it got marked in any way while in my house, I'd have to keep it, blah di blah.

I kept my consumer sanity by imagining stuffing a large bowl of pot pourri down Grumpy's gullet and reversing an empty van over the Marx brothers.

Anyway, after all their "Sorry, Luv, no can do," spiel, my brother and one Black and Decker got the wretched piece of pine in the dining room in 10 minutes. But then, men are from Mars, women from Venus – and my big brother's a Master of the Universe.

*The Western Mail, October 27, 1997*

On the morning of the opening by the Queen of the National Assembly for Wales, *The Western Mail* carried this front-page editorial which spoke of a new Wales standing, at the dawn of the 21st Century, on the threshold of an exciting era.

# Celebration of a Nation

## After 593 years, we have a government whose sole responsibility is to shape the destiny of Wales

FOR TOO LONG Wales has been the nearly nation. Our past is littered with heroes of whom we can say, 'Almost, but not quite.' Even as they lifted the cup of success to their mouths to drink, they found it dashed from their faltering fingers.

And today, as the Queen opens the National Assembly, we should take time to reflect on our people and events which have brought us to the threshold of an exciting new era.

There was Arthur, the greatest warrior in Christendom, who almost succeeded in fighting off the Anglo-Saxon invaders and restoring the glories of Rome to the Ancient Britons.

There were the 13th Century princes, Llywelyn the Great and Llywelyn the Last, who could not quite impose order on their warring vassals and forge a Wales powerful enough to stand up to the English.

And there was Owain Glyndwr, the 14th Century rebel who was so much more than a good guerrilla leader. Against great odds, pressed in on all sides by implacable enemies, he yet managed to create the trappings of a strong Welsh state.

He built an effective civil service, summoned his subjects to Parliaments, planned Wales's first university and schemed to establish a Welsh church free of the control of Canterbury. Yet he and his achievements disappeared like lantern flames in the wind.

Even the Welsh who succeeded, frequently gave the benefits of their great talents to others. Like Henry VII, born in Pembroke, who founded the Tudor dynasty, perhaps the most gifted to have occupied the English throne.

Little wonder that a sense of loss reverberates through our history like a peal of requiem bells. Whether we talk of sport or religion, economics or politics, we constantly hark back to a golden time when the sun shone more brightly, our chapels and churches were packed, our rugby teams beat the world, the coins rattled in our full pockets and we produced leaders who inspired generations.

Today it is time to stop harping on the past and to concentrate on the future. When the Queen opens the National Assembly in its temporary home in Cardiff Bay, she will be ushering in a new Wales, a Wales which the Welsh have at last deemed themselves mature enough to look after.

The brave new world into which we are about to step glitters with opportunities. It offers us a fresh dawn full of the promise of fulfilment – if we have the self-confidence to trust the abilities we have already acquired and to develop the skills our rapidly-changing society demands.

Once, at the beginning of this century, industrial Wales was strong enough, rich enough and enterprising enough to become one of the world's great economies. We were the crucible in which much of the planet's prosperity was created.

Our steel made the railways which opened up continents, our coal fuelled the merchant ships that circumnavigated the globe.

Welsh expertise helped to create the steel mills and furnaces of the mighty United States. The skills of Welsh engineers laid the foundations of the steel industry in Russia.

Is it too much to ask that at the dawn of the 21st Century, with the support of the Assembly, we can recapture a little of that prestige and influence?

With political maturity comes, of course, accountability. It will no longer be acceptable to bemoan our bad luck, to blame others for our failures. Taking charge of our future also means taking responsibility for our fate.

The new Wales stands on the threshold of an exciting era. For the first time for nearly 600 years, since Glyndwr and his Parliament slipped into the shadows of history, we have a government whose sole responsibility is to shape the destiny of Wales.

It is time to write an end to the nearly nation and to take our full place on the international stage.

*The Western Mail, May 26, 1999*

# GRADE THREE

# Electric Guitar Playing

compiled by

## Tony Skinner

on behalf of

*Registry of Guitar Tutors*

A CIP record for this publication is available from the British Library

ISBN 1-898466-53-X

© 2001 & 2009 The Registry of Guitar Tutors
The Guitarograph is a trade mark of The Registry of Guitar Tutors

Published in Great Britain by

Registry Mews, 11 to 13 Wilton Road, Bexhill, Sussex, TN40 1HY

Music and text typesetting by

54 Lincolns Mead, Lingfield, Surrey RH7 6TA

Printed and bound in Great Britain

# Contents

# Introduction

This handbook is primarily intended to give advice and information to candidates considering taking the Grade Three examination in electric guitar playing, although undoubtedly it will be found that the information contained within will be helpful to all guitarists whether intending to take the examination or not.

## GUITAROGRAPH

In order that scales, arpeggios and chords can be illustrated as clearly as possible, and made available for all to understand regardless of experience, notation and fingering are displayed via the use of the *guitarograph*.

The *guitarograph* uses a combination of tablature, traditional notation and fingerboard diagram – thereby ensuring clarity and leaving no doubt as to what is required.  In the example shown above, all three notations refer to the same note, i.e. A on the 2nd fret of the 3rd (G) string, fretted with the 2nd finger.  Each of the notation methods used in the *guitarograph* is explained below:

### Tablature

The tablature is shown on the left of the guitarograph, with horizontal lines representing the strings (with the high E string being string 1), and the numbers on the string lines referring to the frets.  A '0' on a line would mean play that string *open* (unfretted).

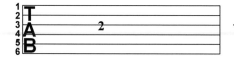
This means play at the second fret on the third string.

## Musical notation

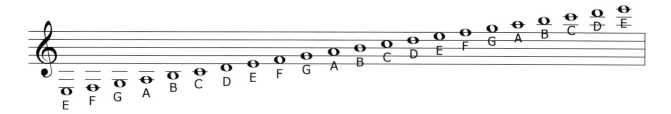

Notation on the treble clef is shown in the centre of the guitarograph.

A sharp (♯) before a note would raise its pitch by a semitone i.e. one fret higher, whilst a flat (♭) before a note would lower the pitch by a semitone, i.e. one fret lower. A natural sign (♮) before a note cancels a sharp or flat sign.

## Fingerboard diagram

The fingerboard diagram is shown on the right of the guitarograph with horizontal lines representing the strings. Vertical lines represent the frets, with fret numbers shown in Roman numerals. The numbers on the horizontal lines show the recommended fingering. Fingerings have been chosen that are likely to be the most effective for the widest range of players at this level, however there are a variety of alternative fingerings and fingerboard positions that could be used and you can use any other systematic fingerings that produce a good musical result.

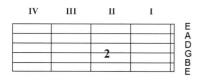

This means play with the second finger at the second fret on the G string.

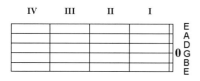

This means play the G string *open*, i.e. without fretting it.

## Interval spellings

Above each guitarograph is an interval spelling. This lists the letter names of the notes within the scale, arpeggio or chord, together with their interval numbers. The interval numbers shown are based on their comparison to the major scale with the same starting pitch. The scale, arpeggio and chord spellings will help you identify the differences in construction between the various scales and chords, and will help you learn the names of the notes that you are playing.

For example:

| A major scale | | | | | | | | | A natural minor scale | | | | | | | |
|---|---|---|---|---|---|---|---|---|---|---|---|---|---|---|---|---|
| A | B | C♯ | D | E | F♯ | G♯ | A | | A | B | C | D | E | F | G | A |
| 1 | 2 | 3 | 4 | 5 | 6 | 7 | 8 | | 1 | 2 | ♭3 | 4 | 5 | ♭6 | ♭7 | 8 |

---

### ALTERNATIVE FINGERING

Whilst the notes indicated in the guitarographs are precise and definitive, the fingering given in all cases is only one possible recommended suggestion: any alternative systematic and effective fingerings will be acceptable. There is no requirement to use the exact fingerings shown within this book.

### TUNING

The use of an electronic tuner or other tuning aid, *prior to, or at the start of the examination*, is permitted; candidates should be able to make any further adjustments, if required during the examination, unaided. The examiner will, upon request, offer an E or A note to tune to.

For examination purposes guitars should be tuned to Standard Concert Pitch (A=440Hz).

Candidates who normally tune to non-standard pitch (e.g. A=442Hz) should revert to Standard Concert Pitch for examination purposes. Candidates who normally tune a full tone or semitone higher/lower should either revert to Standard Pitch for the examination or should be prepared to transpose immediately upon request all requirements to Standard Pitch.

---

# Scales and arpeggios

At this grade candidates should be able to play the following two octave scales in *any* key:

- major
- pentatonic major
- pentatonic minor
- blues
- natural minor

In addition, candidates should be able to play the following two octave arpeggios starting from *any* note:

- major
- minor

Below are examples of the scales and arpeggios required for the Grade Three examination, all illustrated with a starting note of A. All these utilise transpositional finger patterns, so each shape can be moved up or down the fingerboard to a new pitch without the need for a change of fingering. The table below lists the frets on the sixth string that could be used to start each scale and arpeggio, depending upon the pitch required.

| F | F#/Gb | G | G#/Ab | A | A#/Bb | B | C | C#/Db | D | D#/Eb | E |
|---|---|---|---|---|---|---|---|---|---|---|---|
| 1 or 13 | 2 or 14 | 3 | 4 | 5 | 6 | 7 | 8 | 9 | 10 | 11 | 12 |

### A MAJOR SCALE – 2 OCTAVES

| A | B | C# | D | E | F# | G# | A |
|---|---|---|---|---|---|---|---|
| 1 | 2 | 3 | 4 | 5 | 6 | 7 | 8 |

### A PENTATONIC MAJOR SCALE – 2 OCTAVES

| A | B | C# | E | F# | A |
|---|---|---|---|---|---|
| 1 | 2 | 3 | 5 | 6 | 8 |

7

## A PENTATONIC MINOR SCALE – 2 OCTAVES

| A | C | D | E | G | A |
|---|---|---|---|---|---|
| 1 | ♭3 | 4 | 5 | ♭7 | 8 |

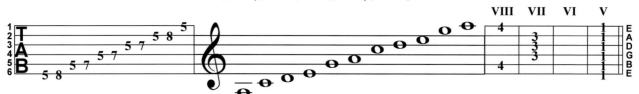

## A BLUES SCALE – 2 OCTAVES

| A | C | D | E♭ | E | G | A |
|---|---|---|----|---|---|---|
| 1 | ♭3 | 4 | ♭5 | 5 | ♭7 | 8 |

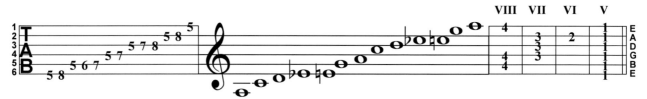

## A NATURAL MINOR SCALE – 2 OCTAVES

| A | B | C | D | E | F | G | A |
|---|---|---|---|---|---|---|---|
| 1 | 2 | ♭3 | 4 | 5 | ♭6 | ♭7 | 8 |

## A MAJOR ARPEGGIO – 2 OCTAVES

| A | C♯ | E | A |
|---|----|---|---|
| 1 | 3 | 5 | 8 |

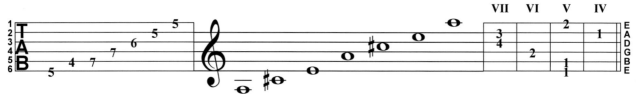

## A MINOR ARPEGGIO – 2 OCTAVES

| A | C | E | A |
|---|---|---|---|
| 1 | ♭3 | 5 | 8 |

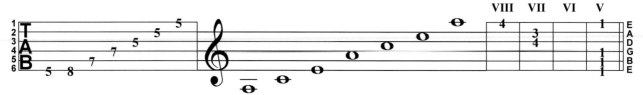

8

# INFORMATION AND ADVICE

A maximum of 12 marks may be awarded in this section of the examination.

The examiner may request you to play, from memory, any of the required scales and arpeggios. Each should be played once only, ascending and descending (i.e. from the lowest note to the highest and back again) without a pause and without repeating the top note. Candidates using acoustic guitars will not be asked to play in inaccessible fingerboard positions.

As a guideline, scales should be played at a tempo range of between 160 and 176 beats per minute (one note per beat), with arpeggios a little slower at between 120 and 138 bpm. Choose a tempo at which you feel confident and comfortable and try to maintain this evenly throughout; evenness and clarity are more important than speed for its own sake.

## Fretting-hand technique

Press the tips of the fretting-hand fingers as close to the fretwire as possible. This minimises buzzes and the amount of pressure required – enabling you to play with a lighter, clearer and hence more fluent touch.

Try to keep all the fretting-hand fingers close to the fingerboard, and have them ready to press in a 'hovering position', as this minimises the amount of movement required. Always have the fretting hand spread, with the fingers correctly spaced and ready in position hovering, before you start to play.

## Picking-hand technique

Although it is not essential to use a plectrum (or pick) for this examination, you may find that not using one has a detrimental effect on speed, attack, volume and tone – or at least more effort will be required to achieve the same effect. However, the use of the fingers, rather than the plectrum, does offer greater flexibility. Ultimately the choice is personal. Both methods are acceptable, providing a strong clear tone is achieved.

If using a plectrum alternate between downstrokes and upstrokes. Grip the plectrum between the index finger and thumb. Position the plectrum so that its tip is just beyond the fingertip. If an excessive amount of plectrum tip extends beyond the finger a lack of pick control will result as the plectrum will flap around when striking the strings – this would consequently reduce fluency and accuracy. Be careful not to grip the plectrum too tightly as excessive gripping pressure can lead to muscular tension in the hand with subsequent loss of flexibility and movement.

# Chords

At this grade, candidates should be able to play all major and minor chords using *barre chord shapes*, in *two* different fingerboard positions.

The barre chords below are illustrated with a root note of C, however, because they utilise transpositional shapes they can be moved up or down the fingerboard to any pitch without the need to change fingering.

This table lists the fret position needed to produce chords at different pitches.

| First finger on fret number | 1 | 2 | 3 | 4 | 5 | 6 | 7 | 8 | 9 | 10 | 11 | 12 |
|---|---|---|---|---|---|---|---|---|---|---|---|---|
| Chords with root on E string | F | F#/Gb | G | G#/Ab | A | A#/Bb | B | C | C#/Db | D | D#/Eb | E |
| Chords with root on A string | A#/Bb | B | C | C#/Db | D | D#/Eb | E | F | F#/Gb | G | G#/Ab | A |

### C minor (root on E string)

C    Eb    G

1    b3    5

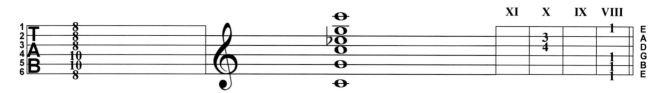

### C minor (root on A string)

C    Eb    G

1    b3    5

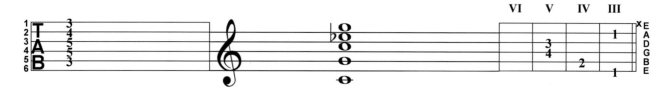

**C major (root on E string)**

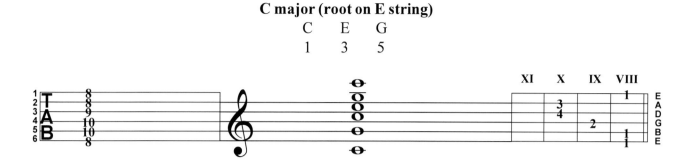

**C major (root on A string)**

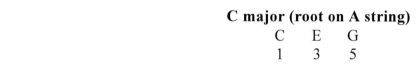

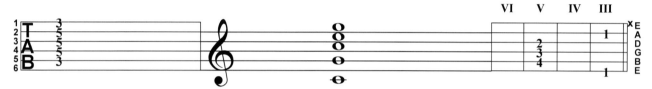

# INFORMATION AND ADVICE

A maximum of 8 marks may be awarded in this section of the examination.

The examiner may request you to play, from memory, any of the required chords in two different fingerboard positions. Each chord shape should be played once only, using a single downstroke. Make sure that your fingers are carefully and correctly positioned before playing the chord. In the fingerboard diagrams, strings that should be omitted are marked by an X – so be careful not to strike these strings when playing the chord.

# BARRE CHORDS

At this grade, chords are required in 'barre' form – where the first finger effectively replaces the nut and acts as a 'bar' across all strings. In chords with the root note on the fifth string, although you can still place the first finger barre over all six strings, you are advised to omit the sixth string in your strum.

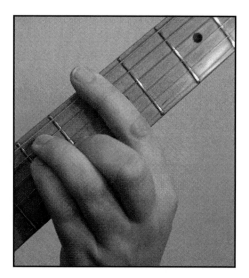

To ensure that your barre chords ring clearly you should observe the following advice:

(i)     The first finger should be straight and in-line with the fret, rather than at an angle to it.

(ii)    The first finger need not be completely flat: it can be tilted very slightly away from the fret toward its outer side.

(iii)   Position the first finger so that the creases at its joints do not coincide with the strings. If necessary adjust the barre until you find the optimum position.

(iv)    All fingers should be positioned as close to the fretwire as possible.

(v)     Do not exert excessive pressure with either the first finger or the thumb.

(vi)    Ensure that fretting fingers, other than the first finger, remain upright and press against the strings with their tips.

# Rhythm playing

In this section of the examination, the candidate will be shown a chord chart and will be allowed a short time (of about 30 seconds) to study it before being asked to play it. The chord chart will only contain chords that are required for Grade Three.

After playing the first chord chart candidates may, at the examiner's discretion, be given an additional chart to play; this will be of similar difficulty to the first.

Some examples of the *type* of chart that may be presented at this grade are given below. The tempo markings are intended only as broad guidelines.

(i)  Not too slow

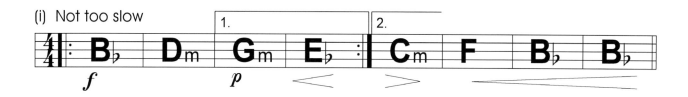

(ii)  Slow ballad

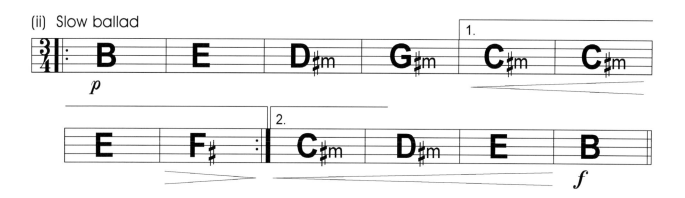

(iii)  Fairly slow

In practice, musicians may write out chord charts not only on staves (as shown previously) but sometimes chords are written above staves instead, or quite commonly just with bar lines (as in the example below). In the examination, to achieve maximum visual clarity, all chord charts will be presented in the style shown below.

(iv)  Moderate tempo

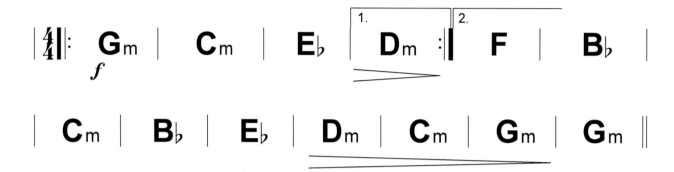

# INFORMATION AND ADVICE

At this grade the time signature is limited to either $\frac{3}{4}$, $\frac{4}{4}$ or $\frac{6}{8}$ time. Whilst the time signature should be evident by generally maintaining a regular pulse and even tempo, candidates are expected to be far more imaginative than simply strumming on each beat of the bar.

The musical style that is used is left to the discretion of the candidate. Fingerpicking can be used, rather than strumming, if preferred by the candidate.

## $\frac{6}{8}$ TIME

$\frac{6}{8}$ is a *compound time* signature: although in $\frac{6}{8}$ time there is an equivalent of six eighth notes in a bar, there are only two main beats.

1 23 2 23

As well as the first beat, the second beat (which falls on the fourth of the six pulses) is usually accented in $\frac{6}{8}$ time.

# Gaining marks

A maximum of 30 marks may be awarded in this section of the examination. The examiner will award marks for accuracy (including attention to time signature, repeats and dynamics), clarity, fluency and inventiveness.

Chord changes should be as smooth and fluent as possible and lack any sense of hesitation. Care should be taken when choosing which barre shape to use (i.e. one based on the E string or one based on the A string) so that large fingerboard jumps between chords are avoided whenever possible. Chords should ring clear, i.e. free of fret-buzz or the unintended muting of notes with the fretting-hand fingers.

During the time given to look over the chord chart, candidates should try to discover the overall structure of the progression. At this grade, the only indications on the chart, other than the time signature and tempo, are repeat and dynamic marks.

*Repeat marks*

Passages to be repeated are indicated by two vertical dots at the start and end of the section to be repeated.

For example:

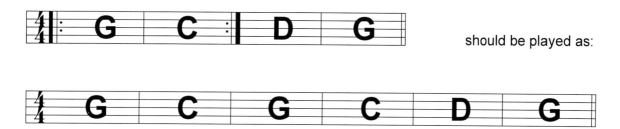

should be played as:

*1st and 2nd time endings.*

Bars marked | 1. | are included in the first playing, but omitted on the repeat playing and replaced with the bars marked | 2.

For example:

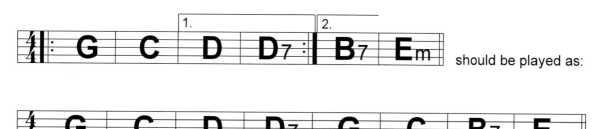

should be played as:

---

**15**

*Dynamic markings*

These indicate the changes in volume to be made:

$p$      – play softly        $f$      – play strongly

       – become louder        – become softer

---

## RHYTHM PLAYING TIPS

### Strumming hand

- It will aid fluency of rhythm playing if the strumming hand pivots from the wrist: a fluid and easy strumming action is best achieved this way, with the wrist loose and relaxed.

- If the wrist is stiff and not allowed to move freely then excessive arm movement will occur as the strumming action will be forced to come from the elbow instead. As this can never move as fluently as the wrist action there will be a loss of smoothness and rhythmic potential.

### Fretting hand

- Be careful not to overgrip with the fretting-hand thumb on the back of the guitar neck as this will cause muscle fatigue and tend to limit the free movement of the thumb.

- It is essential that the fretting-hand thumb is allowed to move freely when changing chords. If the thumb remains static this restricts the optimum positioning of the fingers for the next chord, which may result in unnecessary stretching and the involuntary dampening of certain strings (as the fingers are not positioned upright on their tips).

- For the fingers to move freely, the wrist, elbow and shoulder must be flexible and relaxed: try to ensure that this is not inhibited by your standing or sitting position.

# Lead playing

In this section of the examination, the candidate will be shown a chord progression containing chords chosen from those listed in Section 2 of this book. The examiner will then play this progression (either live or recorded) and the candidate should improvise over this using an appropriate scale selected from Section 1 of this book.

Some examples of the *type* of chord chart that will be presented at this grade are shown below. The scale suggestions are given for guidance in this book, but will NOT appear in the examination.

(i) The A♭ major scale could be used to improvise over the following progression...

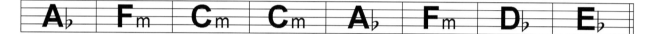

(ii) The E♭ pentatonic major scale could be used to improvise over the following progression...

(iii) The F♯ pentatonic minor scale could be used to improvise over the following progression...

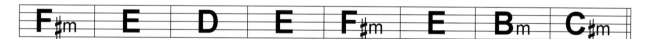

(iv) The B natural minor scale could be used to improvise over the following progression...

# INFORMATION AND ADVICE

The progression will be played a total of three times; during the first playing the candidate should not play, but rather listen and digest the progression, before improvising over the next two cycles. After the final playing the progression will end on the key chord.

To ensure accuracy it is essential that the candidate selects the most appropriate scale with which to improvise. The examiner will NOT advise on this. At this grade each progression will always start on the key chord.

At the examiner's discretion an additional progression may be selected for the candidate to improvise over. Although this will again contain chords only from Section 2 of this book, the candidate may need to select a different scale from Section 1 to improvise with.

## Gaining marks

A maximum of 30 marks may be awarded in this section of the examination. The examiner will award marks for:

- accuracy
- fluency
- phrasing and melodic shaping
- stylistic interpretation
- inventiveness and creativity
- clarity and tone production
- the application of specialist techniques

Although you will need to select a scale to improvise with, be aware that the purpose of the scale is only to set the series of notes that will be in tune in a particular key. Endeavour to make your improvisation melodically and rhythmically inventive and imaginative rather than sounding scale-like.

The style of lead playing should enhance and empathise with the chordal accompaniment, which may be from a range of musical styles such as rock, pop, soul and blues etc. Try to create interesting melodic and rhythmic phrases within your improvisation and avoid inappropriate use of continuous scalic playing. Playing should be fluent, but without the need for speed for its own sake; more important is the overall musical effect that is achieved.

At this grade candidates are not expected to have a high level of fluency in the practical application of arpeggios, but the demonstration of some musically appropriate and accurate use of arpeggios during a performance will be reflected in the marks awarded.

# SPECIALIST TECHNIQUES

At this grade, when musically appropriate, candidates should use some of the following techniques during their improvisation:

## String Bending

Candidates should be reasonably adept in executing ascending whole-tone bends, i.e. bending a note upwards by the equivalent of two frets. This is particularly useful for bending up to the octave from the ♭7th, or up to the 5th from the 4th.

Example taken from A Blues Scale:

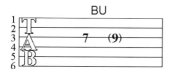

Bend D on the 7th fret, 3rd string, until it reaches the pitch of E – i.e. equivalent to playing on the 9th fret, 3rd string.

It is important to bend the string to exactly the right pitch. The pressure that is needed to bend a string will vary according to the string gauge and the fret position, so candidates will need to rely upon their aural abilities to pitch the note accurately. When bending a string with the third or fourth finger, keep the lower fingers on the string to give support and control. Using the power of the whole arm, pivoting from the elbow, will make string bending easier.

## Vibrato

Vibrato is the wavering of the pitch of a note. It is differentiated from string bending in that the variation in pitch with vibrato is of a much smaller range. There are various methods by which vibrato can be executed whilst fretting a note:

(a)  Horizontal vibrato: achieved by moving the fretting finger and hand from side to side whilst fretting a note.

(b)  Vertical vibrato: achieved by moving the fretting finger vertically up and down to repeatedly shift the note slightly above pitch and back again.

(c)  Wrist vibrato: whilst the first finger frets the note, the pitch of the note is altered with the rotation of the wrist.

# Slurs

A slur is the sounding of two or more notes from the single pick of a string. Slurs can be used to facilitate fluency and speed, but equally importantly to add smoothness and subtlety. Candidates should be able to demonstrate ability with two types of slurs:

(a)  *Hammer-on:* a note is played, then a higher note on the same string is sounded without being picked again but by a hammering action with a fretting-hand finger.

For the hammered note to be clear, it is important to use a certain amount of force and attack when bringing down the hammering finger.

Hammer with the tip of the finger as close to the fretwire as possible.

(b)  *Pull-off:* fret a note and pick the string, then pull the fretting finger lightly downwards until it plucks the string and the lower note is sounded – i.e. without the string being picked again. If the lower note that is required is not an open string, then you need to have another finger in position fretting the lower note *before* executing the pull-off.

For the pull-off to be clear, it is important that the pressure is concentrated on the lower finger anchoring the string (otherwise the note may be pulled out of tune when the higher finger plucks the string).

The plucking action should come from the tip of the finger with a downward pulling action and not simply by lifting the finger off the string.

---

## LEAD PLAYING TIPS

### Phrasing

- Try to create interesting melodic and rhythmic phrases within your improvisation.

- Avoid the inappropriate use of continuous scalic playing by not being afraid to leave gaps between, and within, phrases.

### Resolving notes

- When improvising from a scale you will find that some notes sound better, and more 'resolved', against certain chords than others. However, as long as you stay within the correct scale, no notes will be 'out of tune'. If you play a note that sounds 'unresolved' against a particular chord simply move up or down one note within the scale.

- Rest assured that none of the notes from the correct scale will totally clash with the backing chords; let your ears guide you as to which scale notes sound best over particular chords.

### Interpretation

- Listen carefully to the chord progression and try to make your solo relate to the rhythm and style of the backing.

# Spoken tests

A maximum of 10 marks may be awarded in this section of the examination.

## FINGERBOARD KNOWLEDGE

In order to establish a solid musical foundation, it is important that candidates should be aware of the notes that they are playing rather than merely duplicating finger patterns. At this grade, candidates will be expected to promptly name any note on any string, up to the 12th fret, as selected by the examiner.

Candidates may also be asked to name the notes contained within any major or minor arpeggio as selected by the examiner.

During this section of the examination candidates will be expected to *know* the names of the notes they are asked about and give a prompt response. Candidates will not be permitted to take a long time, or to play the guitar, to 'work-out' answers to these tests.

## CLARITY AND FLUENCY

Candidates may be asked questions about the optimum positioning of the fretting-hand fingers, in regard to achieving clarity and avoiding fret buzz: the most important factor being to press very close to the fretwire, and (except when holding a barre with the first finger) to use the tips rather than the pads of the fingers.

Candidates may also be asked questions about the optimum methods of achieving fluency when picking the strings: the most important factor being that plectrum strokes should generally alternate between down and up strokes in order to facilitate fluency and speed. Care should be taken to have an appropriate amount of plectrum tip protruding from the grip between the index finger and the thumb. Whilst this will vary with the size of fingers and the plectrum used, in general, too much plectrum showing will drag or even snag on the strings thus hampering fluency and articulation, whilst too little increases the chances of missing the correct string altogether.

# KNOWLEDGE OF THE INSTRUMENT

Candidates should have knowledge of the ways in which the tone can be varied on their own instrument. This should include:

(i)    A practical understanding of the use of tone controls and pick-up selectors (where appropriate).

(ii)    An understanding of the effect of changing the strumming hand position: playing at the bridge end generates the brightest tone, whilst movement towards the fingerboard tends to mellow the tone.

(iii)    Knowledge of the effect of plectrum gauge on tone production: a thicker plectrum can produce a fuller, harder tone.

Candidates should have an understanding of the mechanism and anatomy of their guitar, including such terms as:

(i)    *Action* – the distance between the strings and the frets, which determines the ease of fretting notes.

(ii)    *Marker dots* (fret markers) – the dots, or blocks, inlaid into front and/or side of the fingerboard to act as a reminder as to the position of certain frets. These normally include at least frets 3, 5, 7, 9 and 12.

(iii)    *The nut* – a slotted piece of material (normally plastic or brass), situated at the headstock end of the fingerboard, in the grooves of which the strings lie.

(iv)    *The saddle* – the seat upon which the strings rest at the bridge end of the guitar. It is from this point that the vibrating section of the string starts. Electric guitars tend to have an individual saddle for each string, which form part of the bridge.

(v)    *Machine Heads* – the turning keys, normally positioned on the guitar headstock, which when rotated increase or reduce string tension and so raise or lower the pitch of the string.

# Aural assessments

A maximum of 10 marks may be awarded in total during this section of the examination. The candidate will be given a selection of the following tests, which will include a rhythm test and at least two other tests.

## REPETITION OF RHYTHMS

The examiner will twice tap, or play (on a single note), a four bar rhythm in either $\frac{3}{4}$, $\frac{4}{4}$ or $\frac{6}{8}$ time. The note range will be limited to half notes (minims), dotted quarter notes (dotted crotchets), quarter notes (crotchets) and eighth notes (quavers) – except for the last bar, which will contain only one long note. The candidate should reproduce the rhythm by clapping, tapping or playing. Some examples of the *type* of rhythm are given below. Note that the first and third bars will be identical.

# REPETITION OF MELODIC PHRASES

The candidate will be asked to look away while the examiner plays a one bar phrase in $\frac{4}{4}$ time. This will consist of notes, within a range of one octave, from a scale listed in Section 1 of this book. The candidate will be told which scale is to be used, and the keynote will be played. The phrase will start on the keynote and will consist of three quarter notes (crotchets) and two eighth notes (quavers).

The examiner will play the phrase twice before the candidate makes a first attempt to reproduce the phrase on the guitar. If required, the candidate can request the examiner to play the phrase one further time, prior to the candidate's second attempt, with no reduction in marks. However, the candidate will then be expected to reproduce the phrase promptly and will not be permitted any further attempts at 'working it out'. Some examples of the *type* of phrase are shown below.

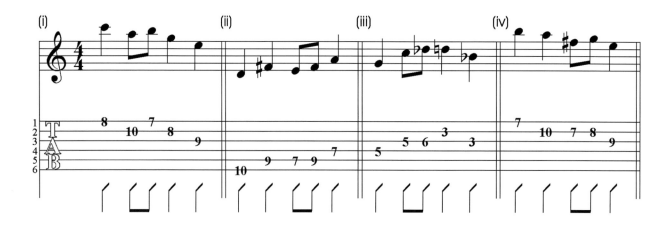

These phrases are taken from the following scales :

(i) C major

(ii) D pentatonic major

(iii) G blues

(iv) B natural minor

# KEEPING TIME

The examiner will twice play a four bar melody in either ¾, ⁴₄ or ⁶₈ time. During the second playing the candidate should clap the main pulse, accenting the first beat of each bar. Two examples are given below, with the rhythmic pulse to be clapped by the candidate shown below both the notation and tablature.

(i)

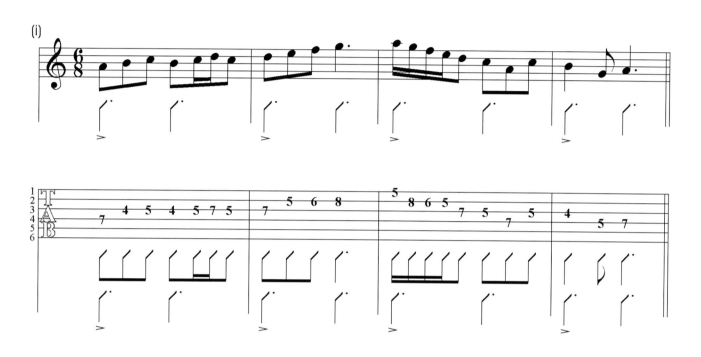

(ii)

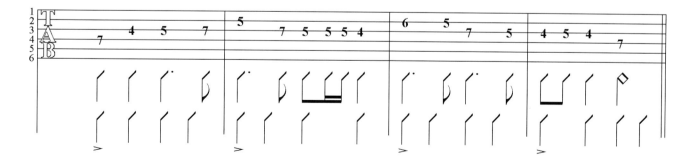

# PITCH TEST

The candidate will be asked to identify any note from any one octave major scale. Whilst the candidate looks away, the examiner will state and play the keynote followed by another note from a major scale. The candidate will then be asked to identify the second note either by letter name or interval number.

Here is an example of the note choices from the C major scale.

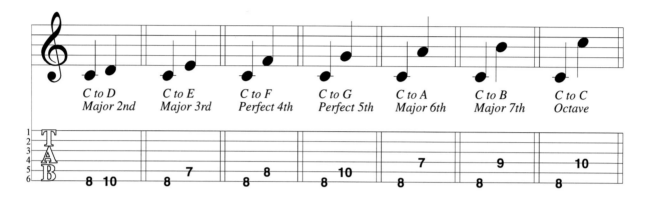

# HARMONY TEST

Whilst the candidate looks away the examiner will twice play either a major chord or a minor chord. The candidate will then be asked to identify whether the chord was major or minor.

$\frac{2}{4}$ ‖ G ‖ = major

$\frac{2}{4}$ ‖ Gm ‖ = minor

# RGT
*Registry of Guitar Tutors*

# EXAMINATION ENTRY FORM
# ELECTRIC GUITAR
# GRADE THREE

## ONLINE ENTRY – AVAILABLE FOR UK CANDIDATES ONLY

For **UK candidates**, entries and payments can be made online at www.RGT.org, using the entry code below. You will be able to pay the entry fee by credit or debit card at a secure payment page on the website.

Your unique and confidential examination entry code is:

## EC-5879-ED

*Keep this unique code confidential, as it can only be used once.* Once you have entered online, you should sign this form overleaf. **You must bring this signed form to your exam and hand it to the examiner in order to be admitted to the exam room.**

*If NOT entering online, please complete BOTH sides of this form and return to the address overleaf.*

SESSION (Spring/Summer/Winter): _____ YEAR: _____

Dates/times NOT available: _____

Note: Only name *specific* dates (and times on those dates) when it would be *absolutely impossible* for you to attend due to important prior commitments (such as pre-booked overseas travel) which cannot be cancelled. We will then endeavour to avoid scheduling an exam session in your area on those dates. In fairness to all other candidates in your area, **only list dates on which it would be impossible for you to attend.** An entry form that blocks out unreasonable periods may be returned. (Exams may be held on any day of the week including, but not exclusively, weekends. Exams may be held within or outside of the school term.)

**Candidate Details:** *Please write as clearly as possible using BLOCK CAPITALS*

Candidate Name (as to appear on certificate): _____

Address: _____

_____ Postcode: _____

Tel. No. (day): _____ (evening): _____

(mobile): _____ Email: _____

**Teacher Details** *(if applicable)*

Teacher Name (as to appear on certificate): *CHRISTIAN LLOYD*

RGT Tutor Code (if applicable): _____

Address: *9 ANNANDALE ROAD, CHISWICK, LONDON, W4 2HE*

_____ Postcode: _____

Tel. No. (day): _____ (evening): _____

(mobile): *07980 710744* Email: *christian_lloyd_@hotmail.com*

*x Ref : RGT03-1090-1265039174*

# RGT Electric Guitar Official Entry Form

**The standard LCM entry form is NOT valid for Electric Guitar exam entries.**

**Entry to the examination is only possible via this original form.**

**Photocopies of this form will not be accepted under *any* circumstances.**

- Completion of this entry form is an agreement to comply with the current syllabus requirements and conditions of entry published at www.RGT.org. Where candidates are entered for examinations by a teacher, parent or guardian that person hereby takes responsibility that the candidate is entered in accordance with the current syllabus requirements and conditions of entry.

- If you are being taught by an *RGT registered* tutor, please hand this completed form to your tutor and request him/her to administer the entry on your behalf.

- For candidates with special needs, a letter giving details should be attached.

Examination Fee: £_____    Late Entry Fee (if applicable): £_____

Total amount submitted: £_____

**Cheques or postal orders should be made payable to Registry of Guitar Tutors.**

**Details of conditions of entry, entry deadlines and examination fees are obtainable from the RGT website: www.RGT.org**

**Once an entry has been accepted, entry fees cannot be refunded.**

## CANDIDATE INFORMATION (UK Candidates only)

In order to meet our obligations in monitoring the implementation of equal opportunities policies, UK candidates are required to supply the information requested below. *The information provided will in no way whatsoever influence the marks awarded during the examination.*

Date of birth: _____ Age: _____ Gender – please circle: male / female

Ethnicity (please enter 2 digit code from chart below): _____ Signed: _____

**ETHNIC ORIGIN CLASSIFICATIONS** (If you prefer not to say, write '17' in the space above.)

White: **01 British**      **02 Irish**      **03 Other white background**

Mixed: **04 White & black Caribbean**      **05 White & black African**      **06 White & Asian**      **07 Other mixed background**

Asian or Asian British: **08 Indian**      **09 Pakistani**      **10 Bangladeshi**      **11 Other Asian background**

Black or Black British: **12 Caribbean**      **13 African**      **14 Other black background**

Chinese or Other Ethnic Group: **15 Chinese**      **16 Other**      **17 Prefer not to say**

I understand and accept the current syllabus regulations and conditions of entry for this examination as specified on the RGT website.

Signed by candidate (if aged 18 or over) _____ Date _____

If candidate is under 18, this form should be signed by a parent/guardian/teacher (circle which applies):

Signed _____ Name_____ Date_____

## UK ENTRIES

See overleaf for details of how to enter online OR return this form to:
**Registry of Guitar Tutors, Registry Mews, 11 to 13 Wilton Road, Bexhill-on-Sea, E. Sussex, TN40 1HY**
(If you have submitted your entry online do NOT post this form, instead you need to sign it above and hand it to the examiner on the day of your exam.)
To contact the RGT office telephone 01424 222222 or Email office@RGT.org

## NON-UK ENTRIES

To locate the address within your country that entry forms should be sent to, and to view exam fees in your currency, visit the RGT website **www.RGT.org** and navigate to the 'RGT Worldwide' section.